Research and Statistics Made Meaningful in Counseling and Student Affairs

Research and Statistics Made Meaningful
in Counseling and Student Affairs

Rebecca M. LaFountain
Robert B. Bartos

Shippensburg University

with contributions by

Jan L. Arminio
Kurt L. Kraus

Shippensburg University

BROOKS/COLE

THOMSON LEARNING

Australia • Canada • Mexico • Singapore • Spain • United Kingdom • United States

BROOKS/COLE
THOMSON LEARNING

Sponsoring Editor: *Julie Martinez*	Interior Design: *Tessa Avila*
Editorial Assistant: *Cat Broz*	Cover Design: *Christine Garrigan*
Marketing: *Caroline Concilla/Megan Hansen*	Cover Photos: *Photo Disc*
Production Editor: *Tessa Avila*	Print Buyer: *Kris Waller*
Production Service: *GEX Publishing Services*	Typesetting: *GEX Publishing Services*
Manuscript Editor: *GEX Publishing Services*	Printing and Binding: *Webcom, Limited*
Permissions Editor: *Sue Ewing*	

For more information about this or any other Brooks/Cole product, contact:
BROOKS/COLE
511 Forest Lodge Road
Pacific Grove, CA 93950 USA
www.brookscole.com
1-800-423-0563 (Thomson Learning Academic Resource Center)

Printed in Canada

10   9   8   7   6   5   4   3   2   1

Library of Congress Cataloging-in-Publication Data

LaFountain, Rebecca M.
    Research and statistics made meaningful in counseling and student affairs /
Rebecca M. LaFountain, Robert B. Bartos.
        p. cm.
    Includes bibliographical references and index.
    ISBN 0-534-58167-6
1. Educational counseling—Research—United States. 2. Student affairs services—Research—United States.
3. Education—Research—Statistical methods. I. Bartos, Robert B. II. Title.

LB1027.5 .L26 2002
370'.7'2—dc21

To the students who used and critiqued the initial draft of this text, with special acknowledgment to my graduate assistant, Johanna Jones
R.L.

To the many hundreds of students who have helped me to understand the importance of research and statistics to the human services
R.B.

About the Authors

Rebecca LaFountain is a Professor in the Department of Counseling at Shippensburg University of Pennsylvania. She is a licensed psychologist, certified clinical mental health counselor, and certified school counselor. She brings her previous experiences as a school counselor, mental health counselor, and residence life professional into her teaching of research and statistics. She received her M. S. in counseling from Iowa State University and her Ed.D. in Counseling from the College of William and Mary. Her primary professional interests are in the areas of Adlerian psychology, solution-focused counseling, and making research and statistics enjoyable for students.

Robert B. Bartos is presently Dean of the College of Education and Human Services at Shippensburg University of Pennsylvania. He has had extensive experience both in teaching undergraduate and graduate coursework in the area of research and statistics and as an administrator in higher education for the past 17 years. He earned a M.Ed. in Administration and Supervision from University of Cincinnati and a D.Ed. in Educational Psychology from West Virginia University. He has published widely in the area of assessment and research methodologies with special interests in middle school research.

About the Contributors

Jan L. Arminio is an Assistant Professor in the Department of Counseling at Shippensburg University of Pennsylvania. Prior to her present position she served as a student affairs professional for 17 years in residence life, campus activities, multicultural student affairs, and judicial programs. She earned her M.A. in College Student Personnel from Bowling Green State University and her Ph.D. in College Student Personnel from the University of Maryland in College Park. Her scholarly writing focuses on multicultural justice in higher education.

Kurt L. Kraus, Ed.D., NCC, ACS, is an Assistant Professor in the Department of Counseling at Shippensburg University of Pennsylvania. In his current position he brings a wealth of varied counseling experience and prior university teaching. He received a M.Ed. in Counseling and an Ed.D. in Counselor Education and Supervision from University of Maine. His scholarship includes phenomenology, ethics, group work, and child and adolescent counseling.

Preface

We wrote this book to help you become statistically literate consumers of research, and to provide you with introductory skills in conducting statistical computation and research projects. We attempted to present a balance of theory and practical application by guiding you through the development of a research proposal, and by including sample quantitative and qualitative research proposals. Since some instructors prefer to emphasize program assessment and evaluation or grant writing, we included some guidelines for their development as well.

When writing this book, we specifically had students in the field of counseling and student affairs in mind. We wrote this book to be consistent with the standards of the Council for the Accreditation of Counseling and Related Educational Programs (CACREP) as well as preparation materials designed for national counseling exams. Additionally, we included practical examples applicable to the field of counseling and student affairs in a variety of settings such as schools, community mental health agencies, and universities.

Throughout the book, we encourage you to use technology in the research process, particularly as you survey the literature and perform statistical analyses. As we introduce new statistical procedures, however, we advocate that you first perform hand computations in order to increase your understanding of computer-generated statistics. You will find that we provide practice activities that guide you through these procedures.

To provide a quick overview of the book: Chapters 1–6 cover the research process while Chapters 7–10 emphasize statistics. Chapter 11 brings together both of these aspects in an activity that challenges your research and statistical literacy.

In Chapter 1 we help you understand the relevance of research and statistics to the fields of counseling and student affairs and emphasize the parallel between research and counseling. Additionally we present ethical standards from the profession as they relate to research. We encourage you to apply your research skills by designing either a research proposal, a program assessment and evaluation, or a grant proposal. In this chapter we provide an overview of each assignment and set the tone for accomplishing the project through the use of process goals.

Chapter 2 summarizes the various types of research and provides vignettes to clarify each. As in all chapters, we include practice activities that reinforce the concepts and guidelines for the development of the research proposal (and alternate projects). Additionally, in this chapter we introduce you to reviewing literature and we provide technological assistance in research.

Since systematic research begins with a question, selecting and formulating a research question is one of the most important aspects of doing research. Chapter 3 highlights the research question and provides practice activities that are designed to help you develop a good research question.

Central to Chapter 4 is a discussion of the hypothesis, which is a powerful tool in scientific inquiry. The practice activities guide you in the writing of strong hypotheses.

Chapter 5 addresses the issue of validity: whether what the researcher says is happening in a study is a result of the independent variable or some other factors not controlled for in the study. The practice activities and research proposal guidelines are designed to challenge you regarding the potential threats to the validity of your study.

An important issue in quantitative research is the process of sampling, discussed in Chapter 6. We provide a rationale for sampling and illustrate the various types. We also include an overview of research designs. Both the practice activities and research proposal guidelines involve the selection of sampling type and research design.

Descriptive statistics are covered in Chapters 7 and 8. We provide practice exercises for hand computation with each new concept and build up to more difficult problems at the end of the chapter. Additional problems for practice are available on the website. Please visit the Counseling Website at http://wadsworth.com/counseling_d and look under Student Resources for this text's webpage. This website contains a glossary of terms found in the text, sample problems and answers, InfoTrac keywords, and a list of statistical symbols found in the text.

Since, for the most part, you will be selecting instruments to measure the outcome of your studies, we present to you in Chapter 9 a theoretical understanding of reliability as well as formulas for estimating reliability.

In Chapter 10 you will learn how researchers use what they observe in samples and what is known about sampling error to reach fallible but reasonable decisions about populations. This process is called inferential statistics. Through practice exercises that are executed by hand and by computer, you will learn to compute and analyze t-tests and chi squares.

Critical to the research process is the accurate summatization and reporting of results. In Chapter 11, you will be exposed to reporting results. Additionally, you will have the opportunity to demonstrate your understanding of the research process and statistics by analyzing a research article.

We'd like to thank the following reviewers for their invaluable feedback: Kia J. Bentley, Virginia Commonwealth University; Steve Culver, Radford University; Joshua M. Gold, University of South Carolina; Mark S. Kiselica, The College of New Jersey; Vergel L. Lattimore, Methodist Theological School, Ohio; Diane McDermott, University of Kansas; Rachelle Perusse, State University of New York at Plattsburgh; and Annette Woodruffe, Wayne State University.

It was important to us to create a book that would diminish any undue anxiety about research and statistics and would bolster your interest in the subject. In order to do this, we attempted to present the material in a nonthreatening manner, with the occasional use of humor. Additionally, we tried to make the examples relevant to your profession. We hope we have met these objectives and that you will not only come to enjoy the subject, but find it meaningful in your work as well.

Rebecca LaFountain
Robert Bartos

Brief Contents

Contents

7   Descriptive Statistics: Describing Single Distributions   104

9   Reliability   149

1

The Research Process

Individuals are making exciting changes through the process of counseling! College students are benefiting greatly from university services! Counselors and student affairs professionals who have serendipitously discovered successful approaches will continue to use them. Unfortunately, others in their profession may never learn about these possibilities. Research and subsequent publication of the findings are the means to promote change and garner professional confidence and respect.

The knowledge you will gain about the research process in this book is twofold. First, as a consumer you will be able to make informed judgments about the worthiness of published studies. Second, as a researcher you will have a solid foundation from which to plan and carry out your studies. It is imperative that counselors and student affairs professionals conduct and publish only reputable research. Faulty conclusions based on substandard research will not only be harmful to the students and clients served but will also greatly diminish the credibility of the profession.

The skills you will learn in this research and statistics book are easily transferable to counseling. These same skills are applicable to the student affairs professional. For instance, students respond to the question, "What skills do you need in order to be an effective counselor?" by saying they need:

- a knowledge base
- competency in gathering information
- effective listening skills
- ability to establish rapport
- good observation skills (as they notice nonverbal communication)
- the ability to help students or clients state their problems
- proficiency in understanding what is going on
- knowledge of how to devise a plan for improvement
- skills in carrying out the plan
- effective communication skills
- organizational skills
- competency in evaluation
- a belief in the process
- a commitment to the process

Whether discussing possible majors with an undecided student, assessing a student program, or doing training for resident assistants, many of these same skills apply to student affairs professionals.

Later in the chapter we will examine some of the similarities between the research process and counseling and student affairs work. Before we discuss the parallel, however, we need to examine what the research process is.

The Research Process

We believe that the best way to understand the research process is through the development of a research proposal. We will introduce you to the research process with the goal in mind of guiding you through the creation of a proposal. So that you will not feel overwhelmed in writing the research proposal, be assured that we will assist you through the process. Some instructors may choose not to have students develop a research proposal, or they may decide that other activities are more appropriate for the goals of their courses or programs. Therefore, we have also provided goals at the end of each chapter to help students with the process of program assessment and evaluation or grant writing.

Research is defined as "the empirical, systematic investigation of the relationship between two or more variables" (Association for Advanced Training in Behavioral Sciences, 1996, p. 1). In order to better understand the research process, we will first examine the key concepts of empirical and systematic investigation found in this definition. Later in the chapter we will explore the meaning of variables.

Empirical Investigation

By **empirical investigation** we mean that the approach will be based on our practical sensory experiences (e.g., observation) as opposed to being a study based on theological or philosophical inquiry. For example, correlating the stress levels of parents with their specific philosophy of parenting would be an empirical or scientific inquiry, while examining philosophy on a theoretical level would not. Likewise, assessing the factors that contribute to college freshmen's retention would be considered an empirical study, while theorizing about the developmental issues that freshmen face would be a philosophical discussion.

Systematic Investigation

By **systematic investigation** we mean that research has several discreet characteristics that appear sequentially. These steps, taken together, constitute a particular approach to the discovery of truth, which we call research. Research begins with a *question* in the mind of the researcher (Bartos, 1992). You can probably think of some baffling behavior that compels you to ask the question why only some persons display certain behavior while others do not. For example, you might question why some people seem to easily overcome adversity while others are traumatized by it. By asking the right questions, researchers find both relevance and direction in their quest for knowledge.

The direction for the research is provided by a *plan.* Research is not haphazard searching for the knowledge you seek; rather, research entails a definite method with a planned direction and design. Research thus consists of an orderly procedural and logical plan based on the *statement of the problem.*

Successful research begins with a clear *statement of the problem.* Before you can begin, you must understand the problem and look at it objectively. You must see clearly what it is you are attempting to research. According to Leedy (1997), researchers focus every step of their research around the problem. They ask themselves constantly what they are doing and for what purpose. Researchers are aware that at the conclusion of their study they will analyze the data to discern what the data says regarding the resolution of the problem.

Research seeks direction through *appropriate hypotheses.* A **hypothesis** is a logical supposition, a reasonable guess that may give direction to the researchers' thinking with respect to the problem and thus aid in solving it.

Research deals with facts and their meaning. Once these steps are taken, we as researchers can begin to interpret the results with a degree of confidence. These interpretations will eventually lead to more questions, which will lead to further research.

It should be evident that the process of research is circular. It really is a never-ending process (Bartos, 1992). However, as the research process continues, many questions can be answered that may bring about a more logical way of accomplishing tasks, thus benefiting all concerned.

The Parallel Between the Research Process and Counseling and Student Affairs Work

Just as researchers approach the research process in a systematic way, as described above, counselors and student affairs professionals need a methodical plan for dealing with their clients, students, and programs. A solid knowledge base and organizational skills are essential.

Just as researchers begin their research with a *question* in mind, counselors and student affairs professionals organize their interventions around the question to be answered. For example, counselors may be aware of certain problems and subsequently ask: What is the relationship between the client's level of stress and her loss of all interest in her work? What skills are needed by the second grade boy in order to get along with his classmates? Student affairs professionals may ask these questions: Based on a student's interests and abilities, what is an appropriate choice as a major? What is the utilization rate of the new game rooms in the student union?

By asking the right questions and investigating available information, researchers focus their plan of study by clarifying it with a statement of the problem. Out of the statement of the problem the researcher develops a hypothesis, which provides direction to the research.

Likewise, counselors design their treatment *plan* after gathering background information related to their clients' presenting *problem.* In order to accomplish this, counselors need skills in listening effectively, establishing rapport, observing, and assisting clients in stating their difficulties. Student affairs professionals use these identical skills to help clarify problems, relating both to students and programs, in order to develop their *plan* for intervention. Let us suppose that after conducting an intake, a counselor verifies that the client's loss of interest in work is due to stress related to her inability to keep up with new technological demands on the job. If the counselor *hypothesizes* that the client's career interests are not matched with her aptitude, then the counselor may provide career counseling. On the other hand, if the counselor suspects that the client is generally anxious, the counselor will take a very different approach.

Similarly, student affairs professionals will choose the direction of their inquiries based on the *hypotheses* that they make. For example, if they want to assess the utilization rate of the new game rooms in the student union as a routine procedure, the approach will be much different than if they want to determine how specifics about the game room (e.g., the facilities, the hours, etc.) affect utilization rates following a period of little use.

The skills that researchers use to design methodology, carry out studies, and analyze and interpret data are very similar to those skills counselors and student personnel professionals use to devise plans, carry them out, and evaluate them. Just as research findings eventually lead to more questions and subsequently more research, counseling and student affairs work is ongoing. Through the process of research, counselors and student affairs professionals gain knowledge and discover new approaches to solving problems, thus benefiting society.

The Need to Conduct Research

The betterment of society is a very significant reason for conducting research. Noted psychologist Alfred Adler (1931/1992) considered that the true meaning of life depends on contributions through the generations. When speaking of our ancestors he stated that "The fruits of their experience of life are communicated to us in traditions, philosophies, the sciences and the arts, and in techniques for dealing with our human situation" (p. 21). He referred to this feeling of cooperation, this benefiting of society, as social interest.

Although research provides new information that advances knowledge and develops professional skills, unfortunately many of the discoveries counselors and student affairs professionals experience with their clients and students are not promoted beyond their offices. Herman (1993) found that few counselors used research in justifying their treatment approaches. This can be attributed to Willett and Singer's (1992) contention that most non-statistics majors see statistics as "a necessary evil." Many graduate students who take courses in research and statistics merely "go through the motions" but have little intention of retaining and utilizing their research and statistical skills in their professional endeavors.

A commitment to conducting more research would bolster the counseling and student affairs profession. According to VanZandt (cited in Herman, 1993), while the counseling profession attempts to garner public confidence and respect by associating its methods with scientific psychology, the large majority of counseling currently practiced is not scientifically based. Research is the avenue by which counselors and student affairs professionals can determine which interventions and programs are most effective, and which approaches and services should be discontinued. *— like Adler*

Many counselors and student affairs professionals prefer practice to research; they tend to identify with a practitioner role rather than with a research one. Actually the two activities complement each other. For example, a counselor who conducts research can immediately put the findings into practice.

We agree with Hadley and Mitchell (1995) that discovering new knowledge is exciting! It is rewarding to come up with a new idea, test it, and confirm its efficacy. They provide additional reasons why counselors conduct research, such as course requirements, grant funding, professional recognition, justification for administrative decisions, influence in legislation, and career advancement.

Variables

In revisiting our definition of **research,** "the empirical, systematic investigation of the relationship between two or more variables" (Association for Advanced Training in Behavioral Sciences, 1996, p. 1), we see that we have thoroughly examined what an empirical, systematic investigation is. We will now consider the concept of **variables.** We spoke earlier of the need to formulate a research question based on the problem (which will be discussed in more detail in Chapter 3). The characteristics or events that comprise the focus of study are the variables (the characteristics or events that are capable of existing in at least two different states or on at least two different levels). Type of teaching method would be a variable in a study that examines the teaching of two sections of a research and statistics course using different pedagogy (the traditional lecture-discussion method in one and an online computer approach in the other). If the course was offered using only one method of instruction, there would be no variation, and the teaching approach would be considered a **constant.**

In research we differentiate between **independent variables** and **dependent variables.** The independent variable is the variable that is thought to affect or change the dependent variable. The dependent variable (just as its name implies) appears to depend on the independent variable. In our example of the research and statistics course, the *type* of research and statistics course (traditional or online) is considered the independent variable. The independent variable is commonly termed the treatment or intervention variable. Suppose we use students' learning (as measured by final course grades) to ascertain which *type* of course is more effective. Student learning *depends* on the *type* of course; therefore, student learning (measured by final course grades) is the dependent variable.

A research study may have one or more independent variables. In the example above there is one independent variable, the *type* of research and statistics course. (A common mistake students make is to consider *each level* of an independent variable an independent variable; thus, in this case they would erroneously consider traditional method as one independent variable and online method as a second independent variable). A second independent variable in this example could be sex of the student (male or female). The dependent variable (student learning) is one dependent variable with many possible variations. An easy way to visualize each variable is to imagine a light switch. In this example the two independent variables are represented by two separate toggle (on-off) light switches. The dependent variable is represented by a dial light switch (such as a dimmer switch) that has variable settings.

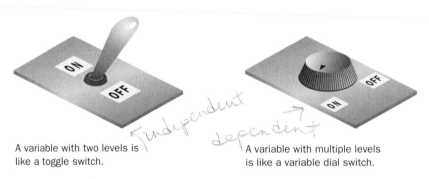

A variable with two levels is like a toggle switch.

A variable with multiple levels is like a variable dial switch.

Figure 1.1 Levels of a Variable

An easy way to identify the independent and dependent variables is to fill in the blanks using one of the following questions:

Question One:
    "What is the effect of *the independent variable* on *the dependent variable*?"
Using the above example we would ask,
    "What is the effect of *the type of course* on *the students' learning*?"

Question Two:
> "What is the relationship between *the independent variable* and *the dependent variable?*"

Using the above example we would ask,
> "What is the relationship between *the type of course* and *the students' learning?*"

In this discussion we introduced you to the concept of variables, specifically independent and dependent variables. In Chapter 3 we will examine additional variables that may affect the results of a study. Below is an activity to help you identify independent and dependent variables.

A   C   T   I   V   I   T   Y

Identifying Independent and Dependent Variables

1.1

Please read the descriptions of the following three studies. In each of the descriptions please identify the independent and dependent variable(s).
The answers are found in Appendix F.

Study #1/Intensive Study Skills
Program for High-school Seniors
At Risk for Failure

A school counselor has designed an intensive study skills program for seniors in high school who were at risk for failure to graduate. The intensive study skills program included small group counseling, small group instruction in study skills, and personal tutoring. The school counselor predicts that involvement in the intensive study skills program will improve the graduation rate of at-risk seniors. She plans to test her hypothesis by comparing the graduation rate of at-risk seniors who participate in the intensive study skills program with those at-risk seniors who do not participate in the program.

Independent Variable(s): *partic. in st. sk. prog.*
Dependent Variable(s): *grad. rate (of those who part. vs those who don't)*

Study #2/Play Therapy
Approaches for Encopresis

A mental health therapist wants to assess the effectiveness of four approaches to play therapy (Child-centered, Adlerian, Psychodynamic, and Behavioral) on encopresis (soiling) in latency age children. Specifically, the therapist wants to measure the rate of occurrence as well as the children's level of responsibility for cleanup on a continuum from high (where the child cleans self and clothing) to low (where the child attempts to hide evidence of the soiling).

Independent Variable(s): *type of play therapy used*
Dependent Variable(s):

rate of occurrence of encopresis
level of respon. for clean-up of self, clothing

continues

continued

Study #3/Committed Resident
Assistants

A director of residential living on a large university campus is concerned about the large turnover rate in resident assistants. In recent years many resident assistants have left their positions before completing even 1 year in their assignments. The director wants to identify factors that predict commitment as a resident assistant (defined as continuing in the position a minimum of 2 years). The director decides to assess knowledge of the position, attitude toward residential policies, and ability to handle conflicts as predictors for commitment to the position.

Independent Variable(s): *knowledge . . . , attit . . . , abil . . .*

Dependent Variable(s): *commit. as r.a.*

Defining and Demystifying Statistics

Since this is a book for a course in research and statistics, let us take a moment to discuss statistics. Many students shudder at the idea of statistics. However, there is a 75% chance that you have heard or spouted a statistic in your casual conversation today. Examples might include discussion about: sports (e.g., a .500 batting average), weather (e.g., 30% chance of rain), or polls (e.g., 22% of Americans [with a margin of error of plus or minus 3%] approve of the president's decision).

Individuals regularly use statistics in their work. Examples of everyday uses of statistics include a teacher computing class averages, a mental health counselor providing required reports, and an admissions counselor preparing a demographic report about the freshman class. A **statistic,** then, is merely a numerical summary about a group of observations. In later chapters we will introduce you to statistics and **statistical procedures.**

Some Ethical Considerations

The matter of ethics is important for researchers in counseling and student affairs. Because their subject of study is primarily human beings, often children, the nature of such research may embarrass, hurt, frighten, impose on, or otherwise negatively affect the lives of the people who are making the research possible by their participation. To deal with this problem, organizations such as the American Counseling Association, the American College Personnel Association, and the National Association of Student Personnel Administrators have developed codes of ethics for research with human subjects (see Appendix D). Also, most universities and institutions have established human subjects committees or institutional review boards who have developed screening procedures based on ethical grounds for evaluating a researcher's proposal to conduct a study. These procedures usually include the review of all consent forms and instruments to be used. In addition, federal law has established requirements concerning the accessibility and inaccessibility of personal information.

Of course it is possible to ask, "Why do research at all if even one person might be compromised?" However, the human services researcher must begin by asserting, and accepting the assertion, that research has substantially contributed to the body of scientific knowledge and all the human and technological advances that have been made based on this knowledge. Thus, research has the potential to help people improve their lives and themselves and, therefore, must remain an integral part of human endeavor. Accepting the assertion that research has value in contributing to knowledge and, ultimately to human betterment, one still must ask: "What ethical considerations *must* the researcher take into account in designing experiments in order not to violate human rights?" The specific ethical research and evaluation guidelines produced by the American Counseling Association, the American College Personnel Association, and the National Association of Student Personnel Administrators are found in Appendix D. Many authors such as Heppner, Kivilighan, and Wampold (1999) focus on the researcher's role in two areas: ethical issues related to participants and ethical issues related to professionalism. Some general considerations related to participants are outlined below.

Informed Consent

Informed consent refers to giving individuals the opportunity to choose whether or not to participate in research. *Voluntarism*, a crucial aspect of informed consent, refers to an individual's ability to decide whether or not to participate without any explicit or implicit coercion or pressure. A common example of coercion occurs when students are expected to participate in a study because of their enrollment in class. In situations where professors offer students bonus credits for involvement in a study, they must offer alternative activities and assignments to students who do not wish to participate in the study but who wish to earn additional points. Researchers must make it clear to individuals who agree to participate in their study that they have the right to withdraw at any time. It must be determined that the individual has the capacity to make an informed decision about their participation. *Capacity* includes one's legal age and the mental ability to process the information needed in deciding to participate. Additionally, researchers must provide potential subjects all relevant information about a study, including risks and benefits, so that they can make an informed decision (Heppner et al., 1999).

Debriefing

While the process of informed consent occurs prior to the study, **debriefing** takes place at the conclusion of the study (Wilkinson & McNeil, 1996). Debriefing includes informing participants of any information that was withheld from them prior to the study (considered as acts of omission) or correcting any false or misleading information that was introduced (referred to as acts of commission) to deceive participants. Deception is a controversial issue in research. However, in situations where deception is justified, the researcher has the responsibility to provide a rationale for it (Wilkinson & McNeil) and to debrief the participants as soon as possible.

The Right to Privacy

The **right to privacy,** in general, refers to the right of participants in a study to keep from the public certain information about themselves. For example, many people would regard questions that ask about religious convictions or personal feelings about parents as an invasion of privacy. To safeguard the privacy of the subjects, the researcher should take care to avoid asking unnecessary questions and those questions customarily regarded as private (Bartos, 1992).

The Right to Remain Anonymous

All participants in human research have the **right to remain anonymous,** that is, the right to insist that their individual identities not be a salient feature of the research. To insure anonymity, two approaches are often used. First, researchers are usually interested in group data rather than individual data; thus scores obtained from individuals in a study are pooled or grouped together and reported as averages. Since an individual's scores cannot be identified, such a reporting process provides each participant with anonymity. Second, wherever possible, subjects are identified by number rather than by name.

Before starting the testing in quantitative research, the researcher should explain to the subjects that they have not been singled out as individuals for study, but rather, that they have been randomly selected in an attempt to study the population of which they are representatives. Thus, they need not fear that the researcher would have any reason to compromise their right to anonymity (Bartos, 1992).

The Right to Confidentiality

Similar to the concerns over privacy and anonymity is the concern over **confidentiality**: Who will have access to the data? In school, agency, and university settings, students and clients, as well as counselors and student affairs professionals, are concerned with others having access to research data and using them to make judgments about character or performance. Certainly participants have every right to insist that data collected from them be treated with confidentiality. To guarantee this, the researcher should: (a) roster all data or code all interviews by number rather than by name; (b) destroy the original test protocols or interview tapes as soon as the study is completed; and (c) whenever possible in survey research, provide participants with stamped, self-addressed envelopes to return questionnaires directly to the researcher (rather than to their counselor, professor, resident assistant, etc.).

The Right to Expect Experimenter Responsibility   *cause no harm*

Finally, every participant in a study has the right to expect that the researcher is sensitive to human dignity and well-meaning in his or her intentions. Researchers should reassure potential participants, particularly assuring them that they will not be "hurt" by their participation (Bartos, 1992).

Research Proposal

As discussed earlier, we believe that the best way to understand the research process is by developing a research proposal, the plan that was discussed earlier in the chapter. The proposal will provide you with a definite plan that offers direction and the methodology for carrying out a proposed study. (A sample proposal is found in Appendix B.) We will help you make this a more manageable process by providing you specific suggestions at the end of each chapter in order to help you develop goals (specifically process goals, discussed later in the chapter) for developing the research proposal.

Alternate Activities

Some instructors may choose not to have students develop a research proposal, or they may decide that other activities are more appropriate for the goals of their courses or programs. With this in mind we have also provided process goals at the end of each chapter to guide students in the process of program assessment and evaluation or grant writing. Although professionals draw upon research and statistical knowledge in order to conduct program assessment and evaluation and to prepare grant proposals, an in-depth discussion of these activities are beyond the scope of this book. A brief overview of program assessment and evaluation and grant writing follows.

Program Assessment and Evaluation

More than ever before, human services professionals are expected to assess and evaluate the programs in which they work. This trend is the result of an increase in the importance placed on accountability and greater competition for grants and governmental funding. Although some authors vary in their use of the terms assessment and evaluation, Upcraft and Schuh (1996) define and link the two. They define **assessment** as "any effort to gather, analyze, and interpret evidence which describes institutional, departmental, divisional or agency effectiveness" (p. 18). They define **evaluation** as "any effort to use assessment evidence to improve institutional, departmental, divisional, or agency effectiveness" (p. 19). This process may take place in one or more of the following: the planning of new program, the implementation of a new program, or the evaluation of an existing program.

From our discussion so far on research, the commonalties between research and program assessment and evaluation are quite evident. In fact, Hadley and Mitchell (1995) define program evaluation "as a form of applied research distinguished by its relationship to a service program" (p. 62). They state that a **service program** is a set of service activities that can range in any size from a national organization to one individual's work with one client or student.

Let us consider an example involving a mental health agency that has increased the number and types of counseling groups offered during the past 12 months in an effort to serve more clients. Assessment would include the documentation of the number of clients served during the 12-month period and a comparison of those numbers with data from the previous year. Evaluation would involve using the assessment in order to determine whether to continue, modify, or eliminate the group offerings.

In the area of student affairs, an example of an assessment might involve tracking the participation of students in activities sponsored by the Office of International Student Services. Using the assessment as the basis for revamping services is an example of evelution.

According to Hadley and Mitchell, the same skills and techniques needed to carry out all research are also necessary for program assessment and evaluation. Additional skills, specific to program assessment and evaluation, are also needed. We will briefly discuss these skills, where applicable, throughout the book.

Grant Writing

In times when demands for educational and human services programs are increasing and resources dwindling, grants are an option that counseling and student affairs professional should not take for granted (pun intended)! **Grants,** for the most part, provide the resources to institutions and organizations for the purpose of providing the services described in the grant proposal. According to Lauffer (1983), **resources** are the means and commodities needed to achieve an objective or provide a service (such as money, personnel, facilities, and equipment). Usually the purpose of a grant request is to either maintain or augment existing programs.

Many grants seem to represent social interests and are outgrowths of political action designed to address societal concerns (Rowh, 1992). For example, let us assume that Congress reacts to a rash of school shootings by making federal funds available to school districts who wish to implement violence prevention programs. After Congress passes the law, they will authorize the funds, write guidelines for the grant applications, and announce the grant competition.

The operative word is competition. In most cases the grant process is just that! The funding agency selects those proposals that most convincingly build a case that a need exists and demonstrate the ability to implement the plan.

According to Rowh (1992), in order to succeed in developing a persuasive proposal, authors need to understand what constitutes an impressive proposal and then demonstrate their knowledge through their proposal writing. Although proposal guidelines vary, the basic elements are the same. They include such components as need and problem, goals and objectives, methodology, and evaluation strategy. These elements closely parallel the parts of both the research proposal and the program assessment and evaluation Again, the skills required to develop and implement a grant proposal are the same as those needed for the previously described research. In the concise grant proposal section of each chapter, additional techniques specific to grant writing will be included.

Process Goals

Several times throughout the chapter we have mentioned that we would guide you through the development of your proposal by providing **process goals** at the end of each chapter. A process goal is terminology derived from solution-focused therapy, a type of brief therapy. A process goal differs from an end goal, the type for which most people normally strive. Usually when people talk about goals they are talking about the end result. Process goals, on the other hand, focus on what needs to be done in order to achieve that end result. For example, if Jack sets an end goal to lose 20 pounds between the first of January and spring break, he will measure his progress by whether or not he lost all 20 pounds by spring break. If instead he sets a process goal, he might say, "Each day I will exercise 30 minutes and limit my fat intake to 20 grams." *process goal* Each day Jack can experience success in the process by exercising and watching his fat grams as he has proposed. Process goals, then, are well-defined goals based on the following criteria: (a) presented in the positive about what the individual will do, instead of what the individual will not do (e.g., "I will limit myself to one snack a day" instead of "I won't eat junk food"), (b) presented in process form about what the individual will be doing instead of as an end goal (e.g., "I will limit myself to one snack a day" instead of "I will lose 10 pounds"), (c) stated in the here and now, (d) stated in specific terms, (e) designed within the individual's control, and (f) stated in the individual's language (Walter & Peller, 1992).

As you can see, process goals can help make an overwhelming task more manageable. Beginning with Chapter 2, each chapter will end with a process goal activity, which will help you progress in your writing of a research proposal, a program assessment and evaluation, or a grant proposal.

A C T I V I T Y

Scaling

1.2

Scaling is another technique derived from solution-focused therapy. It is a time-effective way to assess one's feelings or position about something. It is a behavioral strategy, which allows someone to become less vague and more specific. With this in mind, we would like to ask you a scaling question: On a scale of one to five, how are you feeling about being in this Research and Statistics class? Mark your answer:

1	2	3	4	5
Very anxious	Anxious	So-so	Relaxed	Very relaxed

We hope that now that you have had an introduction to research and statistics that you are looking forward to pursuing the topic in more detail. Often at the very beginning of a research and statistics course we ask students to respond anonymously on an index card to a more open ended question, "When I think of taking this course, I feel _____." We then read the responses out loud. (This is an adaptation of an activity, "Statisticophobia," done by Kathleen Dillon [1982] at Western New England College.) We do this activity in an effort to normalize the feelings that students may be experiencing and to clarify any misconceptions they have about the course. Students who are feeling some anxiety are usually relieved to learn that others in the class are experiencing the same emotions that they are. Research and statistics seems to be the subject that graduate students in human services approach with the most anxiety and least interest. According to Knowles (1974), students often perceive statistics as the most difficult and most feared aspect of their program. It is our hope that you now have a better understanding of the importance of conducting research in the areas of counseling and student affairs. We want to reassure you also that we wrote this book for counseling and student affairs students who have little or no research and statistics in their backgrounds. The exercises and activities are designed to teach basic skills to beginning students and to serve as a refresher for more advanced students.

Summary

In this chapter we attempted to excite you about the process of research and statistics by helping you understand the relevance of research and statistics to the fields of counseling and student affairs and by discussing how statistics are used on an everyday basis. We emphasized the parallel between research and statistics and your fields of study. Hopefully, you have gained respect for the need to conduct research as well as an understanding of the research process, independent and dependent variables, and ethical considerations. We introduced you to process goals, which will guide you through the writing of either a research proposal, a program assessment and evaluation, or a grant proposal.

Key Terms

assessment	hypothesis	scaling
capacity	independent variable	service program
confidentiality	informed consent	statistic
constant	process goal	statistical procedure
debriefing	research	systematic investigation
dependent variable	resource	variable
empirical investigation	right to privacy	voluntarism
evaluation	right to remain	
grant	anonymous	

2

Research Approaches and the Literature Review

There are numerous approaches to research. Each method in its own way is advantageous for gathering specific types of information. This chapter summarizes the various types of research and provides practical examples for each type. In addition, this chapter introduces the methodology and resources for selecting a topic to research in counseling and student affairs, beginning with the literature review. The design for any research begins with an idea, a question, or a topic. These come from a variety of experiences the researcher may have had. The topic may evolve first as a question, then as an idea as to how it might be answered, and finally as a topic of discussion that collectively demands additional action. This process leads to the development of a model. These schemata, in the human sciences help develop our understanding of the phenomena surrounding our thoughts and actions. They will also individually and collectively advance our understanding about the social world and how we can best conduct research through legitimate problems and subsequent "proofs." These schemata encompass theory and method. You have had experiences with these designs in your academic fields. They have been discussed widely in the literature. They have been debated as to their appropriateness. They are quantitative and qualitative models.

Types of Research

Under each of these fundamental types of research are various approaches for conducting studies. Since the number of approaches are too numerous to cover in any one chapter, we chose to illustrate those types included in an adapted model by Crowl (1993), as shown in Figure 2.1.

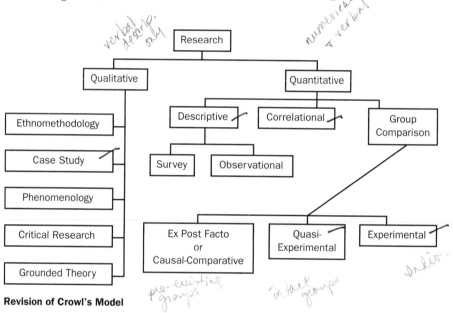

Revision of Crowl's Model

Figure 2.1 Major Types of Educational Research. *Source:* From *Fundamentals of Educational Research,* Third Edition, by T. K. Crowl, p.6. Copyright ©1997 The McGraw-Hill Companies. Reprinted with permission of The McGraw-Hill Companies.

Crowl (1993) differentiates the quantitative and qualitative models by saying that in **quantitative** research "findings are reported in numerical form as well as in terms of verbal description" (p.413), while in **qualitative** studies findings are reported only in terms of verbal description. In the descriptions below, the differences are readily apparent.

Quantitative Research

Quantitative research is generally characterized by the **statistical** testing of hypotheses. The primary purpose of quantitative research is to test hypotheses in order to answer research questions. In these studies statistical methods are used to examine relationships between the independent and dependent variables stated in the hypotheses.

We will examine the quantitative types of research from the perspective of a student who is in the process of reviewing the literature in an attempt to come up with a topic to explore. Our purpose is twofold: (a) to present an overview of various types of quantitative studies, and (b) to provide an example of how someone might approach the selection of a topic.

Greg is in his first semester of study in a graduate program of counseling. He came into the program thinking he would like to be a school counselor. However, in another course, Introduction to the Helping Services, he is exploring the various concentrations that the counseling department offers. He finds that he is confused about his original choice since he is gaining interest in mental health counseling and student affairs work as well. He uses the opportunity of reviewing literature for his research and statistics class to further acquaint himself with the kind of work being done in all three areas since he knows that after he completes his core courses he will need to declare his area of specialization.

As he begins to review the literature, he remembers that his professor pointed out that they will need to take some existing research in the literature and attempt to add to it through their own proposed study. Essentially, one of the purposes of their literature review is to look for a "missing link." Because attention deficit/ hyperactive disorder (AD/HD) has always interested Greg since his younger brother was diagnosed AD/HD in elementary school, Greg decides to focus his review on that topic. Greg begins his literature review by conducting a search on the electronic databases. He inputs the following descriptors: attention deficit/hyperactivity disorder and school, attention deficit/hyperactivity disorder and mental health, and attention deficit/hyperactivity disorder and college. He gets numerous "hits" as a result of each entry. This exhilarates him because while exploring his topic of interest he will be able to explore school counseling, mental health counseling, and student affairs.

Initially, he finds the task of reading the countless articles overwhelming. He realizes that many studies have been done on medication versus no medication, various treatments, dietary influences, and teaching approaches, among other topics. It is quite clear that the majority of the research has focused on children. He becomes frustrated because initially nothing ignites an idea in him.

After much more review Greg comes across an article in a student personnel journal that grabs his attention. The author wrote that on college campuses there seems to be an increase in the number of students having interpersonal problems. Two of the examples mentioned were an increase in roommate problems in the residence halls and students having difficulty in their work-study positions because of inappropriate interpersonal skills (rather than inability to do the job). Greg begins to wonder if students with AD/HD are among the group of students having problems. He remembers reading that one of the arguments for medicating children with AD/HD is that the medication usually makes children more available for learning social skills and helps them control their impulsivity (e.g., cutting in lines, blurting out words). Thinking about this, Greg is reminded of a number of his classmates (primarily boys) in elementary school who used to go to the nurse's office at lunchtime for their medication. He is not surprised when he notes in the literature that the use of medication escalated during the period of time that he was in elementary school. He begins to wonder how some of these former classmates fared in college and in their social lives. He decides that he would like to somehow explore the present social skills level of adults who were diagnosed AD/HD as children.

Since Greg enjoys working with numbers, he decides to examine the right side of Crowl's diagram first as he attempts to formulate his study. He is relieved that for the purpose of his course he only has to write a research proposal but does not have to actually carry it out.

Descriptive Research. **Descriptive research** is research that describes the distribution of a variable throughout a population. As mentioned in Chapter 1 variables are characteristics that take on different values and are the focus of a study. In Greg's case he wants to measure the social skills of adults who were identified with AD/HD as children. Descriptive research includes **surveys** and **observational approaches.**

Survey Research. **Survey research** is a distinctive research methodology that owes much of its recent development to the field of sociology. When considered as a method of systematic data collection, though, surveys have a long historical tradition. As far back as the time of the ancient Egyptians, population counts and surveys of crop production have been conducted for various purposes, including taxation. The contribution of twentieth-century sociologists such as Lazarsfeld, Hyman, and Stouffer was to link instruments of data collection (e.g., questionnaires and interviews) to logic and to statistical procedures for analyzing these kinds of data (Bartos, 1992).

If you are to perform a research project for completion of an advanced degree, you might consider employing the survey approach to investigate a particular counseling or student affairs problem. However, you should be aware that surveys involve considerably more than administering a questionnaire to describe "what is." It is unfortunate but true that many researchers in the field hold surveys in low esteem because they believe that surveys are limited to description. In fact, survey research utilizes a variety of instruments and methods to study relationships, effects of treatments, longitudinal changes, and comparisons between groups.

There are three basic kinds of surveys (Association for Advanced Training in Behavioral Sciences, 1996). **Cross-sectional surveys** permit researchers to examine the distribution of a variable of various segments of the population at *a given point in time*. **Longitudinal surveys** examine possible changes in the distribution of a variable *at several different points in time*. Lewis Terman's classic study of children with exceptionally high IQs (Terman, 1925) is a well-known longitudinal study. He followed the individuals from their elementary school years into adulthood. While cross-sectional studies are easier to conduct, they are prone to **cohort (or generation) effects.** Cohort effects occur due to subjects' differences in factors such as experience rather than increasing age. For example, if findings from a cross-sectional study show that elderly subjects' reflex rate (as measured by clicking the computer mouse every time a designated symbol appears on the computer screen) is slower than that of young adults, the slower response rate of elderly subjects may actually be due to their inexperience with computers rather than their age. **Cross-sequential (cohort sequential) studies** can overcome the problems that arise with cross-sectional and longitudinal studies. Cross-sequential studies combine methodologies from both cross-sectional and longitudinal studies by assessing subjects of two or more age groups at two or more different times.

Suppose Greg wants to carry out a cross-sectional survey to determine the level of social skills of individuals who were identified with AD/HD as children and subsequently took medication. At one given point in time, Greg could select individuals who were diagnosed AD/HD as children and are currently at specific ages (e.g., 10, 15, 20, 25). He could proceed to measure their present level of social skills.

If Greg is interested in determining how social skills of individuals diagnosed with AD/HD have changed over time, he could carry out a longitudinal survey by measuring the social skills of individuals in 2005, and 2010, 2015, and 2020. If the same individuals are not available for the assessment, some will contend that a representative group could be measured at each point in time.

Greg could make this a cross-sequential study by measuring a group of adolescents and a group of adults in their late twenties (all having been diagnosed with AD/HD as children) in the year 2005 and then again in the year 2015. This procedure will help researchers detect cohort effects, will require less time, and will reduce the generalizability problem.

Observational research is the act of gathering data on which to base research conclusions. An observation is the result of the process of observing. In many cases, direct observation may be the preferred method of measurement rather than paper-and-pencil tests or questionnaires. If Greg is interested in assessing social skills ability in adults who were diagnosed with AD/HD as children, he is likely to acquire more valid information by observing these individuals in social situations than by asking them to describe their level of social skills. While actual observation by a trained rater is likely to be more objective than self-reporting, the opportunity for Greg to observe spontaneous social situations may not exist. Greg could arrange contrived observation periods, but, again, the logistics would be quite challenging.

Correlational Studies. In **correlational studies** researchers investigate the extent to which variations in one factor correspond with variations in one or more other factors, using correlation coefficients. More specifically, researchers determine within a population the degree to which one distribution of values associated with a variable is related to a second distribution of values associated with another variable for the same population. Most correlational studies focus on **continuous variables.** A continuous variable is measured quantitatively and can hypothetically take on an infinite number of values. Let us suppose Greg wants to determine among the adults who were diagnosed with AD/HD the extent of their social skills in relationship to the amount of time (measured in years) that the individuals took medication. Social skills would be considered a continuous variable when measured by a test or instrument. (Test scores are typically considered continuous data.) Similarly time is a continuous variable. Therefore, determining the relationship between the level of social skills and length of time the subjects took medication is an example of a correlational study.

Group Comparison Studies. Group comparison studies include experimental, quasi-experimental, and ex post facto or causal-comparative. While correlational studies explore the association among two or more variables within a single group of people, group comparison studies are concerned with the comparison of two or more groups with respect to one or more variables.

In group comparison studies the investigation involves two or more groups that differ on at least one variable. An example would be if Greg decides to compare the social skills level of adults who have been identified as having AD/HD as children and subsequently took medication with adults who have been identified as having AD/HD as children who did not take medication. In Greg's study the level of social skills is the variable being studied. The two groups are mutually exclusive. The adult has either taken or not taken medication as a child.

According to Crowl (1993), group comparison studies are classified into three types: (a) ex post facto, or causal-comparative; (b) experimental; and (c) quasi-experimental. The way in which the group is formed determines the type of group comparison.

The **causal-comparative method** is aimed at the discovery of possible causes for variations found in a variable of interest, among two groups. For example it is useful for uncovering the causes for a behavioral pattern by comparing subjects who possess this pattern with similar subjects who present this pattern to a lesser degree or not at all. This method is sometimes called **ex post facto research** since causes are studied after they have presumably exerted their effect on another variable. In other words, the study is carried out after the fact (the Latin for this is *ex post facto*). In a causal-comparative study, researchers investigate preexisting groups.

A classic example of the causal-comparative method is the research on juvenile delinquency by Sheldo and Eleanor Glueck (1957). They located subjects who were and were not juvenile delinquents, as defined in that era. Characteristics that were present more frequently among the delinquent subjects than among the nondelinquent subjects were examined as possible causes of juvenile delinquency.

The causal-comparative method is often used instead of the experimental method because many of the cause-and-effect relationships that we wish to study in counseling and student affairs do not permit experimental manipulation. For example, Greg can only identify whether or not the adults took medication after being diagnosed with AD/HD; he cannot apply a selection process.

According to Crowl (1993), the major characteristic that distinguishes an experiment from an ex post facto study is that researchers are able to establish groups to be investigated rather than using already established groups. Researchers first identify the population from which they are going to select individuals to participate in the experiment and then they form two or more groups through **random assignment.** This process involves randomly assigning each person to one group or another until all of the participants have been placed. Another difference between experiments and ex post facto studies is that experiments use control groups.

The purpose of **true experimental design** is to investigate cause-and-effect relationships by exposing one or more randomized experimental groups to one or more treatment conditions and comparing the results to one or more randomized control groups not receiving the treatment.

Greg's proposed ex post facto study that compared adults who were diagnosed with AD/HD as children and received medication with adults who were diagnosed with AD/HD as children and received no medication could theoretically be changed into an experiment, but not very practically. Greg would have to have been around when the current adults were children, and he would have had to use the process of individual random assignment to place students diagnosed with AD/HD into one of two groups. One group of students would have been given medication, while the other group would not have received medication. After a given amount of time had elapsed, Greg would have measured the social skills level of each child. The formation of groups by random assignment and the use of control groups, therefore, are characteristic of true experiments.

> Greg decides to consider this scenario further since his professor has encouraged the students to write their research proposal using a true experimental or quasi-experimental design. His professor said that this is not to indicate that the other examples of studies are not legitimate research; however, experimental or quasi-experimental design requires students to demonstrate the widest range of research concepts (e.g., sampling, randomization, etc.) in the quantitative area. Since the above scenario is not practical, Greg returns to the literature to gain additional information so that he can formulate an experimental design. In his reading he discovers that more and more individuals with AD/HD who went undiagnosed AD/HD as children are being identified in adulthood. He wonders what percentage of students he read about as having interpersonal problems in college meet the criteria for AD/HD but went undiagnosed as children. He decides that, for his population, he prefers to work with young AD/HD adults, first identified in college, who are experiencing interpersonal problems. He decides that, for the purposes of his study, he would like to offer some kind of training focused on the acquisition of social skills (instead of the medication he was previously considering) as the treatment.

A C T I V I T Y

Experimental Design

2.1

Based on the new way that Greg conceptualizes his research, how will he go about setting up an experiment? (Do not be concerned at this time about how Greg will find subjects. This will be covered in a discussion on sampling in Chapter 6.)

Quasi-experiments differ from true experiments in that researchers form the groups to be studied by randomly assigning intact groups rather than individual persons. **Intact groups** are groups that are already formed prior to the researchers' involvement or in situations where individual randomization is not feasible or ethical. In quasi-experimental research "the comparison involves **nonequivalent groups** that differ from each other in many ways other than the presence of a treatment whose effects are being tested" (Barlow,

Haynes, & Nelson, 1984, p. 51). For example, if a researcher were to wait until August to approach the director of residential life at a university to request permission to do a study involving random assignment, it would not be feasible at such a late date. The request may be more reasonable if made in the spring. Likewise, a request to conduct a project requiring random assignment in a high school would need to be done well in advance of the school year.

Greg would need to use the quasi-experimental design if students were already grouped in some manner prior to his involvement. Let us suppose the following scenario:

> Greg finds out that the campus counseling center at his large university held a program "Dispelling Myths of AD/HD," which attracted numerous students, who thought they might have AD/HD. As a result of learning that it is a myth that AD/HD goes away at adolescence, many of the attendees made appointments for further assessment and assistance. Out of the 24 students who were diagnosed with AD/HD, 20 of the students indicated interest in attending an educational group focused on social skills. The group is to be co-led by a college counselor and the assistant dean of student affairs. Of the 20 students who signed up, 10 preferred a morning group, while 10 favored an evening group. Greg discusses his proposed study with the counseling center director. After the director weighs the risks and benefits of involving half of the students in a group during fall semester and the remaining students in a group during the spring semester, the director grants permission. Greg flips a coin, and it is decided that those who signed up for a morning session will be the experimental group while those preferring the evening group will be the control group during fall semester.

In the above scenario, decisions had to be made in an effort to compromise neither ethics nor research design. These issues will be addressed further in Chapter 5 in a discussion on threats to validity. In Greg's quasi-experimental study, then, half of the students will receive the educational group, while the remaining students will receive no training during fall semester, as a result of the random assignment of groups of students. After a specific amount of time elapses, Greg will measure the social skills level of the students (both those students who receive the educational group and those students who do not).

The following chart from Crowl (1993, p. 15) summarizes how each type of group is formed.

Type of Study	Method of Forming Groups
Ex Post Facto	Groups Already Formed
Experiment	Random Assignment of Individuals
Quasi-Experiment	Random Assignment of Intact Groups

Figure 2.2 Method of Forming Groups. *Source:* From *Fundamentals of Educational Research,* Third Edition, by T. K. Crowl, p. 15. Copyright ©1997 The McGraw-Hill Companies. Reprinted with permission of The McGraw Hill Companies.

Format for Quantitative Studies

Below is an outline of the format for quantitative studies. A sample research proposal following this outline is found in Appendix B.

Introduction and the Problem and Procedures

Research question, hypotheses, identification of variables

Significance of the problem

Definitions

Assumptions, limitations

Review of the Literature

Methodology

Population, sampling

Measurement devices

Data collection methods

Statistical methods

Research design and procedures

Time scheduling

Reporting and analysis of the data

Tables and figures

Level of significance

Research findings

Summary, Interpretations, Conclusions, and Implications

Statement of the problem

Procedures

Findings and interpretations

Conclusions

Implications

Recommendations

Qualitative research

Jan L. Arminio and Kurt L. Kraus, Contributing Authors

This text teaches you how to conduct research using quantitative approaches. The purpose of this section, however, is to whet your appetite for conducting qualitative research. The remainder of this section introduces key terms and concepts of qualitative research. The broad title "qualitative research" reflects a very different way of exploring issues of interest. It is a process of inquiry. The specific process depends upon the qualitative methodology you select as a roadmap for the exploration. There are a number of methodologies that you may select, depending on the nature of what is to be explored. We describe some of these approaches below and offer sources and examples for each. In Appendix C we provide a sample qualitative research proposal.

Broadly speaking, qualitative research explores a phenomenon by using words as data. Contrary to the popular notion that research designs fall into the two broad exclusive categories of quantitative and qualitative methods, Coomer and Hultgren (1989) wrote that approaches to inquiry actually fall into three modes: empirical/analytical, interpretive, and critical. Through statistical analysis, empirical/analytical modes measure what is observable for the purpose of explanation, prediction, and control. Interpretive approaches explore purpose, motives, intentions, and truths through the shared understanding of communication and/or observation to better understand or make the meaning of complex phenomena clear. Critical approaches through discourse expose social contradictions and social injustices and thus seek to enlighten and emancipate. It is important that researchers discern the philosophical foundation of the approach they are choosing and ensure that the approach is appropriate for what is being explored.

There are many philosophical differences among research approaches. Two important distinctions include the role of researchers in relation to the participants and the philosophical view of the nature of reality. In empirical/analytical designs, researchers are to remain objective observers. In interpretive methods, researchers do not claim objectivity; in fact, many interpretive researchers believe that no researcher can remain truly objective. In this regard, researchers explore a phenomenon in which they are passionate and disclose their current assumptions about the phenomenon before the inquiry begins. Researchers then serve as interpreters of the data (text). Researchers not only explore what is obvious but, more importantly, expose that which is not obvious. Unlike empirical/analytical researchers, who believe that reality is "out there" to be observed, then measured, and counted, interpretive researchers believe that reality is veiled. The role of interpretive researchers is to go beyond the veil and lay open what is not yet discovered. The "knower" is not detached from the known.

In critical research, researchers work with participants to solve a social injustice. Clearly, researchers cannot be objective observers here! Researchers work with participants to: expose an injustice, become knowledgeable on how that injustice came to exist, reflect on the influence of the injustice on the self, and collaborate with participants to redress the injustice. The notion that self-reflection and morally responsive action liberates people is paramount to this approach.

Another important philosophical foundation of interpretive and critical research methods is that the results cannot be universally generalized. The results are not probable (as in empirical/analytical methods) but are possible. Interpretive and critical research depart from the notion that there is "knowledge as representatives" (Darroch & Silvers, 1982, p. 5). Rather, researchers share reflections in common. They "distinguish between the truth of what people say and the fact that they have said something" (Brown, 1989, p. 260). Universal truth is not assumed. "We can never speak on behalf of another…we can only account for how we are speaking for that other" (Darroch & Silvers, p. 4). Consequently, there are no specific sample sizes or requirements. Rather, the study is continued until the researcher can legitimately report new or increased insight. Also, the rigor of the study is gauged by its trustworthiness (if the reader and participants find the results enlightening while believable) not by numerical measures of reliability and validity.

These differing philosophical underpinnings are demonstrated in many ways, including how the research is conducted and how it is written. For example, researchers write interpretive and critical research in the first person. Proposal and thesis formats are flexible and may differ from the five-chapter "quantitative" format. This approach to research is not just interviewing! It is often more time-consuming than empirical research because the data consists of reams of transcriptions and notes that must be read, studied, analyzed, and described through the written word.

There are many specific methods and philosophical underpinnings of interpretive and critical research. For example, in phenomenology there is both philosophical phenomenology and psychological phenomenology. It is important that you are well versed and skilled in the particular approach you select and ensure that it is appropriate for what you are seeking to study.

In this next section we will introduce you to several types of methods that fall under the broad headings of interpretive and critical research methods mentioned above. We briefly describe each method or approach by answering two questions:

1. What or whom do researchers intend to investigate?
2. How does this approach uniquely enable researchers to accomplish their task?

Throughout this section you should be asking yourself, "How would Greg (whom you met earlier in this chapter) possibly utilize each of these qualitative methodologies to further explore the complex phenomena that he is interested in learning more about?"

Ethnomethodology.   While some research approaches are designed to examine the most intricate, complex, and nuance-laden aspects of some phenomena, ethnomethodology typically investigates the "ordinary, the routine, the details of everyday life" (Patton, 1990, p. 74). The methods of ethnomethodology are composed of researchers investigating the norms (the everyday experiences of, usually, everyday people) by thrusting someone or something out of the ordinary on them. The process employed by researchers is to explain the obvious, those everyday ground-rules people operate by, under which all other experiences take place. How is this done?

Ethnomethodologists often disrupt the status quo. They interrupt the norms in order to better understand what the "usual" shields from our eyes. A very common example of an ethnomethodologist process (often called an "experiment") is facing the back wall of an elevator filled with forward-facing passengers (Garfinkle, 1967 as cited in Patton, 1990). The knowledge gained from such an approach is not gleaned through respectful introspection about what might happen, but rather from our responses or reaction as our awareness is jolted by the disruption of the everyday operating norms of the culture. The method allows researchers to help us understand the meaning of events or experiences that no one otherwise would likely notice.

Imagine that Greg is interested in what "tensions" are created in the residence halls of college campuses due to impulsive behavior (e.g., similar to the characteristic AD/HD impulsive behaviors). What ethnomethodological study could you design to explore this topic? With such an investigation, what would Greg be better able to understand about the phenomenon he is studying?

Case Study. You will recall that one of the most important aspects of quantitative research is statistical significance. Typically significance is strengthened when sufficient numbers are considered. Hence, adequate "sample size" is always a consideration for statistical analysis. **Case study,** however, looks at significance quite differently. Researchers who employ a case study approach first find the "perfect example" of whatever they are interested in learning more about. Such an "exemplar" is located because it embodies what investigators seek to learn more about. Be reminded, however, of something that "good" case researchers are well aware of: Small numbers defy confident generalization. The purpose of this methodology is not to offer generalizable conclusions, nor is it to merely illustrate some statistically significant finding; it is to provide vibrant, rich, accounting of another's experience. Case studies are very capable of standing all by themselves, providing that we do not make universal conclusions that were never intended by researchers.

Researchers of a case study typically engage in a personal way with the "case." For a time-limited but intensive study period, researchers may interview, observe, interact, experience, or use any combination of these research tools in order to investigate what interests them. The "richness" of the case study is often thought to lie in the character of the person or event. Consider how one might use a case study methodology for investigating truly unique experiences. Recall the recent story of a woman who chose to live high in the canopy of a tree for over a year in order to "speak out" against lumbering that was endangering an "old growth forest" in the Pacific Northwest. Here one cannot find a significant number of such activists, but the "case" is certainly none the less rich just because it is infrequent.

When the individual experience or event is best told by one person, case study is a powerful research approach. Whom do you think Greg might choose to study in order to richly portray the phenomenon he is interested in, using the approach described here?

Phenomenology. As mentioned at the beginning of this section, sometimes things in the world of research become complex. Phenomenology is a great example of this. A **phenomenological approach** to research intends to investigate the "essence of experience." The study of essence is typically thought of as a philosopher's endeavor; however, it has grown to mean much to psychologists, physicians, theologians, and counselors as well. Phenomenology investigates, unapologetically, phenomena (Patton, 1990). The focus of the phenomenological researcher's inquiry may be an event, such as giving birth, a feeling, such as jealousy or rage, an experience, such as living with cerebral palsy, or even the relationships people have.

Rooted quite firmly in philosophical writings, this research methodology embraces the notion that people can only know what they live. This methodology, then, looks at the essence of what is contained within the lived experience. Essence is often thought to be the most basic and immutable meaning we ascribe to something.

Consider Greg, once again. What questions might be answered by investigating the "lived experience," "essence," or "meaning" of living on a college campus, or having an attention deficit, or feeling socially misfit? Here, though, rather than as in the previously discussed research methodologies, Greg could look at what is shared by many individuals who share a common experience. His task would be to uncover the most basic ingredients that every person who "lives" this AD/HD phenomenon experiences.

Critical Research. When the intent of researchers is to influence, to have an affect on, or to move or forward a cause, they are conducting what is often called critical research. Here, no distance is maintained between the author and the subject. Critical researchers become "explicitly and purposefully" part of the change process by engaging the people in the program or organization, to study their own problems in order to solve those problems (Whyte, 1989). Patton (1990) wrote that the "distinction between research and action becomes quite blurred and the research methods tend to be less systematic, more informal, and quite specific to the problem, people, and organization for which the research is undertaken" (p. 157).

The purpose of critical research is usually problem solving. The process is one of identifying the problem or problems, exposing all of the many facets that make up the problem, and then generating the means to fix whatever aspects of the problem that are possible. Researchers are often passionately involved with the people or organization for whom the research is conducted. Researchers are personally interested in the project, not dispassionate observers free of feelings that might "contaminate" an unbiased "research posture."

Interestingly, the "audience"—who will benefit from the research—is, initially, only those who engage in conducting it. However, there are many people who identify similar problems who would benefit by learning what others did to solve their own. Critical research is not conducted for generalization or even dissemination, but it is often sought after—especially if the way someone solved a problem is notable.

Suppose that Greg was more passionately involved in this "project" than first imagined. Perhaps his brother's experience while in college really affected him. He resolves to "change the odds" with regard to his brother's success in college. Greg engages in critical research. What can you imagine he first attempts to understand? What happens next? Who else might have interest in what Greg "discovers" and the way he is successful in ensuring that his brother and many similar to him find success in college?

Grounded Theory. The last qualitative methodology we will mention in this brief overview has less to do with a "way" of researching than with our basic understanding of the purpose and function of "theory." Research is often intended to create or contribute to the development of—or to deduce—theory. Stanovich (1992) wrote, "theory in science is an interrelated set of concepts that is used to explain a body of data and to make predictions about the results of future experiments" (p. 22). In your education and practice of counseling or student affairs, you have doubtlessly studied a fair number of theories: countless developmental theories (e.g., Betz, Chickering, Erikson, Gilligan, Piaget, Vygotsky), counseling theories (e.g., Rational Emotive Behavior Therapy, Person-Centered Counseling, Gestalt, individual psychology, cognitive-behavioral, existential), theories of resilience, theories of psychopathology, theories of education. An implicit question emerges: What are all these theories attempting to do? They are meant to provide an explanation for some phenomenon worthy of generalization.

Grounded theory is not a way of researching as much as it is a belief about the process of research. Researchers who are creating grounded theory advocate theory generation through discovery (Glesne & Peshkin, 1992). The "theory-generating" process is painstaking in that the theorist/researcher must consider many possible explanations before coming up with a single explanatory statement (p. 19). What is unique about this grounded theory? The process described here is inductive rather than deductive. It is, in fact, in direct opposition to the hypothetical-deductive approach of experimental designs mentioned previously. In grounded theory no variables are defined *a priori*.

Discovery emerges "from the patterns found in the cases under study without presupposing in advance what the important dimensions will be" (Patton, 1990, p. 44). Theory then is "grounded" in the study of what is. This is a methodology where researchers are present and submerged in the world of their subject of investigation. Glaser and Strauss (1967) concluded that qualitative inquiry contributes to basic research through "grounded theory."

Greg never aspired to author any "theory" about the effect of attention deficit/hyperactivity disorder on the social abilities of college students and the qualities of peoples' experiences in college, but, when he was speaking to a friend about what he was thinking, the friend responded, "Interesting theory, Greg!" How can Greg's inductive exploration into this subject create or contribute to "grounded theory"?

Considerations When Choosing a Research Approach

Leedy (1997) offers some criteria you will want to consider when deciding whether a qualitative or quantitative approach is more acceptable for the particular study you are to undertake. The first consideration is the *question*. A quantitative approach is probably more appropriate if you believe there is an objective reality that can be measured and the research question is confirmatory and predictive. If this is the case, you will need to appreciate working within a context of high structure and possess skills in statistics and deductive reasoning. A qualitative approach is more suitable if there are multiple constructed realities and your question is exploratory and interpretive in nature. You need the ability to work with little structure, and attention to detail and inductive reasoning are needed. Second, you will want to consider the amount of *available information* on the topic to be researched. A quantitative approach requires a relatively large volume of literature, and your research focus needs to be broad. On the other hand, you can undertake a qualitative study if there is only a limited amount of literature available, and the focus of your research will be in-depth. Some final *practical considerations* involve: which approach the intended audience is more familiar with, the time available (qualitative approaches are often more time-intensive), your desire to work with people (qualitative approaches require a more interactive style), and writing skills (quantitative reports are more technical and use a scientific writing style, while qualitative reports tend to be literary and employ narrative writing).

As previously mentioned, a sample quantitative proposal is presented in Appendix B and a sample qualitative proposal is given in Appendix C. Recommendations for additional readings are found in Appendix G.

A C T I V I T Y

Types of Research

2.2

Match the following information with the selected type of research listed below.

1. Researchers use intact groups.
2. Researchers attempt to discover possible causes for variations found in a variable of interest among two groups *pre-existing groups*
3. Researchers work with participants to solve a social injustice.
4. Researchers investigate cause-and-effect relationships by comparing one or more treatment groups to a control group.
5. Researchers investigate the norms and the everyday experiences of people.
6. Researchers using this type of research may use surveys or observational approaches.
7. Researchers intend to investigate the "essence of experience."
8. Researchers determine, within a population, the degree to which one distribution of values associated with a variable is related to a second distribution of values associated with another variable.

5 ethnomethodology	1 quasi-experiments	3 critical research
case study	4 true experiments	interpretive research
8 correlational research	2 ex post facto	7 phenemenology
6 descriptive research	survey research	

Action-Oriented Research

The research designs we have described thus far emphasize a knowledge of existing literature and solid planning. **Action-oriented research** (also referred to as **action research**), on the other hand, is "'cutting edge' research which focuses on immediate application, not on the development of theory... its results may be published" (ASCA Research Committee,

1992, p.1). Additionally action research is used when a practitioner seeks to develop new skills or methods for effecting change (Hadley & Mitchell, 1995). Gillies (1993) suggests that action research involves observing the results of planned changes. If you have ever conducted, analyzed, and implemented the results of a needs assessment, then you have been involved in action-oriented research. Other examples include post-graduation surveys to assess the success rates of individuals in obtaining jobs in their field, time studies to analyze employees' tasks, and in-service training programs to help teachers identify students who are at risk for violent behavior.

Individuals conducting action-oriented research are primarily concerned with the local setting (the local school district, the specific university program, or the community mental health services). They want to know if there has been a change in their programs, their clients, or their students after using a specific method or intervention. Researchers following more traditional models, on the other hand, strive to generalize their findings to other settings, clients, and students (although qualitative research may be applied, it may have less of a definitive application to other settings). Applications for action-oriented research beyond the local setting might include professional initiatives by counseling associations on the state or national levels.

Action research often pertains to evaluation and accountability. Evaluation is defined as "collecting information about the effectiveness of services rendered" (Baker, 1983, p. 52), while accountability is "the act of reporting the results of the evaluation" (Baker, 1992, p. 189). Gillies (1993) proposed four approaches to action research: (a) diagnostic, (b) participant, (c), empirical, and (d) experimental.

Diagnostic Action Research

Diagnostic action research is the process of identifying a difficulty, diagnosing the cause, exploring alternatives for remediation of the problem, and making recommendations for resolving it. Whenever goals are established, action research is appropriate. Action research takes place when counselors and student affairs professionals evaluate their approach to resolving problems. For example, counselors might review progress notes of clients to determine which interventions encourage change in clients.

Participant Action Research

Participant action research is an approach in which data are collected from consumers and analyzed in an effort to make recommendations for changes. For example, in an effort to find out what the students, faculty, and staff think of the student union, the director prepares a survey. The director administers the survey to a representative sample of the consumer groups, analyzes the results, and makes recommendations to the student union staff for their implementation.

Empirical Action Research

Empirical action research involves the planning, implementation, and evaluation of programs. Let us consider a career counselor who implements a new computer program to help students in the initial stage of career exploration. After students use the program, the counselor assesses their level of career decisiveness.

Experimental Action Research

Experimental Action Research is an expansion of empirical action research. In order to better determine whether the intervention itself appears to be responsible for the outcome, the professional adds a control group. In the example above, the career counselor would have a control group of students to whom the computer program was not a available, and they would be provided with only the traditional services. The counselor could then compare the career decisiveness of those students who used the computer program with that of those who did not. You may be wondering how this approach differs from true or quasi-experimental design. You will recall that action-oriented research is not so heavily grounded in theory and methodology as traditional research.

The Role of Related Literature in a Research Project

In preparation for planning your research study you need to search the literature to ascertain the current findings and research related to your topic. The literature review stage serves several important functions as summarized below (Bartos, 1992).

First, a knowledge of related research *enables investigators to define the frontiers* of their field. To use an analogy, an explorer might say, "We know that beyond this river there are plains for 2,000 miles west and beyond those plains a range of mountains, but we do not know what lies beyond the mountains. I propose to cross the plains, go over the mountains, and proceed from there in a westerly direction." So the researcher in a sense says, "The work of A, B, and C has discovered this much about my question; the investigations of D have added this much to our knowledge. I propose to go beyond D's work in the following manner."

Second, an understanding of theory in the field *enables researchers to place their question in perspective.* One should determine whether one's endeavors would be likely to add to knowledge in a meaningful way. In general, those studies that determine whether the hypotheses generated by a theory can be confirmed are more useful than studies that proceed completely independently of theory. The latter tend to produce isolated bits of information that are of limited usefulness.

Third, through studying related research *investigators learn which procedures and instruments have proved useful and which seem less promising.* As one proceeds through the related literature and develops increasing sophistication, one may soon find ways in which the studies could have been improved. This point illustrates a major reason for emphasizing the related-literature portion of research studies; both the success and failures of past work provide insight for designing one's own study. If researchers build carefully on past investigations, they can expect increasing sophistication in their knowledge in the field.

Fourth, a thorough search through related material allows *the researcher to avoid unintentional replication of previous studies.* Frequently a researcher develops a worthwhile idea only to discover that a very similar study has already been done. In such a case, the researcher must decide whether to deliberately replicate the previous work or to change the proposed plans and investigate a different aspect of the problem.

Fifth, the study of related literature *places researchers in a better position to interpret the significance of their own results.* Becoming familiar with theory in the field and with previous research prepares researchers for fitting the findings of their research into the body of knowledge in the field.

The Role of Related Literature in Program Assessment and Evaluation

In the initial phase of program assessment and evaluation, you will need to write a description of the program, which requires that you understand the program, its mission, its scope, and its magnitude. Heppner, Kivlighan, and Wampold (1999) encourage researchers to gather program information on a first-hand basis; therefore, it is important that you involve yourselves in all phases of program development from conceptualization to completion. While some programs have missions that include theory, other programs do not. Gottfriedson (1984, cited in Hadley & Mitchel, 1995) promotes an integration of theory and practice in order to form stronger programs, clarify theoretical rationales, identify and measure research variables, and increase the efficacy of the intervention.

The investigation of related literature is crucial if you choose to integrate theory into practice. When surveying the literature, you will need to pay attention to theoretical and philosophical foundations in your area of concern. In your search you will become aware of broad implications that go beyond your agency or institution. You may choose to assess how you can apply such findings to your own programs.

The Role of Related Literature in a Grant Proposal

Just as writing a program description is an initial step in program assessment and evaluation, it is the first step in preparing a grant proposal. Morrell (1996) suggests that you limit your proposal to a specific project rather than creating a multifaceted plan that reviewers are likely to evaluate as unrealistic. The program description responds to the *who* of the project narrative. This description should provide background information about the program (e.g., agency, institution, or organization). In addition, you should emphasize the overall purpose of the program, how long it has existed, its major initiatives, and its special services. You can gather the majority of this program information from in-house documents, such as strategic plans and annual reports, and by interviewing key personnel.

Also it is important to include the entities with which the program has a relationship. Those entities that supply an organization with resources and the legitimacy to use them are called **input publics.** "Resources include concrete items such as money, facilities, and equipment and such ephemerals as expertise, political influence, and energy" (Lauffer, 1983, p. 16). You will find the expertise that Lauffer refers to in such entities as universities, libraries, and professional journals or books. These sources not only provide information on successful programs but also publish abstracts on projects that have been successfully funded; therefore, these sources are indispensable in the grant-writing process.

Through reading the professional literature you have the opportunity to learn about projects in other locales. In addition, you learn about the national organizations with which the projects are affiliated or from which they received funding. Successful grant writers suggest that you write your grant proposal in language that the potential funding source uses. They also suggest that you tailor your proposal to the source's thinking. For example, if the source is solution-oriented, then it is wise for you to present your proposal in solution-oriented language (Morrell, 1996). You can then readily access more information about the affiliate organization through the professional literature or via the Internet.

Resources for Conducting Research in Counseling and Student Affairs

In this section our goal is to acquaint you with print and electronic information available to assist you in your literature review as you prepare your research proposal, program assessment and evaluation, or grant proposal. Since most of you have probably become familiar with the process of accessing print information in your local libraries, the emphasis will be on electronic information related to counseling and student affairs.

Print Information

The process you learned to use to access **print information** (such as books, journals, newspapers) for any subject is the same method you will use to acquire print material in the fields of counseling and student affairs. Since one library significantly varies from another, we encourage you to familiarize yourself with this process in the library you will be using through library orientations, tutorials, and assistance offered by the reference staff. You will find that, although you are accessing print material, technology will play a large part in the process since most library catalogues are now online.

Electronic Information

Information can be accessed through a variety of **electronic sources,** including: **databases, Internet mailing lists,** and **World Wide Web** pages. While the use of electronic information sources can allow researchers to avail themselves to incredible amounts of data, the tremendous volume of information available can easily overwhelm the researcher. Because of space constraints, we will limit our discussion to databases, specifically those databases most often used in the counseling and student affairs fields. It should be noted that many databases can be accessed online from either a computer terminal in a university library or by logging on to the university system from home (or elsewhere) via a modem. Other databases may only be available on CD-ROM, and must to be accessed through a computer in the library. You are encouraged to familiarize yourself with the system available through your university.

Dissertation Abstracts Online. Dissertation Abstracts Online includes dissertations accepted at accredited U.S. institutions since 1861. In addition, selected international dissertations are covered, as well as some master's theses. Beginning in July 1980, abstracts were included for dissertations, and subsequently in spring 1988 they were included for master's theses.

Education Abstracts. Education Abstracts, produced by the H. W. Wilson Company, is a bibliographic database that indexes abstracts of articles of at least one column in length from more than 400 English-language periodicals and yearbooks published in the U.S. and elsewhere. English-language books relating to education published in 1995 or later are also indexed. A wide range of subjects are covered from preschool to higher education. Abstracting coverage begins with January 1994. Full-text coverage begins in January 1996.

Educational Resources Information Center (ERIC). ERIC was established in the 1960s and serves as a clearinghouse, covering all aspects of education and educational research, including abstracts of published and unpublished research. The citations for research published in journals are indicated with accession numbers starting with EJ. Citations and abstracts are indexed from over 750 professional journals. Unpublished documents, including conference proceedings, papers, etc. are indicated with accession numbers starting with ED. Those documents are found on microfiche in libraries.

Health and Psychosocial Instruments (HAPI). HAPI is a multidisciplinary database of instruments in the health and psychosocial areas. HAPI includes comprehensive information on assessment tools that are found in health and psychosocial journals that have been used in studies but are not commercially available. A wide range of instruments are included, such as: questionnaires, rating scales, tests, index measures, computerized simulation programs, and visually oriented materials. The database includes over 45,000 records.

***Mental Measurements Yearbook* Database. *Mental Measurements Yearbook* Database** contains critical review and descriptive information for more than 1,000 commercially available instruments covering educational skills, personality, vocation aptitude, psychology, and related areas. For each instrument, the database provides the name of the test author, publication information, scoring information, and the number of the *Mental Measurements Yearbook* in which the test was originally described. The database provides the text for the most recent editions of the *Mental Measurements Yearbooks*.

PsycINFO. PsycINFO, produced by the American Psychological Association, is a collection of electronically stored bibliographic references—most with abstracts or content summaries. It contains more than 1.5 million references to psychological literature, spanning 1887 to the present day. The references are all written in English, yet the covered literature includes material published in over 45 countries and written in more than 30 languages. PsycINFO is updated monthly with approximately 5,500 new references, including journal articles, dissertations, reports, English-language book chapters and books, and other scholarly documents.

P R O C E S S G O A L	Research Proposal

Conducting a Literature Review

Define a process goal for conducting a literature review. Some suggestions:

> This week I will schedule an orientation session at the university library. ✓

> I will make an appointment this week to meet with a reference librarian to learn about the library databases.

> I will spend 1 hour per day for the next week reviewing the literature of a topic that I am considering for my proposal.

> ✓ I will search one electronic database per day for the next week, looking for literature related to a topic I am considering for my proposal.   *AD/HD*

Galileo password — apocryphal —

Write your own process goal to help you begin to search the literature.

P R O C E S S G O A L	Program Assessment and Evaluation

Preparing to Write a Program Description

Define a process goal for preparing to write a program description on a first-hand basis, based on the literature. Some suggestions:

> This week I will schedule an orientation session at the university library.

> I will make an appointment this week to meet with a reference librarian to learn about the library databases.

> I will spend 1 hour per day for the next week reviewing the literature of a topic that I am considering for my program assessment and evaluation.

> This week I will make an appointment to visit the program (or a similar program) for which I plan to write a program assessment and evaluation.

> This week I will make an appointment to interview the program personnel of the program (or of a similar program) for which I plan to write a program assessment and evaluation.

Write your own process goal to help you begin to search the literature.

PROCESS GOAL	Grant Proposal

Reviewing the Related Literature

Define a process goal for conducting a literature review. Some suggestions:

> This week I will schedule an orientation session at the university library.

> I will make an appointment this week to meet with a reference librarian to learn about the library databases.

> I will spend 1 hour per day for the next week reviewing the literature of a topic that I am considering for my program assessment and evaluation.

> I will search one electronic database per day for the next week, looking for literature related to the grant proposal I plan to write.

> This week I will make an appointment to visit the program (or a similar program) for which I plan to write a grant proposal.

> This week I will make an appointment to interview the program personnel of the program (or of a similar program) for which I plan to write a grant proposal.

Write your own process goal to help you begin to search the literature.

Summary

In this chapter we gave an overview of quantitative and qualitative research. We explained the specific types of research through a case scenario. The case further illustrated the process of conducting a literature review. We described action-oriented research as research that is not as heavily grounded in theory and methodology as traditional research. We designed practice activities to demonstrate knowledge of different research approaches. Finally, we provided you with print and electronic information and encouraged you to establish a process goal to assist you in your literature review.

Key Terms

action-oriented (or action) research

case study

casual-comparative method

cohort (or generation) effects

continuous variables

correlational studies

critical research

cross-sectional surveys

cross-sequential (cohort sequential) studies

databases

descriptive research

diagnostic action research

Dissertation Abstracts Online

Education Abstracts

electronic sources

empirical action research

ERIC

ethnomethodology

experimental action research

ex post facto research

grounded theory

group comparison studies

HAPI

input publics

intact group

Internet mailing lists

longitudinal surveys

Mental Measurements Yearbook Database

nonequivalent groups

observational research

participant action research

phenomenological approach

print information

PsycINFO

qualitative

quantitative

quasi-experiments

random assignment

statistical

survey research

surveys

true experimental design

World Wide Web

3

The Research Problem and the Research Question

Systematic research begins with a **problem.** The problem is an unresolved issue from previous research. Although Leedy (1997) stresses that the problem is "the heart of the research project" (p. 45), he uses problem and question interchangeably, stating, "The problem or question is the axial center around which the whole research effort turns" (p. 45). While some authors like Leedy develop their discussion about the focus of a study around the problem statement, other authors such as Hadley and Mitchell (1995), Heppner, Kivlinhan, and Wampold (1999), and Marlow (2000) make a distinction between the problem and the question. They see the problem statement as broad, expressed in general terms, and containing many questions. The problem is a larger issue that the question seeks to shed light on. Like the latter authors, we speak of the problem statement as the broader concern from which the specific research question is derived.

Research Questions

The Nature of Research Questions

Research questions in counseling and student affairs are questions about the state of affairs in the field. "Research questions explore the relations among or between constructs" (Heppner et al., 1999, p. 36). Although there are different types of research problems, all involve a question, the answer to which is being sought in the research. For example, quantitative research involves a question about the relationship existing between two or more variables. A counselor, perhaps, might ask a question about the relationship that exists between type of counseling intervention and counseling outcome. A researcher could make a study more elaborate by introducing other variables into the question. For instance, one might ask what the effect of the counseling intervention is in various settings (outpatient, partial hospitalization, and inpatient). A student affairs professional might consider the relationship between type of resident assistant training and the resident assistants' effectiveness in managing their assigned areas. The investigation might examine the type of training (an intensive summer retreat, ongoing monthly trainings throughout the academic year, or a combination of both) and the resident assistants' effectiveness.

In qualitative research, questions differ from more traditional quantitative research questions as discussed in Chapter 2. In fact, many qualitative researchers would prefer to say they explore "what is" rather than say they investigate problems. In a qualitative statement, the researcher orients the reader to the question to be explored; however, this is not a specific statement that generates propositions to be tested on a hypothesis that will be generated accordingly. It is primarily a general discussion of this issue or this group that is to be studied. The qualitative question may become more precise as a result of a continued literature review process. It does not generate the opportunity for data collection of a qualitative nature or a hypothesis as presented in a quantitative proposal. For example, a qualitative researcher might interview resident assistants noted for their ability to manage their residence halls and look for trends contributing to their effectiveness.

The Sources of Problems and Questions

The first question most students ask is, "How do I find a research problem?" Although there are no set rules for locating a problem, certain suggestions may help. Three important sources of problems are knowledge and experience, deductions from theory, and related literature. The solution-focused activity at the end of this chapter will assist students in this process.

Formulating a good research problem and subsequent question involves two types of **knowledge**: knowledge of the research process and knowledge of the research topic (Wilkinson & McNeil, 1996). The more researchers know about research design, methodology, types of research, assessment, data collection, data analysis, and statistical techniques, the easier it is for them to identify and formulate good research. An understanding of the specific topic, acquired either through experience or literature, greatly assists the researcher in planning solid research.

For those researchers who rely on **deductions from theory** to provide sources for research problems, an in-depth knowledge of theory in the profession is also imperative. Research in counseling and student affairs deals with such theories as human development, personality, counseling, psychology, and human behavior. According to Heppner et al. (1999) mathematics serves as the methodological traditions of quantitative research. The deductive process from theory to hypothesis testing is syllogistic: "If theory X is true, then result Y will be present, and if result Y is not present, then theory X is not true" (p. 245).

In the activity on page 29 in Chapter 2, we introduced you to conducting a literature review. We encourage you to review related literature as a way to determine what has already been done in the field as well as to serve as a springboard from which you can create new ideas. The goal of a literature review is not only to understand, critique, extend, and improve upon previous research, but also to find an area of study that interests you. Reading widely in professional books and journals, facilitated by the prevalence of electronic databases, will provide you with knowledge of the subject. We discourage you from merely brainstorming topics as you commute to class. Often when students are struggling to find a topic, we will inquire into the depth of reading they have been doing. We regularly find the source of their difficulty: they have not been searching in the literature for guidance. As Heppner et al. (1999) recommend, thinking and reflecting should come after you have collected a wide range of information. You need to consider: What subjects are you most drawn to? What do you like about a certain area of research? What appears to be a missing link in the field of study that you could provide?

We encourage students to think about areas related to the field in which they possess some experience and curiosity. Take for example a counseling student who is doing her practicum in the university counseling center. While doing intakes as part of her practicum experience, she notices a trend in those students who appear depressed. It seems to her that the students who appear depressed lead very sedentary lifestyles. She begins to wonder if there is a relationship between the degree of physical activity of college students and their degree of depression. Through a thorough review of the literature, she gains significant knowledge about the topic and discovers that there is a relationship between exercise and level of depression. She realizes that to merely measure that relationship would be a descriptive study. She decides she would like to make her study experimental by creating an exercise program in which half of the sedentary, depressed students will participate, on a randomly selected basis. At the conclusion of the exercise program she will compare the depression levels of those students who participate in the exercise program to those who do not.

Relationship Between Variables

The type of research question that we deal with in this book examines the relationship between two or more variables. In this kind of question, the researcher manipulates a minimum of one variable to determine its effect on other variables, as opposed to a purely descriptive study in which the researcher observes, counts, or in some way measures the frequency of appearance of a particular variable in a particular setting. For instance, in a descriptive study the question might be: "How many freshmen on a college campus have been identified with an eating disorder?" Since no attempt need be made to deal with a relationship between variables, this question requires only a "bookkeeping" procedure. However, in an experimental study we might ask: "Are freshmen identified as being at risk for an eating disorder less likely to develop an eating disorder if they are involved in counseling?" In this case the question involves the relationship between variables. For the purposes of this book, a research question will require the inclusion of at least two variables and their relationship to each other.

Beginning researchers are often surprised to find that this initial stage often takes up a large part of the total time invested in a research project. There is no way to conduct research until a problem is recognized, thought through, and formulated into a useful question. The process can involve a wide range of **creativity.** Those researchers who replicate studies or advance previously conducted research in minuscule ways use very little creativity. On the other hand, researchers who investigate original ideas or integrate diverse areas of study in novel ways involve much creativity in their work. No matter what degree of creativity is introduced into research, all such attempts add to the existing knowledge. This furthering of society through research is considered of social interest by noted psychologist Alfred Adler (1931/1992).

A researcher must first of all decide on the general subject of investigation. Such choices are necessarily very personal but should lead to an area that holds deep interest or about which there is a real curiosity. Otherwise, the individual may lack the motivation to carry the research study through to its end. The researcher's own knowledge, experience, and circumstances generally determine these choices: A student affairs professional may want to examine the efficacy of a semester-long orientation program for freshmen. An elementary school counselor may feel a need to investigate whether the conflict resolution program is actually affecting the number of fights occurring in the school.

Once chosen, the general subject is then narrowed down to a very specific research problem. The researcher must decide on a specific question to be answered and must state precisely what is to be done to reach an answer. Much of this chapter focuses on this aspect of research in the field of counseling and student affairs.

Refinement of the Research Question

Most beginning researchers find this task of formulating a researchable question a difficult one. The difficulty is not due to a shortage of researchable questions in the counseling field. In fact, there are so many questions begging for answers that beginners usually have trouble choosing among them. One common difficulty is that a problem must be selected and a question formulated very early, when the beginner's understanding of how to do research is most limited. In addition, uncertainties about the nature of research problems, the isolation of a problem, the criteria for acceptability, and the way to solve the problem often seem overwhelming. Even experienced researchers usually find it necessary to make several attempts before arriving at a research question that meets generally acceptable criteria. A first selection of a formulation may, on closer examination, be found to be unfeasible or not worth doing. Skill in doing research is, to a large extent, a matter of making wise choices about what to investigate. The skill takes time and repeated effort to develop but can be developed by the willing novice. Unlikely as it may seem, once the researcher selects a problem and clearly formulates a question, he or she has accomplished one of the most difficult phases of the research process.

Characteristics of a Research Question

Although selecting a research question is one of the most difficult steps for a student in the research process, it is unfortunately one for which we can give the least guidance. Selection of a research question is not subject to the same degree of technical rules or requirements as is research design, measurement, or statistics; fortunately, however, we can offer some guidelines.

A research question must have the following characteristics, which we will examine in detail:

1. It should ask about a relationship between two or more variables.
2. It should be stated clearly, unambiguous, and in question form.
3. It should be testable by empirical methods; that is, it should be possible to collect data to answer the question(s) asked.
4. It should not represent a moral or ethical position.

Specific Considerations in Choosing a Problem

The following are some critical criteria to apply to a chosen problem before going ahead in its study. Try these questions out on your potential problem to be studied:

1. *Theoretical value.* Does the question, when answered, fill a gap in the literature? Will others recognize its importance? Will it contribute to advancement in your field? Does it improve upon the "state of the art?" Is it publishable?
2. *Practical value.* Will the solution to the problem improve professional practice? Are practitioners likely to be interested in the results? Will the fields of counseling and student affairs be changed by the outcome? Are you likely to change your own counseling and student affairs practices as a result?
3. *Workability.* Is the contemplated study within the limits and range of your resource and time constraints? Will you have access to the necessary sample in the numbers required? Is there reason to believe that you can come up with an "answer" to the problem? Is the required methodology manageable and understandable?
4. *Critical mass.* Is the problem of sufficient magnitude and scope to fulfill the requirement that has motivated the study in the first place? Are there enough variables? Are there enough potential results? Is there enough to write about?
5. *Interest.* Are you interested in the problem area, specific question, and potential solution? Does it relate to your background? Does it involve your career interests? Is it something that excites you? Will you learn useful skills from pursuing it?

Stating the Research Question

After you select the problem and decide upon its significance, there is still the task of formulating the question in a form amenable to investigation. A good research question must (a) clarify exactly what is to be determined or solved and (b) restrict the scope of the study to a specific question. We cannot overemphasize the importance of a clear, concise statement of the question. Beginning researchers often have a general idea of the problem but have trouble formulating it as a workable research question. They find that their initial general ideas, although adequate for communication and understanding, are not sufficiently specific to permit an empirical attack on the problem. They cannot make progress until they can state a concrete question amenable to research (Bartos, 1992).

To illustrate, a beginning researcher states that he or she is interested in studying the effectiveness of parent education on teenage mothers. As stated, one could understand in a broad sense what the researcher wants to do but the problem needs to be specified with much greater clarity.

An essential step involves a definition of the terms involved. What is meant by *effectiveness, parent education,* and *teenage mothers*? The definitions required for research will not usually be supplied by a dictionary. For example, effectiveness is defined as "producing the intended or expected result." This definition describes the general construct *effectiveness* but is not sufficiently precise for research purposes. One needs to be able to specify exactly what indicator of effectiveness one will use or what one will do to assess the presence or absence of the phenomenon denoted by the concept *effectiveness*. The same is true for the other terms. In other words, one must define the variables of the problem operationally. To define concepts operationally, one must designate some kind of overt behavior or event that is directly observable and measurable by oneself and others to represent these concepts. An **operational definition** is one that defines a concept in terms of the operation or processes that will be used to measure the concept.

In this study, the researcher might choose to define *effectiveness* as teenage mothers' increased ability to use logical and natural consequences (as opposed to punishment) with their children. The term *parent education* would be defined as the specific parent education model used such as *Systematic Training for Effective Parenting (STEP) for Preschoolers. Teenage mothers* might refer to those female teenagers who have young children. The original problem now might be written as the following research question, "What is the effect of *STEP for Preschoolers* parenting groups on teenager mothers' ability to use logical and natural consequences (as opposed to punishment) with their preschool children?" The operational definitions serve to focus the scope of a general question to specific observable variables. In addition, operational definitions as an essential component throughout the entire study are described below.

Now that the work is indicated with some clarity and focus, the researcher can proceed to design an experimental study that compares the number of uses of logical and natural consequences by teenage mothers who had the STEP parent education training with those teenage mothers who did not have the training.

Furthermore, in stating the problem, and ultimately the question, the researcher must strive for a balance between generality and specificity. If the stated problem is too broad and too general, one is faced with a vague area with no clear indication of the direction the research is to take. For instance, a question such as, "What is the effect of career counseling on career decisiveness of college students?" is too general. It would be much better to ask, "What is the effect of using DISCOVER, a computerized career program, on undeclared college freshmen's ability to identify career clusters that interest them?" This statement indicates immediately the specific subjects to be included, the variables involved, and the type of data that will be gathered.

On the other hand, the problem must not be so narrow that it becomes trivial and meaningless. One wants a problem that is broad enough to be significant according to the criteria discussed, yet specific enough to be feasible in one's particular situation. As previously mentioned, once the researcher specifies the problem area to be studied, the researcher then formulates it into a research question that asks about the relationship between two or more variables. However, this does not mean that the *exact* words: "What is the relationship between _____ and _____?" have to appear in the statement. The question may appear in that form, or the relationship may only be implied. Students are often confused on this point (Bartos, 1992). For instance, the following questions ask about the relationship between variables but without using those precise words: "How does required study hall attendance affect the academic performance of college athletes?" and "What is the relative effectiveness of cognitive-behavioral therapy and client-centered therapy on impulse control in elementary children diagnosed with attention deficit hyperactivity disorder?"

State the question in such a way that research is possible. Avoid philosophical issues, as well as value or judgmental questions that cannot be answered by scientific investigation.

A C T I V I T Y

3.1

The following are some research questions that former students have submitted. Determine whether or not they meet the characteristics of a good research question.

Yes_✓_ No___ 1. Will there be an increase in retention rates of college students from underrepresented groups when they are placed in classrooms of less than 25 students as opposed to classrooms of 25 or more students?

Yes_✓_ No___ 2. Will there be a statistically significant decrease in the depression scores of adults involved in group therapy as opposed to adults involved in individual therapy?

Yes___ No_✓_ 3. Is there a significant difference between the opinions of professors and the opinions of administrators concerning the need for a diverse campus?   *measured how?*

Yes___ No_✓_ 4. Will there be an increase in nontraditional college students' performance using a mentoring approach as opposed to the traditional orientation program?   *meas. how?*

Yes___ No_✓_ 5. Will students trained in beginning counseling skills over a full academic semester counsel any better than students who receive the training in an intensive 5-week course?

Yes_✓_ No___ 6. Will there be an increase in reading achievement among first grade students taught by the language experience approach as opposed to those taught by the basal reader approach?

Yes___ No_✓_ 7. Are college freshmen in public universities indifferent in their academic achievement compared to college freshmen in private institutions?

Below are descriptions of studies that we used in Chapter 1 to identify independent and dependent variables. From the following descriptions (and keeping in mind the independent and dependent variables) write a research question for each.

Study #1/Intensive Study Skills
Program for High-School Seniors
at risk for Failure

A school counselor designed an intensive study skills program for seniors in high school who were at risk for failure to graduate. The intensive study skills program included small group counseling, small group instruction in study skills, and personal tutoring. The school counselor predicts that involvement in the intensive study skills program will improve the graduation rate of at-risk seniors. She plans to test her hypothesis by comparing the graduation rate of at-risk seniors who participate in the intensive study skills program with those at-risk seniors who do not receive the program.

Research question: *Will there be an increase in grad. rates for at-risk seniors who participate in the intensive study skills program? (small group instr. and counseling + personal tutoring?)*

grad rate (dv) on ss prog (iv)

Study #2/Play Therapy
Approaches for Encopresis

A mental health therapist wants to assess the effectiveness of four approaches to play therapy (child-centered, Adlerian, psychodynamic, and behavioral) on encopresis (soiling) in latency age children. Specifically, the therapist wants to measure the rate of occurrence as well as the children's level of responsibility for cleanup on a continuum from high (where the child cleans self and clothing) to low (where the child attempts to hide evidence of the soiling).

Research question: *What is the effect of play therapy (4 types) on encopresis and the child's responsibility for self clean-up?*

rate of encopresis, etc. (dv) on play ther (iv)

Study #3/Committed Resident
Assistants

A director of residential living on a large university campus is concerned about the large turnover rate in resident assistants. In recent years, many resident assistants have left their positions before completing even 1 year in their assignments. The director wants to identify factors that predict commitment as a resident assistant (defined as continuing in the position a minimum of 2 years). The director decides to assess knowledge of the position, attitude toward residential policies, and ability to handle conflicts as predictors for commitment to the position.

Research question: *factor 3 things; ① retention rate*

level of comm. dv on know. att, mana management confl. management

How do knowledge of 1, 2, +3 determine comm. of RA's to their position?

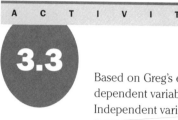

A C T I V I T Y

3.3

Based on Greg's experimental scenario found on page 21, identify his independent and dependent variables. Then write a research question.

Independent variable(s):

Dependent variable(s):

Research question:

A C T I V I T Y

3.4

Based on your interests, write a research question related to a topic you may choose for your research. Initially it may be helpful if you identify your independent and dependent variables.

Independent variable(s):

Dependent variable(s):

Research question:

Writing a Research Question for an Experimental Design

When we have students write a research proposal as a course requirement, we ask students to propose a study that is experimental (true or quasi) in nature. This is not to say that this type of research is the premier type of research; however, experimental research allows you to demonstrate your knowledge of a wide range of research principles (such as control groups and sampling) that are not necessarily utilized in all types of research.

For instance, let us say that in your review of the literature you found that a large amount of research has been done regarding treatment for college females with anorexia nervosa but little has been done with college males with the eating disorder. Your research question might be "What types of treatment are being used with college males identified with anorexia nervosa?" If you decide to send out a questionnaire to a large sample of male college students and ask them: (a) whether they had ever been identified with an eating disorder, and (b) what type(s) of treatment were used, this would be descriptive research. A way to make the research question experimental would be to ask, "What is the effect of inpatient hospitalization versus outpatient counseling on college males diagnosed with anorexia nervosa?" This research question lends itself to setting up a study in which two samples of college males with anorexia nervosa are treated with different approaches in order to assess the relative effectiveness of these treatments.

A C T I V I T Y

3.5

Review the research question that you just wrote. Is it appropriate for setting up a research study that is experimental in nature? If it is not, follow the example above, which should help you rewrite your research question for experimental research.

Rewrite the research question to make it experimental (if necessary). Rewrite the research question regarding direction (if necessary). Refer to the discussion regarding direction below.

Research Questions: Directional or Nondirectional

In the activity where you determined the acceptability of the research questions, you may have noticed that some research questions used words such as *increase*, *decrease*, and *better.* These terms indicate a **direction** to the research question. Terms such as *difference, effect,* and *indifference* are **nondirectional.** It is important for researchers to correctly give direction or not to their research questions, since the statements serve as a preliminary step to formulating the research hypotheses (discussed in the following chapter). Hypotheses should be written consistently (in terms of direction or nondirection) with research questions. If the wrong direction is predicted, significant findings in a study may be missed altogether. Researchers, therefore, are discouraged from generating directional research questions based on intuition alone. Therefore, only when the researcher has sound reasoning for stating the direction of an outcome (e.g., indicators are found in the review of literature, or the researcher has experience with the intervention) should the research question be stated so as to predict the researcher's belief. The **directional** question indicates that one treatment or group will do better than other ones.

When the researcher does not have a rationale for providing a directional research question, then a nondirectional question is warranted. A nondirectional question indicates that there will be a difference between groups or treatments, but the way the differences will occur is not stated. Direction will be discussed further in Chapter 4.

Go back to the page where you wrote out your research question. Is it directional or nondirectional? Based on the above reading, decide if you want to keep your research question as you have it or change it in regard to being directional or nondirectional.

Operational Definitions That Are Essential to the Study

An important component of Chapter 1 in the research proposal or study is a list of operational definitions. The words in this list define the terms that are essential to the study or that are used in a restricted or unusual manner. The operational definition provides the reader of the study with a concrete understanding or working definition of each significant term or construct. According to Heppner et al. (1999) "the operational definition allows the researcher to move from general ideas and constructs to more specific and measurable events" (p. 39). For example, brief therapy is a concept that is found regularly in counseling literature, but it can be used either generically or specifically. Is brief therapy defined by the approach used? The number of sessions? A combination of both? Or neither? In order to understand the purpose of the study, the consumer needs to know the operational definition of brief therapy. Even more importantly, in order to understand the results of the study, it is essential that the reader know what is meant by brief therapy. Results from one study cannot be generalized to other studies unless operationally the same constructs have been studied.

As researchers write their proposals, they need to list and define those terms that are critical to their studies. The list readily supplies the consumer with a "glossary of terms." As mentioned previously, this list appears in Chapter 1. This evolving process, which is ongoing throughout the writing stage, helps researchers to be consistent in their use of the terms and helps them avoid what will be an arduous task if left until the end.

A C T I V I T Y

3.6

List any terms that need to be operationally defined from the research question that you wrote in the previous activity. Next, define the terms. Keep the list current as you come across terms that are essential to your study.

Problems as Related to Program Assessment and Evaluation

All assessment and evaluation activities emanate from a problem; therefore, it is essential that you clearly define the problem you will be investigating (Upcraft & Schuh, 1996). Heppner et al. (1999) discuss the importance of determining the purposes of the evaluation. They emphasize that in the position of researcher, you and program personnel need to agree on your role and what the evaluation should include. This is the *what* of the program assessment and evaluation. It is helpful when you are familiar with the program and its mission, since the problem to be addressed is often based on the program's mission. Many of the same criteria for writing good problem statements and research questions (such as being clear and unambiguous) apply to specifying the problem you are going to investigate through program assessment and evaluation.

Problems as Related to Grant Proposals

A statement of the problem that you are going to address in the grant proposal is usually a standard element of most proposals. You should clearly state the problem early in the proposal. The problem may be one that exists at the present time or one that you may anticipate in the future. According to Lauffer (1983), problems may be apparent in the population, in the service system, or in the program management. It is important that there is agreement on the vision for the program among the program personnel and consumers of the program.

In the writing of the problem statement you should be specific about the problem you want to address. You will want to make a connection between the issue and your program. The characteristics of a good problem statement and research question for research proposals are applicable to writing grant proposals as well.

Karges-Bone (1994) suggests that you highlight the problem that will be addressed in the grant proposal through the use of a catchy title. A carefully chosen title helps you focus your writing of the grant around the problem, write your proposal with flair, and make your proposal memorable to the reviewers.

P R O C E S S G O A L	Research Proposal

Finalizing a Research Problem and Research Question

Define a process goal for finalizing a problem statement and research question. Some suggestions:
Since three important sources of research problems are knowledge and experience, deductions from theory, and related literature, each day for the next week I will do one of the following activities:

1. Think about knowledge I have gained through my experiences in work settings that would lend themselves to possible research problems.
2. Review theories that interest me with the end goal of deducing from one a possible research problem.
3. Read articles from my particular areas of interest with an eye out for a topic appropriate for a research problem.

Write your own process goal to help you finalize your research problem and question. Based on your problem statement, write your research question. (Examples given in the chapter.)

P R O C E S S G O A L	Program Assessment and Evaluation

Defining the Problem to Be Assessed and Evaluated

Define a process goal for finalizing the problem to be assessed. Some suggestions:
Just as knowledge and experience, deductions from theory, and related literature supply
material for research problems, these sources can also serve as the foundation for program assessment and evaluation. Each day for the next week I will do one of the following activities:

1. Think about knowledge I have gained through my experiences in work settings
   that would lend themselves to possible problems to address through program
   assessment and evaluation.
2. Review theories that interest me with the end goal of deducing from one a possible problem to address through program assessment and evaluation.
3. Read articles from my particular areas of interest with an eye out for a topic
   appropriate for program assessment and evaluation.

Write your own process goal to help you finalize your problem to address through program assessment and evaluation.
Write down what problem you will address through program assessment and evaluation.
(Example: Which strategies are the most cost-effective in recruiting and admitting qualified students to the university?)

P R O C E S S G O A L	Grant Proposal

Defining the Purpose of the Grant

Define a process goal for defining the purpose of the grant. Some suggestions:
Just as knowledge and experience, deductions from theory, and related literature supply
material for research problems; these sources can also serve as the foundation for grant
writing. Each day for the next week I will do one of the following activities:

1. Think about knowledge I have gained through my experiences in work settings that
   would lend themselves to possible problems to address through grant writing.
2. Review theories that interest me with the end goal of deducing from one a possible problem to address through grant writing.
3. Read articles from my particular areas of interest with an eye out for a topic
   appropriate for a grant proposal.

Write your own process goal to help you finalize your problem to address through a grant
proposal.
Write down the purpose to be achieved through the grant. (Example: Parent education
classes will be offered in three rural communities through interdisciplinary teams made

up of school counselors from local school districts, mental health therapists from the county mental health agency, and social workers from the county Department of Social Services.)

Summary

This chapter highlighted the research problem and question as the most important aspects of conducting research. The discussion involved defining the research problem and formulating a research question, the nature of research questions, the source of questions, and characteristics of a research question. Since the type of research question that this book deals with examines the relationship between two or more variables, relationships between variables served as the cornerstone to writing good research questions. Practice activities were designed to help you identify and formulate good research questions, culminating in the writing of your own research question.

Key Terms

creativity

deductions from theory

directional

knowledge

nondirectional

operational definition

4

Hypothesis

A hypothesis may be precisely defined as a tentative proposition suggested as a solution to a problem or as an explanation of some phenomenon. It presents in simple form a statement of the researcher's expectations relative to a relationship between variables within the problem (Bartos, 1992). The hypothesis is a powerful tool in scientific inquiry. It enables us to relate theory to observation and observation to theory. The use of hypothesis enables us, in our search for knowledge, to employ both the ideas of the inductive philosophers, with their emphasis on observation, and the logic of the deductive philosophers, with their emphasis on reason. The use of hypotheses has united experience and reason to produce a powerful tool for seeking knowledge (Bartos).

After finding the problem, examining the literature, and stating the research question, the researcher is ready to structure a hypothesis. Hence it is presented only as a suggested solution to the problem, with the understanding that the ensuing investigation may lead either to its retention or to its rejection.

You will recall from Chapter 2 that Greg begins to explore ways to reduce interpersonal difficulties experienced by college students. He may begin with the question, "What is the effect of participation in an interpersonal relationship group on the social skills of college students diagnosed AD/HD?" He might then hypothesize that a positive relationship exists between college students' involvement in an interpersonal relationship group and their social skills. In this example you can see that the hypothesis is a proposition relating two variables: participation in an interpersonal relationship group and level of social skills.

The hypothesis must be constructed before the data-gathering phase of the study for two reasons: (a) A well-grounded hypothesis indicates that the researcher has sufficient knowledge in the area to undertake the investigation. (b) The hypothesis gives direction to the collection and interpretation of that data; it tells the researcher what procedure to follow and the type of data to gather. Thus, constructing a hypothesis may prevent a great deal of wasted time and effort on the part of the researcher. It should be emphasized that this is true for all types of research studies, not just the experimental.

Purposes Served by the Hypothesis

The hypothesis provides:

1. A tentative explanation of phenomena and facilitates the extension of knowledge in an area
2. The investigator with a relational statement that is directly testable in a research study
3. Direction to the research
4. A framework for reporting the conclusions of the study

Characteristics of the Usable Hypothesis

After the hypothesis has been tentatively formulated, but before any actual empirical testing is attempted, the researcher must assess the potential of the hypothesis as a research tool. A hypothesis must meet certain criteria of acceptability. The final worth of a hypothesis cannot be judged prior to empirical testing, but there are certain criteria that characterize worthwhile hypotheses and the researcher should use them to judge the adequacy of the proposed hypothesis (Bartos, 1992).

1. A hypothesis must have explanatory power.
2. A hypothesis must state the expected relationship between variables.
3. A hypothesis must be testable.
4. The literature either supports a strong rationale for the hypothesis or a strong rationale contrary to it.
5. A hypothesis should be stated as simply and concisely as possible.

Stating the Hypothesis

research hypothesis (alternative)

We have already stressed that if hypotheses are to be evaluated, they must be stated in a testable form. This form requires a simple, clear statement of the specific relationship between two variables. This type of hypothesis, with which we usually begin, is called the research hypothesis, or **alternate hypothesis.** It reflects the researcher's expectations based on theory or previous research findings. An example of a research hypothesis is: Oldest children in a family will exhibit more responsibility than youngest children in the family.

Research hypotheses, just as research questions, are sometimes further classified as being directional or nondirectional. As the label indicates, a directional hypothesis is one that specifies the direction of the expected findings. This type of statement is made when the experimenter has definite reasons for expecting certain relationships or certain differences to occur between groups. The research hypothesis, "Oldest children in a family will exhibit a statistically significant higher degree of responsibility than youngest children in the family," is a directional hypothesis because it stipulates the direction of the difference between groups.

A research hypothesis that does not specify the direction that expected differences or relationships might take is termed a nondirectional hypothesis. Stated as a nondirectional hypothesis, our example would read, "There is a difference in the responsibility levels exhibited by oldest and youngest children in a family." Although the hypothesis indicates that a difference is expected, the direction of the difference is not specified.

Null

Generally, the experimenter formulates a **statistical,** or **null, hypothesis,** which is one that states that no relationship exists between the variables of the problem. For example, the foregoing hypothesis stated in null form reads, "There is no difference in the level of responsibility exhibited by oldest children in a family and that of youngest children in a family." In other words, there is no relationship between the variables responsibility and birth order.

Below are two examples of research and null hypotheses derived from research questions. Notice the changes that have taken place between the research question and the hypothesis.

Example One

Research Question.   Will there be a difference in levels of responsibility exhibited by oldest children and youngest children in a family?

statement

Research Hypothesis.   There will be a statistically significant difference in the level of responsibility exhibited by oldest children in a family and that of youngest children in a family as measured by the *Behavior Rating Profile*.

Null Hypothesis.   There will be no statistically significant difference in the level of responsibility exhibited by oldest children in a family and that of youngest children in a family as measured by the *Behavior Rating Profile*.

Example Two

Research Question. Will the level of social skills of college students diagnosed AD/HD increase as a result of being involved in an interpersonal relationship group?

Research Hypothesis. There will be a statistically significant increase in the level of social skills of college students diagnosed AD/HD who are involved in an interpersonal relationship group as opposed to those college students diagnosed AD/HD who are not involved in an interpersonal relationship group as measured by the *FIRO Awareness Scales*.

Null Hypothesis. There will be no statistically significant increase in the level of social skills of college students diagnosed AD/HD who are involved in an interpersonal relationship group as opposed to those college students diagnosed AD/HD who are not involved in an interpersonal relationship group as measured by the *FIRO Awareness Scales*.

In the above examples the hypotheses are much more specific than the research questions. The hypothesis is written in such a way that makes it testable. We use the term "statistically significant" because a difference or increase is not enough; the variance must be at a statistical level (as described in Chapter 10).

A C T I V I T Y

Writing the Hypotheses

4.1

On page 47 of Chapter 3, you wrote your research question. Rewrite it as you now conceptualize it.
Write a research hypothesis based on your research question.
Write a null hypothesis based on your research question.

Identification of Variables

You will recall that in Chapter 1 we defined variables as the characteristics or events that are the focus of study. They are recognized either as measurable in some way or as indirectly affecting the results of the study. There are five basic variables that should be recognized in a research study. They are the independent, dependent, **control, moderator,** and **intervening variables.** The following is a discussion of these variables and their relationships to each other.

Independent Variable

The *independent variable* was introduced to you in Chapter 1 as the treatment or intervention variable. That is because the independent variable, which is a stimulus variable, or input, operates within a person or within his or her environment to affect behavior. It is that factor that is measured, manipulated, or selected by experimenters to determine its relationship to an observed phenomenon. If the experimenters studying the relationship between two variables, X and Y, ask, "What will happen to Y if we make X greater or smaller?" the experimenters are thinking of variable X as the independent variable. It is the variable that they will manipulate or change to cause a change in some other variable. They consider it independent because they are interested only in how it affects another variable, not in what affects it. They regard it as an antecedent condition: a condition required preceding a particular consequence.

Dependent Variable

The *dependent variable* is a response variable, or output. It is an observed aspect of the behavior of an organism that has been stimulated. The dependent variable is that factor that is observed and measured to determine the effect of the independent variable; that is, the factor that appears, disappears, or varies as the experimenters introduce, remove, or vary the independent variable. In the study of the relationship between the two variables X and Y when the experimenters ask, "What will happen to Y if we make X greater or smaller?" they are thinking of Y as the dependent variable. It is the variable that will change as a result of variation in the independent variable. It represents the consequence of a change in the person or situation studied.

The Relationship Between Independent and Dependent Variables

Most experiments involve many variables, not just a single independent and a single dependent variable. The additional variables may be independent and dependent variables, or they may be moderator or control variables. But in this section, for the purpose of explanation, we will deal solely with the relationship between a single independent and a single dependent variable.

In many experiments, the independent variable is **discrete** (that is, categorical) and takes the form of the presence versus the absence of a particular treatment or approach being studied or a comparison between different approaches. In other experiments, the independent variable may be continuous (theoretically having an infinite number of values), and the experimenters' observations of it may be stated in numerical terms indicating its degree. (These terms are related to levels of measurement, which are discussed further in Chapter 7.) When two continuous variables are compared, as in correlational studies, deciding which variable to call independent and which dependent is sometimes arbitrary. They can simply be referred to as variables of interest.

Some Examples of Independent and Dependent Variables

A number of hypotheses drawn from studies undertaken in a research methods course are listed below; the independent and dependent variables have been identified for each one.

1. There will be a statistically significant increase in tolerance scores as measured by the *Tolerance in Diversity Scale* among freshmen college students who are presented a program of skits and discussion on diversity in their English 101 classes as opposed to freshmen college students who are not given the program.

    Independent variable: Exposure to program of skits and discussion on diversity
    Dependent variable: Tolerance score *depends on*

2. There will be a statistically significant difference in graduation rates of at-risk high-school seniors who participate in an intensive study program as opposed to at-risk high-school seniors who do not participate in the intensive study program.

    Independent variable: Participation in intensive study program
    Dependent variable: Graduation rates *depends on*

3. Male veterans seen for depressive symptoms at an outpatient clinic of the Veterans' Administration (V.A.) and prescribed Prozac® have statistically significant lower scores on the *Beck Depression Scale* than male veterans seen for depressive symptoms at an outpatient V.A. clinic who do not receive Prozac®.

    Independent variable: Taking Prozac®
    Dependent variable: Level of depressive symptoms *depends on*

Control Variables

All of the variables in a situation (situational variables) or in a person (dispositional variables) cannot be studied at the same time; some must be neutralized to guarantee that they will not have a differential or moderating effect on the relationship between the independent variable and the dependent variable. These variables whose effects must be neutralized, or controlled, are called *control variables*. They are defined as those factors that are controlled by the experimenter to cancel out or neutralize any effect they might otherwise have on the observed phenomenon. This is often done by making a variable a constant, such as using just women in a study as opposed to both men and women.

Control variables are not necessarily specified in the hypothesis. It is often necessary to read the methods section of a study to discover which variables have been treated as control variables.

Control Var = effects must be neutralized or controlled

Some Examples of Control Variables

The control variables from the above hypotheses are identified below.

1. There will be a statistically significant increase in tolerance scores as measured by the *Tolerance in Diversity Scale* among freshmen college students who are

presented a program of skits and discussion on diversity in their English 101 classes as opposed to freshmen college students who are not given the program.

Control variable: Class level (in this case freshmen)

2. There will be a statistically significant difference in graduation rates of at-risk high-school seniors who participate in an intensive study program as opposed to at-risk high-school seniors who do not participate in the intensive study program.

ref – likely to drop out

> **Control variable:** Status in terms of likelihood of dropping out of school (in this case "at risk" meaning likely to drop out of school)

3. Male veterans seen for depressive symptoms at an outpatient clinic of the Veterans' Administration (V.A.) and prescribed Prozac® have statistically significant lower scores on the *Beck Depression Scale* than male veterans seen for depressive symptoms at an outpatient V.A. clinic who do not receive Prozac.

> **Control:** Gender (in this case male)

Moderator Variables

Moderator var.
the factor measured, manipulated, or selected
Z

The term *moderator variable* describes a special type of independent variable, a second independent variable selected for study to determine if it affects the relationship between the primary independent variable and the dependent variables. The moderator variable is defined as that factor that is measured, manipulated, or selected by the experimenter to discover whether it modifies the relationship of the independent variable to an observed phenomenon. The word *moderator* simply acknowledges the reason that this secondary independent variable has been singled out for study. If the experimenter is interested in studying the effect of independent variable X on dependent variable Y but suspects that the nature of the relationship between X and Y is altered by the level of a third factor Z, the Z can be included in the analysis as a moderator variable.

Some Examples of Moderator Variables

The examples (taken from above) are modified to include a moderator variable in each hypothesis:

1. Freshmen college students from rural areas who are presented a program of skits and discussion on diversity in their English 101 classes tend to get high scores on the *Tolerance in Diversity Scale*, while freshmen college students from urban areas who are not given the program get high scores on the *Tolerance in Diversity Scale*.

> **Independent variable:** Exposure of program of skits and discussion
> **Moderator variable:**   Location of upbringing (rural or urban)
> **Dependent variable:**   Score on *Tolerance in Diversity Scale*

2. At-risk high-school seniors who are below average in intelligence and are offered an intensive study program tend to graduate at a high rate, while at-risk high-school

seniors who are above average in intelligence and do not participate in the intensive study program graduate at a high rate.

Independent variable: Participation in intensive study program
Moderator variable: Level of intelligence
Dependent variable: Graduation rates

3. Female veterans seen for depressive symptoms at an outpatient clinic of the Veterans' Administration (V.A.) and prescribed Prozac® have low scores on the *Beck Depression Scale*, while male veterans seen for depressive symptoms at an outpatient V.A. clinic who do not receive Prozac® have low scores on the *Beck Depression Scale*.

Independent variable: Taking Prozac®
Moderator variable: Sex
Dependent variable: Score on the *Beck Depression Scale*

Intervening Variables

All of the variables described thus far—independent, dependent, moderator, and control—are concrete. Each independent, moderator, and control variable can be manipulated by the experimenter, and each variation can be observed as it affects the dependent variable. What the experimenter is trying to find out by manipulating these concrete variables is often not concrete, however, but hypothetical: the relationship between a hypothetical underlying of intervening variable and a dependent variable. An intervening variable is that factor that theoretically affects the observed phenomenon but cannot be seen, measured, or manipulated; its effect must be inferred from the effects of the independent and moderator variables on the observed phenomenon. You may be familiar with **extraneous,** or **confounding, variables.** Extraneous or confounding variables are examples of intervening variables. When groups in an experiment systematically differ on a variable (other than the independent variable), the variable can be considered extraneous or confounding because the researcher does not know whether differences in the dependent variable are due to the independent variable or not.

In writing about their experiments, researchers do not always identify their intervening variables and are even less likely to label them as such. Oftentimes, it is difficult to identify them. Researchers must take care to avoid confounding variables because they make research results difficult to interpret.

Consider the role of the intervening variable in the following hypotheses (taken from above). One probable intervening variable is given for each example (although there are many different possibilities). Following each example please identify other possible moderator variables.

1. There will be a statistically significant increase in tolerance scores as measured by the *Tolerance in Diversity Scale* among freshmen college students who are presented a program of skits and discussion on diversity in their English 101 classes as opposed to freshmen college students who are not given the program.

Independent variable: Exposure to program of skits and discussion on diversity

> **Intervening variable:** Extent of prejudices
> **Dependent variable:** Tolerance score

2. There will be a statistically significant difference in graduation rates of at-risk high-school seniors who participate in an intensive study program as opposed to at-risk high-school seniors who do not participate in the intensive study program.

> **Independent variable:** Participation in intensive study program
> **Intervening variable:** Attitude toward school *[handwritten: motivation, family support, self-image]*
> **Dependent variable:** Graduation rates

3. Male veterans seen for depressive symptoms at an outpatient clinic of the Veterans' Administration (V.A.) and prescribed Prozac® have statistically significant lower scores on the *Beck Depression Scale* than male veterans seen for depressive symptoms at an outpatient V.A. clinic who do not receive Prozac®.

> **Independent variable:** Taking Prozac®
> **Intervening variable:** Level of family support *[handwritten: age, where served + how long,]*
> **Dependent variable:** Depressive symptoms

A C T I V I T Y

4.2

Intervening Variables

List other possible intervening variables for the above examples.

[handwritten:]
1. race, heritage, language, rural or urban background
2. motivation, family support, self-image
3. age, where served + how long, physical health + wholeness

Causes ⟶ Relationships ⟶ Effects

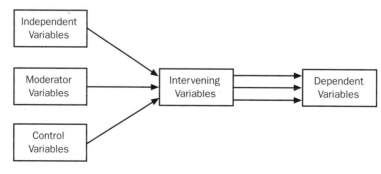

[handwritten in margin: class level, gender, ethnicity]

Figure 4.1 The Relationship of Variables. This figure provides an illustration of the relationship between variables.

Significance of the Problem

No matter if you are proposing to do a study, a program assessment and evaluation, or a grant proposal, you will need to establish the significance for carrying out such a project.

Significance of the Problem in the Research Proposal

In the research proposal the first chapter of the report must present the problem: its nature, scope, and significance. By the significance of the problem, we mean the justification for the proposed study and its implication for practice. You need to document the existence of the problem and its significance by statistics and findings in the professional literature. In addition, the significance of the study includes how the proposed results may contribute to the field.

Significance of the Problem in Program Assessment and Evaluation

The significance of conducting program assessment and evaluation is "to determine whether a program is effective, to what degree, under what conditions, at what financial or social costs, and with what intentional or unintentional outcomes" (Heppner, Kivlighan, & Wampold, 1999, p. 490). The findings gain broader significance when you "seek results that can be generalized to similar programs or to the same program's future" (Hadley & Mitchell, 1995, p. 64).

Significance of the Problem in Grant Proposals

In the project narrative of a grant proposal, you first need to give an overview of the project and build a case for funding it. According to Karges-Bone (1994), justifying why your grant should be funded is the most important aspect of the proposal. The way that you develop the significance for the project is by providing information to demonstrate that a problem exists that could be appropriately addressed if funded. You can best accomplish this by furnishing statistics and citations from professional literature to support your assertions.

Distinguishing Chapter 1 and Chapter 2 in the Research Proposal

You will recall that in Chapter 1 you attempt to build a case for the significance of conducting your study, while in Chapter 2 you present a review of the literature. As you reread the literature you have acquired, try to identify those articles that provide you information related to the significance of the study and those articles that help develop the intervention or approach that you propose. Articles related to the significance of the study would help you write Chapter 1, while articles related to the development of the intervention would contribute to Chapter 2. Another way to distinguish which pieces of literature are related to each chapter is to identify the *dependent and independent variables*. Literature related to the dependent variable usually helps you develop arguments for the significance of the study (Chapter 1), while articles associated with the independent variable help you write the literature review (Chapter 2).

For example, let us pretend that your research hypothesis is "There will be a statistically significant increase in the rate of graduation of at-risk high-school seniors who participate in an intensive study program as opposed to at-risk high-school seniors who receive no intervention." The dependent variable is graduation rate, and the independent variable is participation in an intensive study program. As you attempt to develop the significance of the study in Chapter 1, you will want to concentrate on the literature that discusses the immediate and long-term effects of students dropping out of high school. You will need to cite specific statistics to back up your study. For example, the reviewers may have only a lukewarm response to your stating that an alarming number of students drop out of your high school each year. On the other hand, they are more likely to take action if you specifically state that 20% of the students over the age of 16 in your high school dropped out in the year 2000 compared to 5% in that age group in 1995. Essentially, you are building a case as to why the study needs to be done. In an effort to develop an effective solution, in Chapter 2 you will want to provide a thorough and exhaustive review of approaches that have been tried to increase graduation rates.

P R O C E S S G O A L	Research Proposal

The Significance of the Study

Define a process goal for developing the significance of the study. Some suggestions:

> This week I will find at least five articles related to my dependent variable.

> This week I will identify at least three statistics that will contribute to building a case for doing my study.

> This week I will draft at least two paragraphs related to the significance of the study.

Write your own process goal to help you develop the significance of the study.
As mentioned in Chapter 3 you should keep a list of operational definitions as you identify them. List them below:

P R O C E S S G O A L	Program Assessment and Evaluation

The Significance of the Problem to Be Assessed and Evaluated

Define a process goal for developing the significance of the problem to be assessed and evaluated. Some suggestions:

> This week I will find at least five articles related to the problem to be assessed and evaluated.

This week I will identify at least three statistics that will contribute to building a case for doing my program assessment and evaluation.

This week I will draft at least two paragraphs related to the significance of the program assessment and evaluation.

Write your own process goal to help you develop the significance of the problem to be assessed and evaluated.

As mentioned in Chapter 3 you should keep a list of operational definitions as you identify them.

P R O C E S S G O A L	Grant Proposal

The Significance of the Problem

Define a process goal for developing the significance of the problem for which funding is proposed. Some suggestions:

This week I will find at least five articles related to the problem for which funding is proposed.

This week I will identify at least three statistics that will contribute to building a case for the need to fund such a proposal.

This week I will draft at least two paragraphs related to the significance of the problem for which I am requesting funding.

Write your own process goal to help you develop the significance of the problem for which funding is proposed.

As mentioned in Chapter 3 you should keep a list of operational definitions as you identify them.

Summary

Central to this chapter is the hypothesis, which is a powerful tool in scientific inquiry. We discussed the purposes served by the hypothesis as well as the characteristics of a usable hypothesis. We presented a number of variables (independent, dependent, control, moderator, and intervening) and their importance in writing a hypothesis. In addition we guided you in the writing of your own hypothesis, and we introduced you to writing about the significance of the problem.

Key Terms

alternate hypothesis
control variable
discrete

extraneous (or
    confounding) variable
intervening variable

moderator variable
statistical (or null)
    hypothesis

5

Validity in Research

The term **validity** simply refers to whether what you say is happening in an experiment is a result of the independent variable or some factors not controlled for in the experiment. Achieving validity in research is not an easy task, as the following examples demonstrate.

A statistics professor is designing a new instructional program for graduate students in the helping professions. She has at her disposal computer programs, videos, textbooks, lectures, and group activities. She wants to find out which of these approaches to use and in what combination. To do this she decides to teach the unit on descriptive statistics using the lecture-textbook approach and to teach the unit on inferential statistics using a computer program. She can then see which has the better effect and be guided accordingly—or can she?

Suppose the unit on descriptive statistics were easier than the unit on inferential statistics. If this is the case, students might perform better on the end-of-unit test on descriptive statistics simply because the concepts covered in this unit were easier. It is possible, too, that computer programs are a particularly good way to teach inferential statistics because of the nature of the subject matter but a poor way to teach descriptive statistics. If this were the case, any generalization about the advantage of computers beyond the teaching of inferential statistics would be invalid. It is also possible that the particular computer program that the professor has chosen for teaching inferential statistics is a poor one, and its failure to instruct would not entitle her generally to condemn computer programs for instruction in statistics. Of additional concern is the fact that what the students learned about descriptive statistics might help them learn about inferential statistics, thereby predisposing them to do better on the second unit, regardless of pedagogical technique. Even if the two units were fairly independent in terms of subject matter, the sophistication gained in the first unit might help in mastering the second unit. Furthermore, one of the end-of–the-unit tests might be easier or more representative of the learning material than the other. Finally, the outcome in the two units might occur once but have little likelihood of recurring. It might simply be an unstable outcome due to chance (Bartos, 1992).

What is a researcher to do in dealing with this morass of potential pitfalls? Let us dig the hole a bit deeper with another example before trying to fill it.

A graduate student in student affairs is interested in exploring the similarities and differences in matters of motivation and values between transfer students and disadvantaged high-school graduates making the transition to college. He plans to collect data from 150 transfer students taking summer classes that will get them on track with their major and 150 disadvantaged students attending a university summer program to prepare them for the fall semester. He plans to review the students' responses to open-ended questions and to detect any generalities or trends without any system for data analysis. Needless to say, the representativeness of the samples of the two groups is in serious doubt. Transfer students and disadvantaged students who have the motivation to attend a summer program at a university are probably different in their perceptions and values from those who do not attend such programs. As for drawing conclusions based on visual inspection of some 300 or more responses, aside from the obvious difficulty and tediousness of such an approach, the likelihood that the conclusions would reflect the initial biases of the researcher is great since he may tend to see exactly what he is looking for in the data (Bartos, 1992).

One final example at this point may be helpful. A faculty group is interested in assessing the effectiveness of a new program that allows college seniors who are enrolled in teacher education to begin course work toward their masters degree in school counseling. They are specifically interested in the amount of identification with the school counseling profession that the students in this program make. The students are asked to complete a questionnaire dealing with professional identification during their junior year (prior to the program) and again at the end of their senior year (subsequent to the program). Unfortunately, whatever outcome is obtained is as likely to be a function of the fact that the students had matured a year as it is a function of the program. Another university also wanting to evaluate the new program is fortunate in having two campuses. Since only one campus is to have the new program, the experiment is done by comparing the degree of identification of the students in that program with the degree of identification of students in the old program at the end of their senior year. Sadly, however, it is impossible to be sure that the groups were similar to begin with since the students on the two campuses were known to be different in many ways.

In the real world, as opposed to the laboratory, researchers in the field of education and human services are often confronted by such situations as those described. Because they often lack the opportunity to exercise control over what is to happen and to whom it is to happen, they are often likely to proceed as did the researchers in the examples. It is, however, the contention in this book that the research process, when properly understood, provides a basis for dealing with such situations in a more adequate and logical way. To help you understand the research process we will discuss *internal and external validity* in this chapter. In addition, we will discuss the shortcomings in research situations **(threats to validity)** and how to overcome them.

Internal and External Validity

When researchers conduct quantitative studies, they want to investigate if there is a relationship between independent and dependent variables **(internal validity)** and whether the relationship is generalizable to other people, settings, and circumstances **(external validity).** *Internal validity* asks the question: Did, in fact, the treatments make a difference in this *specific* instance? *External validity* asks the question: To what populations, settings, times, treatment variables, and measurement variables can this effect be *generalized*?

The process of conducting an experiment—that is, exercising some control over the environment—contributes to internal validity while producing some limitation in external validity. As the researcher regulates and controls the circumstances of inquiry, as in an experiment, he or she increases the probability that what is studied is producing the outcomes attained (internal validity). Simultaneously, however, he or she decreases the probability that the conclusions will hold in the absence of the experimental manipulations (external validity). If we do not utilize procedures to provide some degree of internal validity, we may never know what has caused our observed effects to occur. Thus, external validity is of little value without some reasonable degree of internal validity, giving us confidence in our conclusions before we attempt to generalize from them (Bartos, 1992).

Consider again the case of the statistics professor who was designing a new course for graduate students in education and human services. For several reasons her experiment lacked internal validity. To begin with, she should have applied her different teaching techniques to the same material to avoid the pitfall that some material is more easily learned than other material. In fact, she should have taught both units to one group of students using the lecture approach and both units to another group of students using a computer program. Doing so would help offset the danger that computer programs might be especially appropriate for a single unit since this special appropriateness would be less likely to apply to two units than to one. By using two different computer programs and two different lectures, she would also minimize the possibility that the effect was solely a function of the merits of a specific computer program since both computer programs are less likely to be more outstanding (or less outstanding) than one computer program. In repeating the experiment the professor should be extremely cautious in composing her two groups: if one group contains more bright students than the other, obviously that group would have an advantage. (However, the use of two groups is the only way to insure that one teaching approach is not given the advantage of being applied last.) The professor should also, of course, ensure that her end-of-unit tests are representative of the learning material; however, since both groups will take the same tests, their relative difficulty ceases to be as important as it was in the original plan.

A   C   T   I   V   I   T   Y

5.1

Problems in Validity

Review the other two examples and try to identify problems in validity.

Example 2
Transfer students and disadvantaged high school graduates

Example 3
New school counselor program

Discussion of Activity 5.1

Example 2: Transfer students and disadvantaged high school graduates. This example poses some particular problems in external validity. As was pointed out, both the transfer student group and the disadvantaged student group are unrepresentative of the universe of transfer students and disadvantaged students. Thus, it would be difficult to generalize conclusions drawn from this investigation much beyond the specific transfer students and disadvantaged students employed in the study. With such a limitation, the study might not be worth undertaking. The study as described also poses some problems with regard to internal validity. Converting "answers" into "data" is an important part of the research process. In effect the researcher creates a measuring "instrument" to accomplish this conversion. This instrument, like the instruments used in the physical sciences, must possess some consistency. It should generate the same readings when read by different people and when read by the same person at different points in time. If, however, the instrument reflects the researcher's own biases or hypotheses, the researcher may overlook some relevant occurrences to the detriment of internal validity.

Example 3: New school counselor program. This example illustrates a common problem in achieving internal validity: the fact that human beings change over time as a function of the normal course of development and the acquisition of experience. If a study involves the passage of time, then the researcher must use a design that allows for the separation of changes resulting from normal human development from changes resulting from the special experiences of the experimental treatment. It is tempting indeed for a researcher to take measures at Time 1 and Time 2 and conclude that any change was a function of what was introduced during the interim period. If, however, it cannot be proven that the change was a result of the experiment rather than a natural change over time, then the researcher cannot claim to have discovered a change agent.

Threats to Internal Validity

It is important that you are aware of sources of variability that can threaten internal validity so that as you plan your research you can make decisions that will minimize threats to validity. Internal validity is threatened whenever an investigator cannot *maximize* the effects of the independent variable, control the effects of extraneous variables, and *minimize* the effects of random error.

Researchers *maximize* the effects of the independent variable when they make the levels of the independent variable as different as possible so that its effects on the dependent variable can be detected. For example, if the statistics professor above is truly interested in the effect of computer program instruction on graduate students' learning, she would be wise to maximize the impact of computer instruction by teaching the entire course in that way and comparing students' grades to their peers who take a lecture-discussion-taught statistics course. She should ensure that students in the lecture-discussion course do not have any exposure to instruction by computer throughout the course.

Investigators will want to attempt to control extraneous variables as much as possible. An *extraneous variable* is a source of systematic error that confounds results because it correlates with the dependent variable. Again, in the example about the statistics course, graduate students' level of intelligence could be an extraneous, or confounding, variable. If the statistics professor does not have data on the intelligence level of the graduate students, she would not be certain whether an observed difference in the students' grades were due to the computerized instruction or to the students' level of intelligence. Appropriate selection of subjects is one way to control the effects of extraneous variables. This will be discussed further in Chapter 6.

Additionally, researchers need to *minimize* the effects of *random error*. **Random error** is unpredictable error due to fluctuations in such elements as subjects, conditions, and measuring instruments. For example, the statistics professor will want to make sure that the students do not become fatigued or overwhelmed during the computerized instruction.

Researchers need to be aware of the seven extraneous variables that Campbell and Stanley (1963) have identified in their classic research as potential threats to internal validity. These variables can threaten a study's internal validity if they are not controlled. The seven extraneous variables identified by Campbell and Stanley are discussed below.

History. **History** occurs when subjects experience an external event, besides the exposure to the treatment, that may affect their dependent variable. For example, a few years ago, a graduate student in student affairs designed a series of classes on diversity for freshman students. A control group of freshmen were not exposed to the classes. The dependent variable was a measurement in attitude towards diversity. Unfortunately, unknown to the graduate student, a campus committee had arranged a diversity awareness week, including major national speakers and small group sessions that took place concurrently with the study. A number of the participants from both the experimental and control groups attended these activities. As a result, the researcher did not know if any observed effect was due to the diversity courses, the campus-wide diversity initiative, or both.

Researchers can control history by including more than one group in the study. Random assignment of subjects to the groups ensures that subjects in all groups have an equal probability of exposure to external events. The investigator, then, is better able to conclude that an observed difference between groups is due to the independent variable.

Maturation. Maturation is the biological and psychological processes within the subjects that may change during the progress of the experiment and may affect their responses. Maturation processes are a function of time rather than related to the research hypothesis, and they tend to affect most subjects on the dependent variable in a systematic way. Examples of maturation that can limit a study's internal validity are fatigue, boredom, hunger, and physical and intellectual growth. A counselor who involves children in a social skills program over an extended amount of time needs to understand that any improvement in social skills might be due to learning that would have occurred without social skills training rather than to the effects of the procedure.

The best way to control maturation in a study is to include more than one group, using random assignment to form the groups. This procedure will help to ensure that subjects in all groups equally experience maturation and that observed differences between them can be attributed to the independent variable.

Testing. Since tests may serve as a learning experience that will cause subjects to alter their responses on a test when it is readministered, testing is considered a threat to internal validity. For example, let us assume that a researcher pretests subjects before they participate in a study on disability awareness. One participant, who is a biker, is particularly struck by a question asking the purpose of cut curbs. She had always assumed that their primary purpose was for bikers. She now realizes that they are to benefit people with physical disabilities. As she walks around campus after the pretest, she notices the sidewalks, is aware of how difficult it would be to enter many of her classroom buildings, and thinks what a struggle it would be in the cafeteria. If questions such as these serve as a learning experience, they should only be administered as a measurement of the dependent variable once, or they should be designed so as to minimize memory and practice effects. Additionally, researchers can minimize this threat to internal validity by including at least two groups in the study.

Instrumentation. Instrumentation refers to any type of measurement including, but not limited to, testing instruments, human raters, and interviews. Changes in the accuracy or sensitivity of measuring devices or procedures can affect the obtained measurements. If one test is more difficult than another test, or if a different person rates subjects on the rating scales, these factors rather than the treatment can cause the difference in the two scores. As raters become more experienced, their judgment may vary due to higher levels of discrimination or as a result of fatigue or boredom. Let us suppose that a rater is to record episodes of aggression during recess at an elementary school for 1 week prior to the implementation of a peer mediation program and for 1 week after the program has been in place a week. If the incidents of aggression decrease in the second week of observation, we want to be assured that the decrease is due to the intervention rather than a change in the rater's accuracy. Again, including more than one group in the study is a way to control for threats to internal validity. The researcher should also ensure that all groups are subject to the same instrumentation effects. This is accomplished by using the same measuring devices and procedures with all subjects, and by making sure that they do not change during the course of the study.

Statistical regression.   Statistical regression is the tendency of extreme scores on a measure to regress toward the mean when the measure is readministered to the same group of people. Whenever subjects are selected because of extreme scores or their extreme status on the dependent variable (or a related variable), we can predict that they will not score that way again. In some educational research, particularly in remedial education, groups are selected on the basis of their extreme scores. When this selection procedure is employed, the effect of what is called statistical regression may be mistaken for the effect of the intervention. Suppose that students who do exceptionally poorly or exceptionally well on one test are selected to receive an experimental treatment. The mean (average score) of either of these groups will move toward the mean of the population on the second test whether or not the treatment is applied. If the mean for the top 10 students in a class is 90, the scores of these subjects will fan out on the retest—some will be higher and some will be lower—but the mean of the group will be almost inevitably lower. Similarly, the mean for the lowest 10 subjects on the second test will almost inevitably be higher.

Upon retesting, low initial means go up toward the population mean, and high initial means go down toward the population mean. Why? Regression toward the mean occurs because of random imperfections in measuring instruments. The less-than-perfect capacity of the tests to measure the dependent variable will cause a variation of subjects' outcome. Students are likely to vary within a given range because there is a less-than-perfect correlation between the two tests. The more deviant (extreme) students' scores are from the population mean, the more they are likely to vary. Random instability in the population may also account for regression toward the mean. Some subjects may obtain low scores on the first test because they are upset or careless on that day. On the second test they may have better "luck," feel better, or strive harder to bring themselves up to their natural level. As a result, their higher scores will pull up the mean of their group on the second test (Bartos, 1992).

Statistical regression tends to occur at even a higher degree when a group is selected for their extreme status on one variable (i.e., giftedness) and then tested on an unrelated variable (social skills). This tendency is further demonstrated and explained in the activity that follows.

Statistical regression is avoided by including in the study individuals with a wide range of scores rather than only extreme scorers, unless justified by the research question or sampling strategy. In the event that all subjects are of extreme status, then the researcher should include more than one group and ensure that all groups consist of subjects who are similarly extreme. Although no test has perfect reliability, researchers should attempt to use only measurements with sound reliabilities and should use measures that are highly correlated with the variable upon which the subjects are extreme.

5.2

Statistical Regression

Joel Levin (1982) devised the following activity as a modification of Cutter's earlier demonstration of the statistical phenomenon regression toward the mean. While Cutter used dice, Levin used playing cards. The procedure follows:

Setting up the Demonstration and Establishing the "Classification" Measure

The class will use two decks of playing cards, designated decks A and B. The instructor is to remove all of the 7s from deck A and then divide the deck into two partial decks: deck A_1 (made up on all Aces, 2s, 3s, 4s, 5s, and 6s) and deck A_2 (made up of 8s, 9s, 10s, Jacks, Queens, and Kings). The class is to keep deck B intact.

Five students will each select three cards from A_1, and another five students each will select three cards from A_2. The students in group A_1 will add up their three cards (counting Aces = 1) and record the sums of their cards. They will then find the mean for group A_1 (which should be close to the theoretical value of 10.5). Students in group A_2 will repeat the procedure (counting Jacks = 11, Queens = 12, Kings = 13). Their mean should be close to the theoretical value of 31.5. The difference between the two means will be approximately 21 and constitute the "classification" measure. It will be readily apparent that there is no overlap between the two groups.

Demonstration One

The two groups will repeat the procedure, but this time they will select only two cards from their respective A decks and the third card from deck B. Following the calculation of the resulting sums, the students will immediately notice a reduction in the original mean difference (theoretical means are 14 and 28, for a difference of 14).

Demonstration Two

Students will repeat the process by selecting one card from their respective A decks and two cards from deck B. The students will notice that the mean difference shrinks to about 7.

Demonstration Three

Finally, the students will draw three cards from deck B only. The mean difference will essentially vanish.

Discussion

The demonstration can be easily related to real-world situations where researchers make repeated measures on subjects. Demonstration one illustrates what would be expected to happen to extreme-group differences if the measures are highly correlated (e.g., measuring intelligence on two different occasions). Likewise demonstration two shows what would be expected to happen to extreme-group differences if the measures are moderately correlated (e.g., measuring intelligence on one occasion and academic achievement on another). While demonstration three illustrates probable results when the measures, which are taken at different times are uncorrelated (e.g., measuring intelligence and social skills).

Selection.   When the method of assigning subjects to treatment groups results in systematic differences in the make up of the groups at the beginning of the study, then **selection** is a threat to the study's internal validity. Selection is often a problem when intact groups are used. Recently a graduate student proposed to study the effect of group counseling on the academic achievement of nontraditional students who commuted to campus. She held a meeting to recruit interested students. Her plan was to randomly select 15 students in attendance to participate in the group as well as 15 students as the control group. Unfortunately, only 16 commuting students came to the planning session, and, of those, only 14 students chose to participate. The graduate student selected 14 nontraditional commuting students to serve as a control group through a process called **matching** (described in Chapter 6). Her experimental group as well as the control group are **intact groups,** formed on the basis of whether or not they showed up for the meeting. We know that the groups differed in terms of their willingness to sign up for a group. The participants may also vary on other variables. Since selection is often a threat to internal validity when intact groups are used, random assignment is the best method of controlling for this threat. When this is not possible, it is important to administer a pretest to subjects to determine if the groups differ initially in reference to the dependent variable.

Attrition (Mortality).   **Attrition,** or **mortality,** has to do with the loss of subjects during the research study between pretest and posttest or between the groups. As mentioned in the discussion in Chapter 1 on ethics, subjects have the right to drop out of a study at any time. Attrition poses a threat to a study's internal validity when subjects who drop out from one group differ significantly from subjects who drop out from other groups. Suppose that in a study on depression subjects with the highest levels of depression in the experimental group drop out, while subjects with the lowest levels of depression drop out of the control group. The remainder of the experimental group may show a greater gain at the end of the study, not because of its exposure to the intervention, but because the most depressed subjects are missing.

Attrition is also a problem in longitudinal studies since the make up of the final sample may not be comparable to the initial sample when the characteristics of the subjects who dropped out of the study are considered. A researcher is more likely to end up with groups that are representative of the population when large randomized samples are initially used. Pretesting can help determine if dropouts and nondropouts differ regarding their initial status on the dependent variable.

Interactions with Selection.   When researchers study groups that are initially nonequivalent, the problems related to selection, alone or interacting with other factors, can threaten the internal validity of a study. When the experimental and control groups have the same pretest scores, some other differences between them (such as intelligence or motivation) rather than the treatment may cause one of them to get higher scores on a posttest. Because of this type of interaction, studies that compare volunteers with nonvolunteers must always be questioned. In the example above regarding nontraditional commuter students, this is a concern since the volunteers may achieve better academically than the nonvolunteers because they are different initially—they are motivated more highly toward self-improvement to begin with. Interaction between selection and history results when an external event affects one group of subjects but not all groups in the study.

Threats to External Validity

Discussion thus far has been confined to checking the internal validity of the design. Experimenters give this task primary consideration, but they are also concerned about *external validity*—the generalizability or representativeness of the experimental findings. Consequently, they ask: What relevance do the findings concerning the effect of the treatment have beyond the confines of the experiment? To what subject populations, settings, independent variables, and dependent variables can these findings be generalized?

When checking the design of an experiment, experimenters may ask: Can the findings be generalized to all college students? All students attending Harvard University? All Harvard freshmen who are enrolled in a particular course? Or must the findings be limited to the particular Harvard freshmen who participated in the experiment? Experimenters can strengthen the external validity of their design if they describe the population to which the results will apply *before* they conduct the experiment. If they draw a random sample from this predetermined population (e.g., Harvard freshmen) and expose the sample to the treatment, they can make the following generalization: The effect that the treatment had on the sample population (50 Harvard freshmen) will be the same for the population that the sample represents (all Harvard freshmen).

Investigators are concerned not only about the generalizability of their findings with respect to a subject population, but also with respect to settings, independent variables, and dependent variables. Investigators may ask: Will the findings be representative of other geographical areas, sizes of schools, times of day, or time of year? Will the findings provide information about situations in which one treatment, no treatment, variations of treatment, or more than one treatment is present? Will the findings be representative of situations in which one or several types of measurement criteria are used?

The representativeness of the setting that is selected for an experiment will determine how extensively the findings can be applied. If the findings of a study are derived from data that are obtained in a deprived rural area, an experimenter cannot claim that the same effect would have been observed if essay tests or oral participation had been used as the measuring instruments.

A study's external validity is always limited by its internal validity. If researchers cannot conclude a causal relationship between variables within the context of the study, then they cannot conclude that there is a relationship that holds for other populations or other circumstances. A high degree of internal validity does not necessarily guarantee external validity. A relationship between variables may very well exist within the context of the study but may not, however, be generalizable to other populations or conditions.

External validity is affected by a number of other factors. Campbell and Stanley (1963) describe four factors that can threaten external validity:

Interaction between Testing and Treatment. The administration of a pretest can serve as an intervention in itself or can sensitize individuals to the purpose of the research study by alerting them to issues, problems, or events that they might not ordinarily notice. This sensitization may alter their reaction to the independent variable; consequently, these subjects may be no longer representative of the unpretested population from which they came. Suppose that 50 Harvard freshmen are exposed to a treatment, a romantic film with racial-prejudice theme. Their responses to a posttest may not reflect the effect of the film as much as the increased sensitivity to racial prejudice that taking the pretest produced. The effect of the film for the experimental subjects may not be representative of its effect for Harvard freshmen who see the romantic film without being pretested. When a study's results have been tainted by a pretest, they cannot be generalized to other populations that have not been pretested.

Interaction between Selection and Treatment. The characteristics of the subjects who are selected to participate in an experiment determine how extensively the findings can be generalized. A random sample of anxious adults receiving therapy from one community will not be representative of all anxious adults receiving therapy. The intelligence, socioeconomic status, or some other characteristic of those particular clients may cause the treatment to prove more effective for them than for all other anxious adults. If the treatment is therapy based on existential theory, it may produce excellent results in Gross Pointe, MI, where more adults of high socioeconomic status live. But an experimenter cannot generalize that existential therapy will produce the same results with all anxious adults, for the intervention may not be equally effective in inner-city Detroit, where the socioeconomic status is lower. Therefore, when subjects in a study have characteristics that contribute to their response to the independent variable, the results of the study cannot be generalized to people not possessing those characteristics.

Reactivity (Reactive Arrangements). The experimental procedures may also produce effects that limit the generalizability of the experimental findings. If the presence of observers and experimental equipment makes subjects aware of the fact that they are participating in an experiment, they may alter their normal behavior. This phenomenon is known as **reactivity.** If they alter the very behavior that is being measured, the experimenter cannot claim that the effect of the treatment for the sample population will be the same for subjects who are exposed to the treatment in nonexperimental situations.

When the subjects have a tendency to perform better because of the attention they are receiving, this is called the **Hawthorne effect.** The term is the result of the experience of researchers involved in productivity studies at the Hawthorne plant of the Western Electric Company in Chicago during the 1920s. Basically the phenomenon says that, if you single out a group of workers for a special research project, you make those individuals feel and act differently from regular workers. What they found was a consistent increase in productivity in spite of the fact that any changes they introduced seemed unrelated to the improvement in any systematic way. Some factors that may be important in this concept are novelty, awareness that one is participating in an experiment, somewhat modified environment involving observers, or special procedures and the knowledge of the results in the form of daily productivity rates.

Along these same lines, **evaluation apprehension** is what causes subjects to act in ways they believe will help them avoid negative evaluations. **Demand characteristics** are cues that inform subjects of the purpose of the study or suggest what behaviors are expected of them. An experimenter can unintentionally provide subjects with demand characteristics, ultimately biasing the study due to **experimenter expectancy.**

Reactivity can be controlled through the use of deception, **unobtrusive (nonreactive) measures,** or a **blind technique.** Subjects do not know which treatment group they have been assigned to in **single-blind studies,** while neither the subjects nor the experimenter know which group subjects have been assigned to in **double-blind studies.** As discussed in Chapter 1 under ethics, deception is ethical if the gains in performing such a practice outweigh the risks, and if upon completion of the study the researcher explains the study to the participants.

Multiple Treatment Interference. When the same subjects are exposed repeatedly to two or more treatments, the effects of the previous treatments are not usually erasable; hence, the findings may be generalized only to persons who experience the same sequence of treatments repeatedly. If subjects are exposed to three types of music throughout the day, they may be more productive when marching music is played; but they might not respond in the same way if marching music were played continuously.

Other Common Sources of Error to Consider in Structuring a Research Study

The Halo Effect. The **halo effect** is a tendency for some irrelevant feature of the individuals involved in a study to influence, in either a favorable or unfavorable direction, the researchers' impressions. For example, a very strong initial positive or negative impression of a person or group or event tends to influence ratings on all subsequent observations. Basically, it is a concept of "first impressions are lasting impressions." For example, let us suppose that a faculty member in a graduate department has been very impressed with the graduates of a local private college and regularly hires those students when he has graduate assistant positions available. The faculty member is later hired to serve as a rater for an experiment that involves graduate students. It is very likely that he will give high ratings to those graduate students in the study whom he knows are graduates of that particular college.

Other tendencies related to the halo effect plague the validity of ratings. You may have an overrater who rates subjects, in general, very leniently or an underrater who rates subjects, in general, on the side of severity, or one of those individuals who simply rate everybody in the middle no matter where they are.

Self-fulfilling Prophecy. **Self-fulfilling prophecy** involves researchers' expectations (Rosenthal & Rosnow, 1969). What researchers expect to see (where researchers direct their attention) and what they ignore or forget, or what they remember or record, may alter the expectations to their own delight.

The Placebo Effect. A **placebo,** as you may know, is something that researchers use as an alternate stimulus for subjects. Although placebos are primarily used in medical research, they have been used in a broader sense to describe a control treatment that gives subjects the same amount of attention as the experimental treatment but unrelated to the dependent variable. For example, Butler, Miezitis, Friedman, and Cole (1980) describe a study for depressed children in which the placebo treatment lasted for the same amount of time and was carried out in the same format as the experimental treatment, but it dealt with problems unrelated to depression.

According to Krathwohl (1993), in many social sciences situations, the placebo effect is an intended part of the treatment. He states that "counseling and psychological therapy can be effective only if the client wants to participate in it and has some hope, however small, of benefiting from it" (p. 493).

A C T I V I T Y

Threats to Validity

5.3

Please match the following descriptions with the appropriate threat to internal or external validity.

1. __ Changes that occur within subjects during a study over time
2. __ Subjects alter their behavior because they are aware that they are being observed
3. __ An external event that occurs during the course of the research and affects subjects' performance on the dependent variable
4. __ Occurs when subjects who drop out of a study differ in a significant way from those subjects remaining in the study
5. __ Occurs when more than one level of the independent variable is administered to each subject
6. __ The tendency for extreme scores to move toward the mean
7. __ Occurs when the method of assigning subjects to groups results in systematic differences between the groups at the beginning of the study
8. __ Occurs when exposure to a test may alter subjects' performance on subsequent tests

a. history
b. attrition
c. maturation
d. selection
e. testing
f. instrumentation
g. statistical regression
h. interaction with selection
i. reactivity
j. interaction between testing and treatment
k. interaction between selection and treatment
l. multiple treatment interference

5.4

Critiquing a Study

As you will recall, Chapter 2 is a literature review that primarily summarizes empirical research regarding the problem you are researching. Look over the articles you have found for your literature review for Chapter 2 and choose one that involves either an experiment or quasi-experiment. Analyze any potential threats to validity that you notice in the design of the study.

Minimizing Error
in Program Assessment and Evaluation

Just as researchers strive to conduct research that eliminates as many threats to validity as possible, when conducting program assessment and evaluation, researchers attempt to choose the method that will most appropriately and accurately gather the information needed. This is the *how* section of a program assessment and evaluation. Researchers must decide whether to use a qualitative or quantitative approach, or both. They need to decide what they will use as their source of information. Additionally, they need to specify the design most appropriate for their purposes.

The most appropriate method for the program assessment and evaluation depends on its purpose.

- Does the researcher plan to track clients' use of services?
- Is a needs assessment in order?
- Is an assessment of satisfaction necessary?
- Does the researcher want to assess the environment, culture, or service outcomes?
- Would it be feasible for the researcher to compare the program's performance against that of other programs or against professional standards?

These decisions will determine whether the researcher will need to: (a) use quantitative methods that use standardized measures for gathering data and giving meaning to the findings through the assignment of numbers, (b) use a qualitative approach that allows the researcher to investigate the issues in depth, or (c) use a combination of both.

This phase of the program assessment and evaluation process involves how it will assess and provide information about the program's effects. Heppner, Kivlighan, and Wampold (1999) discuss a number of useful methods for program assessment and evaluation, including surveys, focus groups, journals, and content testing. Surveys are generally a quick and inexpensive method for gathering information. They can be used to collect data about participants before and after a program so that changes can be determined. Surveys are ideal when participants can respond through a method such as multiple choice, or when they can respond in a simple way that can later be categorized. Interviews or focus groups are more appropriate when the researcher wants to gather more in-depth and detailed information from participants. In focus groups, individuals discuss their experiences or viewpoints as they interact with a small group of people.

Through the use of journal keeping, researchers can acquire the thoughts and reactions of program participants and staff about specific programs. Content testing is useful when program content is assessed, and this would be achieved through a paper-and-pencil format such as a test.

Our discussion on threats to internal and external validity included considerations on how to best avoid them. Likewise, Heppner et al. (1999) state that, in program assessment and evaluation, it is crucial to keep the process in focus. By doing so, researchers will avoid wasting time and collecting data on unimportant aspects of the program, and missing opportunities to collect significant data.

Maximizing the Probability of Getting Grants Funded

Just as researchers attempt to increase the validity of their studies by careful planning, they want to maximize the likelihood of funding through the thoughtful designing of grant proposals. Two important areas are (a) establishing goals and objectives, and (b) seeking funding sources.

In Chapter 4 we addressed the need for demonstrating the significance of conducting your project. Once that is accomplished, the next step is to state the goals and objectives. This is one of the most significant aspects in the development of your proposal. The quality of this section of the proposal will depend on the choice of the words used and the organization of the presentation. Although many people use the terms *goals* and *objectives* interchangeably, their meanings differ. A **goal** tells about a desired change in general terms, while **objectives** are specific, measurable outcomes. Some examples are:

Goal: To improve orientation services for transfer students.

Objective: To provide an orientation program for 100% of all transfer students that recognizes the unique developmental issues of transfer students.

Goal: To make available postsecondary education opportunities for high school seniors who seek technical training.

Objective: To establish an educational fair that includes representatives from at least 20 postsecondary technical schools and serves at least 75 students.

Properly designed objectives will help you develop your proposal in two critical ways. First, they will establish criteria upon which your project can be evaluated. Second, they can lay the groundwork upon which you can design approaches, trainings, or research strategies.

Seeking funds from appropriate sources is a second issue in maximizing the possibility of receiving funding. It is important that you do your homework and research prospective funders. You will want to target funding sources that have an interest in your type of organization and program. In Chapter 2 we pointed out that reviewing the literature is an excellent way to become familiar with organizations that share your interests.

PROCESS GOAL	Research Proposal

Assumptions and Limitatons

As shown in the research proposal outline on page 23, *assumptions* are premises from which the researcher is operating. These assumptions illustrate the researcher's knowledge of proper planning. For example, when a researcher states that it is assumed that all raters will receive intensive training in the rating method, the researcher demonstrates awareness that instrumentation is a threat to validity.

Define a process goal for writing *assumptions* for your research proposal. Some suggestions:

> This week I will identify at least three assumptions related to my research proposal.

> This week I will draft the assumption section of Chapter 1 of my research proposal.

Limitations are the potential weaknesses of the study that will help the reader judge the validity of the conclusions drawn from the results. These limitations illustrate the researcher's knowledge of proper planning. For example, when a researcher notes under limitations that the researcher is also serving as the therapist in the study, the researcher demonstrates awareness of the potential for experimenter bias.

Define a process goal for writing *limitations* for your research proposal. Some suggestions:

> This week I will identify at least three limitations related to my research proposal.

> This week I will draft the limitation section of Chapter 1 of my research proposal.

Write your own process goal to help you write assumptions and limitations for your proposal.

PROCESS GOAL	Program Assessment and Evaluation

Minimizing Error

Define a process goal for minimizing error in writing the program assessment and evaluation. Some suggestions:

> This week I will review the purpose of the assessment and identify which approach (e.g., needs assessment, cultural assessment, program comparison, etc.) is most appropriate.

> This week I will decide whether the best research method to use should be quantitative, qualitative, or a combination thereof.

> This week I will investigate specific methods for gathering the information (e.g., surveys, focus groups, journaling, content testing).

Write your own process goal to help you minimize error in writing your program assessment and evaluation.

P R O C E S S G O A L	Grant Proposals

Maximizing the Probability of Getting Funded

Define a process goal for maximizing the probability of getting funded. Some suggestions:

> This week I will review the purpose of my grant proposal.

> This week I will write at least two goals and objectives based on the purpose of my grant proposal.

> This week I will identify at least two funding sources that appear to have an interest in organizations or programs similar to the one on which I am basing my grant proposal.

Write your own process goal to help you maximize the probability of getting your grant funded.

Summary

In this chapter we stressed the importance of planning your studies in an effort to minimize threats to internal and external validity. Validity simply asks whether what you say is happening in an experiment results from the independent variable or some factors not controlled for in the study. We discussed the threats to internal and external validity and illustrated ways to control for these errors. The practice activities and process goals that we provided dealt with identifying threats to validity, analyzing threats to validity in published research, and considering possible limitations in the project you are proposing.

Key Terms

attrition
blind technique
demand characteristics
double-blind studies
evaluation apprehension
experimenter expectancy
external validity
extraneous (or
  confounding) variables
goal
halo effect

Hawthorne effect
history
independent variable
intact groups
internal validity
instrumentation
matching
maturation
mortality
objective
placebo

random error
reactivity
selection
self-fulfilling prophecy
single-blind studies
statistical regression
threats to validity
unobtrusive
  (nonreactive) measures
validity

6

Sampling and Research Design

Sampling

An important characteristic of inferential statistics is the process of going from the part to the whole. For example, we might study a randomly selected group of 500 students attending a university in order to make generalizations about the entire student body of that university. The small group that is observed is called a **sample** and the larger group about which the generalization is made is called a *population*. A **population** is defined as all members of any well-defined class of people, event, or objects. For example, in a study in which American adolescents constitute the population of interest, one could define this population as all American males and females within the age range of 12–21 (Bartos, 1992).

Statistical inference is a procedure by which one estimates **parameters** (characteristics of *population*), from statistics (characteristics of *samples*). These related terms are easy to remember with their common initial letters: p in parameters is to population as s in statistics is to samples. Such estimations are based on the laws of probability and are best estimates rather than absolute facts. In any such inferences a certain degree of error is involved.

Rationale of Sampling

Inductive reasoning is an essential part of the scientific approach. The inductive method involves making observations and then drawing conclusions from these observations. If we can observe all instances of a population, we can, with confidence, base conclusions about the population on these observations (perfect induction). On the other hand, if we observe only some instances of a population, then we can do no more than infer that these observations will be true of the population as a whole (imperfect induction). This is the concept of sampling, which involves taking a portion of the population, making observations on this smaller group, and then generalizing the findings to the larger population.

Sampling is indispensable to the researcher. Usually the time, money, and effort involved do not permit a researcher to study all possible members of a population. Furthermore, it is generally not necessary to study all possible cases to understand the phenomenon under consideration. Sampling comes to our aid by enabling us to study a portion of the population rather than the entire population.

Since the purpose of drawing a sample from a population is to obtain information concerning that population, it is extremely important that the individuals included in a sample constitute a representative cross-section of individuals in the population. For example, we might assume that the students at Maywood High School are representative of American adolescents. However, this sample might not be representative if the individuals who are included have some characteristics that differ from the population as a whole. The location of their school, their socioeconomic background, their family situation, their prior experiences, and many other characteristics of this group might make them unrepresentative of American adolescents. This type of sample would be termed a **biased sample.** The findings of a biased sample cannot legitimately be generalized to the population from which it is taken.

Steps in Sampling

The first essential step in sampling is the identification of the population to be represented in the study. In a study of the attitudes and values of American adolescents, the **target population** would be all American boys and girls in the age range of 12–21, granted that adolescence is operationally defined as the period between ages 12 and 21. If we are interested in learning about perceptions of student affairs professionals in the United States, all the student affairs professionals within the system constitute the target population.

However, since it is usually not possible to deal with the whole of the target population, we must identify that portion of the population to which we have access—called the **accessible population**—and it is from this group that we will take the sample for the study. The nature of the accessible population is influenced by the time and resources we have as researchers. In a typical study, for example, we might designate all student affairs professionals in Pennsylvania or just those in Philadelphia as the accessible population.

From the accessible population, we select a sample in such a way that it is representative of that population. For example, we would have to sample student affairs professionals from all over the state of Pennsylvania if Pennsylvania student affairs professionals were the accessible population. Or if student affairs professionals working in Philadelphia were the accessible population, then we would draw the sample from this particular group.

How safely can we generalize from a sample to a target population? If the sample selected is truly representative of the accessible population, then there is little difficulty completing this first step in the generalization process. The general principle is: If a sample has been determined to represent the accessible population, findings from the sample can be generalized to that population. For example, if we selected a representative sample of Pennsylvania student affairs professionals, then we could make generalizations concerning the perceptions of all student affairs professionals in Pennsylvania.

However, generalizing from the accessible population to the target population typically involves greater risk. The confidence we can have in this step depends upon the similarity of the accessible population to the target population (Bartos, 1992). In the example above, we could have more confidence making generalizations about American student affairs professionals if we designated student affairs professionals throughout the country as the accessible population rather than those in Pennsylvania alone. In this way all sections of the United States would be represented and a more adequate sampling of perceptions would be possible.

It is true that we must make an inferential "leap of faith" when estimating population characteristics from sample observations. The likelihood that such inferences will be correct is largely a function of the sampling procedure employed. Various sampling procedures are available to researchers for use in the selection of a subgroup of a population that will represent that population well and will avoid bias.

According to Leedy (1985) there are five basic types of sampling that we associate with random sampling. We have described them below with their advantages and disadvantages. Corresponding diagrams further illustrate the sampling procedures.

Types of Sampling

Simple Random Sampling. **Simple random sampling** is a procedure in which all individuals in the defined population have an equal and independent chance of being selected as a member of the sample. By "independent chance" it is meant that the selection of one individual does not affect in any way the selection of another. Let us say, for example, that a mental health counselor is conducting some research and decides that she does not want more than one member of any family in the research. She could not use random sampling, then, since the criteria of independent chance is not being met. Likewise, if a resident assistant decides that he will limit his study to include no more than one resident from each room, then he cannot use simple random sampling.

Various means can be used to derive a simple random sample. These include picking names from a fish bowl, box, etc.; using a table of random numbers (see Appendix E); or generating numbers (with each number representing a name) from a computer or calculator.

For example, if members of a state-level school counseling professional organization decide to survey school counselors, they could get a list of school counselors (the population) from the state department of education. They could cut up the list of names, put the slips in a container, and randomly select the number of school counselors desired by picking out one name at a time. (They need to make sure that they write down each selected name and return it to the container before picking the next name in order to keep the probability for selection constant). An alternate means would be to number names on the list and put corresponding numbered slips in a container. This numbered list would also be useful when using a table of random numbers or with computer-generated number lists.

Systematic Random Sampling. As with random sampling, **systematic random sampling** is used to obtain a sample from the defined population. This technique can be used if all members in the defined population have already been placed on a list in random order. By random order we mean that there is no relationship between the order in which the subjects are listed and the characteristic being measured. If a researcher were to study the effect of caseload size on counselor burnout, an alphabetical list would be considered random while a list of counselors arranged in order of size of caseload would not be random (meaning that every nth individual shares a certain characteristic). Researchers then divide the number in the population by the number needed for the sample. For example, if there are 3,000 school counselors on the list provided by the stated Department of Education, and the researcher wants to sample 300 (or 10%) of the population, the researchers will count every 10th school counselor.

Stratified Random Sampling. Researchers use **stratified random sampling** when they want certain subgroups to be represented in the sample. Stratified random sampling is particularly appropriate in studies in which the research problem requires a comparison among various groups, such as among high-school, middle-school/junior-high-school, and elementary-school counselors. This technique is illustrated in Figure 6.1. **Proportional stratified random sampling** occurs when individuals are selected in proportion to their numbers in the population itself. Let us suppose that out of the 3,000 school counselors in the state, the state department of education determines that 1,500 of them are working at the high-school level, 500 are employed at the middle-school/junior-high-school levels, and 1,000 are counseling at the elementary-school level. As indicated in Figure 6.2, the researchers will need to first **stratify,** or separate, the population according to levels: high school, middle school/junior high school, and elementary school. Then they will randomly select subjects from each **strata** in proportion to the number they represent in the overall population. In this example the following number of counselors would be selected: 150 high school, 50 middle school/junior high school, and 100 elementary.

Cluster Random Sampling. **Cluster random sampling** is used when it is more feasible to select groups of individuals than it is to select individuals from a defined population. Let us suppose that the researcher wants to personally administer the surveys to the subjects. It is unrealistic for the researchers to think that they can select 300 school counselors from around the state and be able to personally visit all of the subjects. What they may need to do is to get lists of counselors that are arranged by districts, counties, regions, instructional units, etc. Then, instead of selecting individuals for the study, they will select groups or **clusters** of individuals. This procedure allows researchers to visit only those regions where groups of counselors are selected. This process is illustrated in Figure 6.3. Interestingly enough, when we examine the clusters by strata, we notice that they proportionally represent their overall numbers in the population.

Purposive Sampling. Purposive sampling is also called judgment sampling or polling. It represents a deliberate selection of a sample, manipulated by a researcher in such a fashion as to obtain a representative cross-section of the population. This type of sampling can be very biased and is often not recommended.

The 3,000 Counselors in the State

```
MHHEEMHMHEHHHMEHEMEHEMEHMMEEEEHHHHHHHHHHH
EMEHEMEHEMEEEHHHHHHHMMMHHEEMHEMHEEEHEMEHEME
EEEEHEEMMMHHEEMHEMHEEHMEHEMEHEMEHEHEMEHEMMH
HHHHHHHHHHHMEEHHHEHHEEHHHHHHHEMHHMEHHHHHHHEH
HHEEMHEMHEMEEHEEHEEHEMEHEMEHEMEHEMEEEEHHHHHH
HHEEEHHHHHHHHHHHHHHHHHHHHHHHHHHHMMHHHHHHHH
```

The 3,000 Counselors in the State Stratified by Level

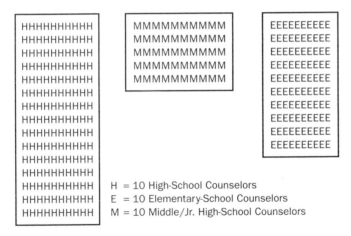

```
HHHHHHHHHH        MMMMMMMMMM        EEEEEEEEEE
HHHHHHHHHH        MMMMMMMMMM        EEEEEEEEEE
HHHHHHHHHH        MMMMMMMMMM        EEEEEEEEEE
HHHHHHHHHH        MMMMMMMMMM        EEEEEEEEEE
HHHHHHHHHH        MMMMMMMMMM        EEEEEEEEEE
HHHHHHHHHH                          EEEEEEEEEE
HHHHHHHHHH                          EEEEEEEEEE
HHHHHHHHHH                          EEEEEEEEEE
HHHHHHHHHH                          EEEEEEEEEE
HHHHHHHHHH                          EEEEEEEEEE
HHHHHHHHHH
HHHHHHHHHH
HHHHHHHHHH        H = 10 High-School Counselors
HHHHHHHHHH        E = 10 Elementary-School Counselors
HHHHHHHHHH        M = 10 Middle/Jr. High-School Counselors
```

Figure 6.1 Stratified Random Sampling

Ten Percent of the 3,000 Counselors in the State Stratified by Level

```
HHHHHHHHHH        MMMMM        EEEEEEEEEE
HHHHH
```

H = 10 High-School Counselors
E = 10 Elementary-School Counselors
M = 10 Middle/Jr. High-School Counselors

Figure 6.2 Proportional Stratified Random Sampling

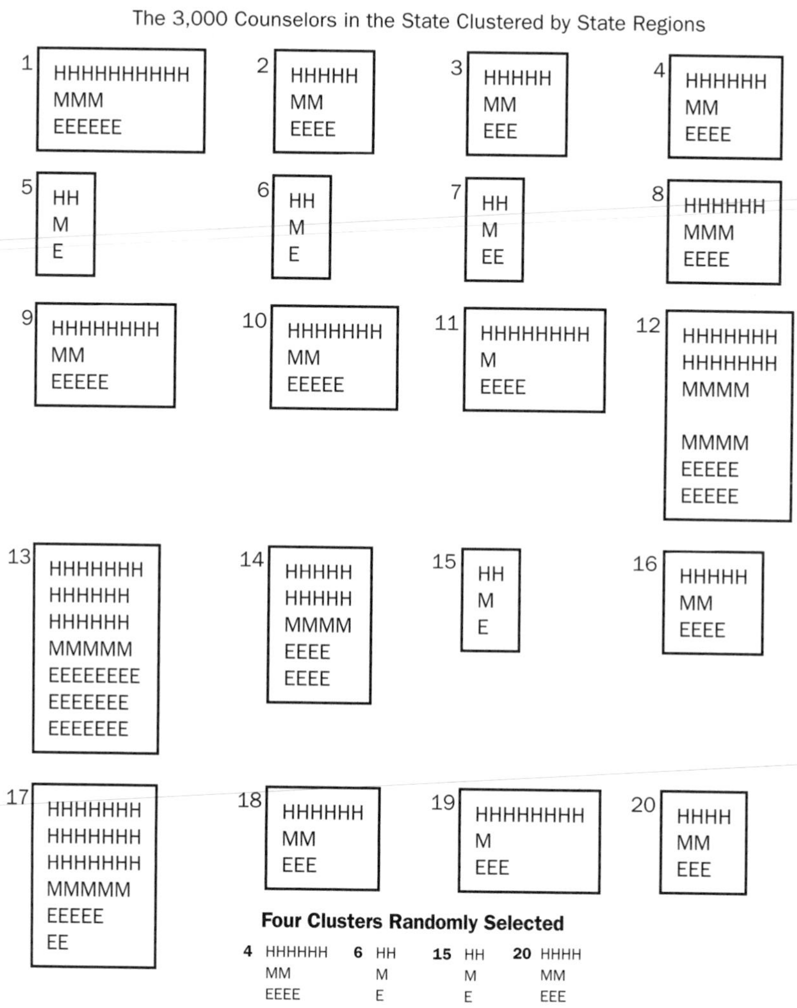

The 3,000 Counselors in the State Clustered by State Regions

1 | HHHHHHHHHH
MMM
EEEEE

2 | HHHHH
MM
EEEE

3 | HHHHH
MM
EEE

4 | HHHHHH
MM
EEEE

5 | HH
M
E

6 | HH
M
E

7 | HH
M
EE

8 | HHHHHH
MMM
EEEE

9 | HHHHHHHH
MM
EEEEE

10 | HHHHHHH
MM
EEEEE

11 | HHHHHHHH
M
EEEE

12 | HHHHHHH
HHHHHHH
MMMM

MMMM
EEEEE
EEEEE

13 | HHHHHH
HHHHHH
HHHHHH
MMMMM
EEEEEEEE
EEEEEEE
EEEEEEE

14 | HHHHH
HHHHH
MMMM
EEEE
EEEE

15 | HH
M
E

16 | HHHHH
MM
EEEE

17 | HHHHHHH
HHHHHHH
HHHHHHH
MMMMM
EEEEE
EE

18 | HHHHHH
MM
EEE

19 | HHHHHHHH
M
EEE

20 | HHHH
MM
EEE

Four Clusters Randomly Selected

4 HHHHHH   6 HH   15 HH   20 HHHH
MM   M   M   MM
EEEE   E   E   EEE

Through random sampling of clusters approximately 10 percent of each stratum was selected:

- 140 High-School Counselors were selected out of 1,500 (which is 9.3%).
- 60 Middle/Jr. High-Counselors were selected out of 500 (which is 12%).
- 90 Elementary-Counselors were selected out of 100 (which is 9%).

H = 10 High-School Counselors
E = 10 Elementary-School Counselors
M = 10 Middle/Jr. High-School Counselors

Figure 6.3 Cluster Sampling

Volunteer Samples

Random sampling of populations is much more feasible in survey research than in experimental research since only slight demands are made on the subjects. In nearly all educational research that employs methods other than surveys, volunteer subjects are used. When volunteers are used in research, the *accessible population* is volunteers who share a certain characteristic. For example, if a resident director is conducting a study regarding conflict resolution training among college freshmen living in the residence halls, the resident director will probably need to solicit interested students. The students who consent to participate in the study represent volunteer freshmen resident hall students. All findings, then, can only be generalized to volunteer freshmen resident hall students.

Random Assignment

Let us suppose that the resident director proposes to compare the number of roommate conflicts encountered by freshmen residence hall students who are trained in conflict resolution strategies versus freshmen residence hall students who did not receive the training (the control group). Randomization can still occur as long as all groups are randomly selected from the population of volunteers. In this case the resident director would use the most appropriate of the above sampling methods to randomly select the experimental group and the control group. Instead of calling it *random sampling,* the procedure is called **random assignment** when volunteers are used. Random assignment does not assure that the sample is representative of the accessible population, but it does ensure that the subjects in the different treatment groups are reasonably comparable (Borg & Gall, 1983).

When we use random assignment, some degree of difference is likely to be found between groups. This kind of error can be reduced by means of the following two methods. First, as researchers, we should employ large groups, because the larger the group, the less the error. Second, we need to check the groups for "outliers," subjects who do not seem to fit the group. We should eliminate these subjects from the study.

Characteristics of Volunteers

In the fields of counseling, student affairs, and related social science areas, volunteers primarily serve as research subjects. In a classic study by Rosenthal and Rosnow (1975), the researchers identified a number of characteristics shared by volunteer subjects (with a range of conclusions warranting maximum confidence to minimum confidence). At the maximum confidence level they found that on average when volunteers were compared to nonvolunteers, volunteers tended to be: better educated, of higher social-class status, more intelligent, higher in need for social approval, and more sociable. Rosenthal and Rosnow made the following comparisons at a level warranting considerable confidence. They found that volunteers tend to be more arousal-seeking, more unconventional, less authoritarian, and less conforming than nonvolunteers. In addition, they found that females are more likely to volunteer than males, and Jews are more likely to volunteer than Protestants, while Protestants are more likely than Roman Catholics to volunteer.

Researchers need to be concerned about these qualities to the degree to which these characteristics are related to the variables of the study. For example, the above mentioned study in conflict resolution would probably yield spuriously high results when using volunteers since volunteers appear to have a higher need for social approval than nonvolunteers. Conversely, if the study concerned financial aid knowledge acquired through various means (online instruction, written material, or PowerPoint presentation) the tendency for volunteers to seek social approval might not be an issue.

Suggestions for Recruiting Volunteers

As mentioned above, one way to increase the possibility that the sample of volunteers represents the accessible population is to use large numbers of subjects. The ability to recruit enough volunteers for a study is a concern shared by most researchers, particularly since adequate sample sizes are required (as discussed below). Rosenthal and Rosnow (1975) identified 10 variables that affect the rate of volunteering. They stated that researchers should do the following in order to improve the rate of volunteering. When necessary, researchers need to make the appeal for volunteers as interesting and non-threatening as possible. The appeal for volunteers will probably be more successful if made by an influential person and if monetary compensation is offered for participation. Researchers need to state the theoretical and practical value of the study as well as the benefit it will impart to others. They need to communicate the normative nature of volunteering as well.

Sample Sizes

It is important that researchers use the largest sample possible when conducting a study; however, finances and time restrictions may limit the number of subjects to be studied. Borg and Gall (1983) offer the following guidelines for establishing minimum sample sizes. In causal-comparative and experimental research, a minimum of 15 subjects in each group is recommended. In correlational research a minimum of 30 subjects is desired. In survey research at least 100 subjects in each major subgroup should be studied and 20 to 50 in each minor subgroup. We suggest that a minimum of three clusters be used in each condition when clustered sampling is done. For example, if the researcher is using an experimental group and a control group, at least three clusters should be randomly selected for the experimental group and another three clusters should be randomly selected for the control group.

Matching and Blocking

Matching is the process of selecting subjects for experimental and control groups in an effort to make the two groups comparable on variables correlated with the dependent variables. The primary purpose of using matching is to reduce initial differences between the groups. Matching is helpful in studies where small samples are to be used and when large differences between groups on the dependent variable are unlikely to occur.

When using matching in the pretest-posttest control-group design, the researcher would administer the pretest and then match subjects on the basis of their pretest scores. The researcher would then randomly assign one member of each matched pair to either the experimental or control group. Another method of accomplishing this is to rank order all the subjects based on their measurement on the matching variable. The researcher would then take the first two subjects and randomly assign one to the experimental group and the other to the control group. The researcher would continue this procedure until all subjects had been assigned.

Recently a graduate student who had planned to conduct a study on the effects of a support group on commuting students' adjustment to college had to change her research design to include matching instead of random assignment when only 16 students showed up for the orientation meeting. Originally she had planned to randomly assign commuting students who attended the meeting into either the experimental or control group. Instead she decided to assign all of the attendees who decided to volunteer for the study (14 of 16 who originally showed up) to the experimental group, and to track another 14 closely matched students as the control group. Since she planned to measure adjustment to college by grade point average, she decided to match students on a closely related variable, their high-school grade point average. She gained permission from the administration to review records of commuting students and to select 14 who closely matched the 14 students in her experimental group. In addition to grade point average, she matched the subjects on variables such as sex, age, distance from campus, etc. For example, a 20-year-old female who attended the orientation meeting who had a high-school grade point average of 3.20 and lived 25 miles from campus was matched with a 20-year-old female who had a high-school grade point average of 3.05 and lived 20 miles from campus. One limitation in the matching process was the researcher's inability to match subjects on levels of motivation. Those subjects who attended the orientation session demonstrated a different level of motivation from the students who were selected according to their academic records. The graduate student then planned to compare semester grade point averages between the commuting students who participated in the support group and those who were selected as the comparison group at the end of the semester.

Blocking is a method of matching that involves pairing by strata rather than by individual. For example, if a school counselor elicits teachers to participate in a violence prevention study and gets numerous responses, the school counselor will want to ensure that the experimental group and the control group are comparable in terms of grade level involvement. This could be accomplished by randomly assigning an equal number of classes from each grade level to either the experimental or control groups. Let us suppose that only three teachers respond (one at the second grade level, one at the third grade level, and one at the fifth grade level). The counselor may decide to use those three classrooms as the experimental group and to match them with three classrooms at the same grade levels as control groups. Again, this researcher will need to be cautious when reporting any findings since randomization did not take place.

Cultural Considerations When Selecting Populations to Research

Students will probably notice that a significant amount of research is conducted on college student populations because of their easy accessibility. Although universities are making gains in the diversification of college campuses, the majority of the subjects involved in these studies are traditional-aged white college students. Even when diversity among the subjects is noted in the description of the sample, there is usually a disregard for within-group or intracultural differences. We encourage students to consider these cultural aspects when selecting their populations to research. In fact, we state that in their review of the literature students are to identify a missing link. A missing link in much of the literature in the field of counseling and student affairs is the lack of research in populations other than the majority culture. We not only encourage students to plan for diversity in the studies they are creating but to replicate studies that have already been done with the addition of using diverse populations. By conducting a replication study the students already have a research plan to work from, but they are specifically challenged by using populations that are not so easily accessible. Finding psychometric instruments that have been normed on minority populations offers an additional challenge.

Group Experimental Research Designs

In this section we present nine common designs for group experimental research. We organize the presentation around the sources of invalidity developed by Campbell and Stanley (1963) as discussed in Chapter 5. We have defined research as the empirical, systematic investigation of two or more variables. Each design offers the researcher the specific procedures for carrying out a study. Selection of a given design dictates such factors as whether there will be a control group, whether subjects will be randomly assigned to groups, whether each group will be pretested, and how the results will be analyzed. Researchers must choose the appropriate design for their particular hypothesis and consider which design controls the most sources of internal and external validity since models vary widely in the degree to which they control the various threats.

There are two major classes of experimental designs, **single-variable designs,** which involve one independent variable (which is manipulated) and **factorial designs,** which involve two or more independent variables (at least one of which is manipulated). Single-variable designs are classified as **pre-experimental, true experimental,** or **quasi-experimental** depending upon the control they provide for sources of internal and external invalidity. Since pre-experimental designs do not adequately control threats to validity they should be used cautiously. The true experimental designs provide a high degree of control of threats to validity. Quasi-experimental designs do not offer as much control as true experimental designs but are preferable to pre-experimental designs. Factorial designs are basically elaborations of true experimental designs and permit the investigation of two or more variables, individually and in interaction with each other.

As you examine the research designs in Figure 6.4, which are based on the work of Campbell and Stanley, you will notice that treatments are indicated by X, while measurement or testing is represented by O. If the design is known to control for the source of invalidity (as indictated across the top of the chart) a plus sign (+) has been assigned. If the design does not control for the source of invalidity, then a minus sign (−) denotes it. A question mark (?) indicates that it is questionable whether or not the design controls for the source of invalidity. A brief discussion of all of the designs presented by Campbell and Stanley follows.

Pre-Experimental Designs

The One-Shot Case Study. The **one-shot case study** involves one group that is exposed to a treatment and then posttested. An example of this might be a school counselor who presents a decision-making unit to a ninth grade class and then administers an instrument that measures the students' decision-making skills. None of the relevant threats to validity are controlled through this design.

The One-Group Pretest-Posttest Design. The **one-group pretest-posttest design** involves one group which is pretested, exposed to a treatment, and posttested. In the above example concerning the decision-making unit, the school counselor would administer a pretest in addition to the posttest. Although this design controls several sources of invalidity not controlled by the one-shot case study, a number of additional factors are relevant to this design, which are not controlled for.

The Static-Group Comparison. The **static-group comparison** involves at least two groups: one receives a new, or unusual, treatment, and both groups are posttested. In the example of the ninth grade decision-making unit, one class would receive the treatment, while another class would not. The counselor would administer a posttest to both groups. Since subjects are not randomly assigned to groups, and since there is no pretest data, it is difficult to determine just how equivalent the groups are.

True-Experimental Designs

True-experimental designs have four characteristics:

- The true-experimental designs control for nearly all sources of internal and external validity.
- All of the true-experimental designs have one characteristic in common, which none of the other designs has—random assignment of subjects to groups.
- Ideally, subjects should be randomly selected and randomly assigned; however, to qualify as a true design, at least random assignment must be involved.
- All true designs also involve a control group.

Sources of Invalidity

Research Design	Internal								External			
	History	Maturation	Testing	Instrumentation	Regression	Selection	Mortality	Interaction of Selection and Maturation	Interaction of Testing and X	Interaction of Selection and X	Reactive Arrangements of X Situations	Multiple-X Interference
Pre-Experimental Designs:												
1. One-Shot Case Study X O	–	–				–	–			–		
2. One-Group Pretest-Posttest Design O X O	–	–	–	–	?	+	+	–	–	–	?	
3. Static-Group Comparison X O — O	+	?	+	+	+	–	–	–		–		
True Experimental Designs:												
4. Pretest-Posttest Control Group Design R O X O R O O	+	+	+	+	+	+	+	+	–	?	?	
5. Solomon Four-Group Design R O X O R O O R X O R O	+	+	+	+	+	+	+	+	+	?	?	
6. Posttest-Only Control Group Design R X O R O	+	+	+	+	+	+	+	+	+	?	?	

R = Randomized
X = Treatment
O = Testing/Measurement

+ = Design is known to control for source of invalidity
– = Design is not known to control for source of invalidity
? = It is questionable whether or not design controls for source of invalidity.

Figure 6.4 Research Designs According to Campbell and Stanley. *Source:* Campbell, D.T., & Stanley, J.C. (1963). *Experimental and quasi-experimental designs for research.* Chicago: Rand McNally.

Sources of Invalidity

	Internal								External			
	History	Maturation	Testing	Instrumentation	Regression	Selection	Mortality	Interaction of Selection and Maturation	Interaction of Testing and X	Interaction of Selection and X	Reactive Arrangements of X Situations	Multiple-X Interference
Quasi-Experimental Designs:												
7. Time-Series $0\ 0\ 0\ 0X0\ 0\ 0\ 0$	−	+	+	?	+	+	+	+	−	?	?	
8. Equivalent Time Samples Design $X_1 0\ X_0 0\ X_1 0\ X_0 0$, etc.	+	+	+	+	+	+	+	+	−	?	−	−
9. Equivalent Materials Samples Design $M_a X_1 0\ M_b X_0 0\ M_c X_1 0\ M_d X_0 0$, etc.	+	+	+	+	+	+	+	+	−	?	?	−
10. Nonequivalent Control Group Design $0\ X\ 0$ / $0\ \ \ 0$	+	+	+	+	?	+	+	−	−	?	?	
11. Counterbalanced Designs $X_1 0\ X_2 0\ X_3 0\ X_4 0$ / $X_2 0\ X_4 0\ X_1 0\ X_3 0$ / $X_3 0\ X_1 0\ X_4 0\ X_2 0$ / $X_4 0\ X_3 0\ X_2 0\ X_1 0$	+	+	+	+	+	+	+	?	?	?	?	−
12. Separate-Sample Pretest-Posttest Design $R\ 0\ (X)$ / $R\ \ \ \ X\ \ 0$	−	−	+	?	+	+	−	−	+	+	+	

R = Randomized
X = Treatment
0 = Testing/Measurement

+ = Design is known to control for source of invalidity
− = Design is not known to control for source of invalidity
? = It is questionable whether or not design controls for source of invalidity.

Figure 6.4 *continued* Research Designs According to Campbell and Stanley. *Source:* Campbell, D.T., & Stanley, J.C. (1963). *Experimental and quasi-experimental designs for research.* Chicago: Rand McNally.

2 groups
random assign
pre + post tests both
DV
one group-trtmt

The Pretest-Posttest Control Group Design.   The **pretest-posttest control group design** involves at least two groups, both of which are formed by random assignment. Both groups are administered a pretest of the dependent variable. One group receives a new, or unusual treatment, and both groups are posttested. According to this design, the school counselor would need to form the groups by randomly selecting the individuals in each. The school counselor could accomplish this prior to the finalization of schedules by randomly selecting from the entire ninth grade class 25 students who would receive the decision-making unit and 25 students who would serve as a control group. Then the counselor could assign each group of students to separate health classes and teach the decision-making unit through the health curriculum. In the event that the school counselor did not have the opportunity to do randomization prior to the finalization of schedules, the counselor could select 25 students from the entire freshman class to serve as the experimental group and 25 students from the freshman class to be the control group. The counselor would then have to schedule times in the school day when the 25 experimental subjects could come together for the unit and the posttesting. The control group members would have no need to come together, except perhaps for the posttesting.

The combination of random assignment and the presence of a pretest and a control group serves to control for all sources of internal invalidity. The only definite weakness with this design is a possible interaction between the pretest and the treatment, which may make the results generalizable only to other pretested groups. The best approach to data analysis is to simply compare the posttest scores of the two groups. The pretest is used to see if the groups are essentially the same on the dependent variable. If they are, posttest scores can be directly compared using a T-test (discussed in Chapter 10). If they are not essentially the same (since random assignment does not guarantee equality), posttest scores can be analyzed using analysis of covariance (further explained in Chapter 10). A variation of the pretest-posttest control group design involves the random assignment of members of matched pairs to the groups, one member to each group, in order to more closely control for one or more extraneous variables.

Solomon Four-Group Design.   The **Solomon four-group design,** a factorial design, involves random assignment of subjects to one of four groups. Two of the groups are pretested, and two of the groups are not. One of the pretested groups and one of the groups that did not receive the pretest receive the experimental treatment. All four of the groups are posttested. Continuing with the example above, the school counselor would select four groups of freshmen students to study in the decision-making research. Only two of the four groups would receive the training, and of the two groups receiving the training only one of them would be pretested. All four of the groups would receive the posttest. This design combines the pretest-posttest control group design with the posttest-only control group design. As previously mentioned, in the pretest-posttest control group design, a possible interaction may exist between the pretest and the treatment. The posttest-only control group design, which is discussed below, has mortality as a possible threat to validity. The combination of the two designs results in a model that controls for these two threats to validity. Data resulting from the use of this design are best analyzed through a 2×2 factorial analysis of variance (described in Chapter 10). The factorial analysis identifies possible interactional effects between the treatment and the pretest. The best design depends on the nature of the study.

The Posttest-Only Control Group Design.   The **posttest-only control group design** is the same as the pretest-posttest control group design with the exception that it does not include a pretest. The researcher randomly assigns subjects to groups, the experimental group is exposed to the treatment, and the subjects are posttested. The effectiveness of the treatment is determined by comparing the posttest scores of the groups. As mentioned above, because of the absence of pretest data on the subjects, mortality is the one threat to internal validity not controlled for in this design. Again, matched pairs can be randomly assigned, one to each group, in order to more closely control for one or more extraneous variables.

Quasi-Experimental Design

When it is not possible to randomly assign subjects to groups, the researcher can use *quasi-experimental designs*. They provide adequate control of sources of invalidity.

The Time-Series Design.   The **time-series design** is an elaboration of the one-group pretest-posttest design. One group is repeatedly pretested, exposed to a treatment, and then repeatedly posttested. If a group scores essentially the same on a number of pretests and then significantly improves following a treatment, the researcher has more confidence in the effectiveness of the treatment than if just one pretest is administered. History is a problem since something might happen between the last pretest and the first posttest, the effect of which might be confused with the treatment. Let us suppose that the school counselor, as previously mentioned, pretests the freshmen students numerous times on decision-making skills prior to the teaching of the unit. The counselor may then teach the unit and give the posttest and notice significant gains on the posttest. Although it would be likely that the counselor would surmise that the outcome resulted from the unit, it is plausible that the students received instruction in decision making in another course; thus the results were not specifically due to the counselor's unit of instruction. Pretest-treatment interaction is also a validity problem. While statistical analyses appropriate for this design are rather advanced, the researcher determines the effectiveness of the treatment by analyzing the pattern of the test scores.

Variations of the Time-Samples Design.   One variation of the time series design is the **equivalent time-samples design.** It attempts to control history in time designs by intermittently applying the experimental variable. **Multiple time-series design (or control group time series design)** involves the addition of a control group to the basic design. This variation eliminates history and instrumentation as threats to validity, and thus represents a design with no probable sources of internal invalidity.

The Nonequivalent Control Group Design.   The **nonequivalent control group design** looks very much like the pretest-posttest control group design; the only difference is that the nonequivalent control group design does not use random assignment. The lack of random assignment adds a source of invalidity not associated with the pretest-posttest control group design—possible interactions between selection and variables such as maturation, history, and testing. The researcher should make every effort to use groups that are as equivalent as possible. If differences between the groups on any major extraneous variable are identified, analysis of covariance can be used to statistically equate the groups. An advantage of this design is that, since classes are used "as is," possible effects from reactive arrangements are minimized.

Counterbalanced Designs

In a **counterbalanced design** all groups receive all treatments but in a different order. The only restriction is that the number of groups equal the number of treatments. While subjects may be pretested, researchers usually use this design when intact groups must be employed and when administration of a pretest is not feasible or possible. Researchers assess the effectiveness of the treatments according to the average performance of the groups for each treatment. A unique weakness of this design is potential multiple-treatment interference, which can result when the same group receives more than one treatment. A counterbalanced design should really only be used when the treatments are such that exposure to one will not affect evaluation of the effectiveness of another.

Single-Case Experimental Designs

According to Lundervold and Belwood (2000) the **single-case experimental design** is the "best kept secret" in the field of counseling (p. 78). They recommend this model as an objective means to evaluate counseling practice and to conduct clinically relevant research in practice settings. This procedure is explained as it applies in a counseling practice (which could include a wide-range of settings such as, but not limited to, mental health, school, and college).

Single-case experimental design is a method in which information on one or more individuals is obtained concurrently. Single-system design refers to a method that gathers information on any system that serves as a single unit. In a community mental health setting, for example, the single unit may be a person, an entire family unit or a subset of the family system. In single-case designs there are two phases: *baseline* and *treatment*. In single-case design the evaluation of the effectiveness of the intervention (independent variable) is based on comparisons of data in the baseline phase versus the treatment phase.

Let us use an example in which the single case is a single client (as opposed to a larger unit as described above). The client's behavior during the **baseline phase** (labeled "A") is used as the standard upon which to evaluate changes in the **treatment phase.** A minimum of three observations is needed to establish the baseline. Since the baseline phase is considered a period of "control" with no treatment, it is comparable to a no treatment control group used in between-group experimental methods. During this baseline phase counselors are encouraged to limit their interventions to the establishment of rapport and the initial assessment of the targets of change and corresponding measurements for evaluating change. Following the baseline phase, the treatment phase (labeled "B") begins. At this point a change in the counselor's interventions demonstrates a transition into the treatment phase. For example, let us say that in the baseline phase an Adlerian play therapist primarily uses tracking, "You move slowly around the room," and open-ended questioning, "Who is the boss of this family?" Through this initial phase the therapist hypothesizes that the child is fearful of trying new things and relies on others to do things for him. Since the child continually asks the counselor for help in things he could do himself (e.g., open the can of playdough, reach the dollhouse on the shelf, pick up the crayons that fell on the floor), the counselor decides to make age-appropriate, self-reliant behavior the target for change. The identified target(s) for change are considered the dependent variables.

Researchers are encouraged to select directly observable targets (as opposed to indirect measures) as well as multiple targets in order to enhance construct validity. After selecting of the targets, the researcher must choose a means of measuring (quantifying) the targets. Researchers may choose from a variety of means such as standardized instruments, client-observation, and researcher observation. Systematic methods of observation and data collection are necessary and should include how, by whom, how often, etc. These data indicate the degree to which the client is achieving the target. Repeated observation allows the counselor to determine what factors, if any, have contributed to any observed change.

Counselor interventions are considered to be the independent variables since the assumption in counseling theory is that certain counselor interventions effect change in client behavior. Lundervold and Belwood (2000) compare this to the manipulation or the independent variable in laboratory-based research. In order to increase internal validity, the counseling intervention needs to be specific and have construct validity. In addition, when researchers specifically define their counseling intervention, they allow other counselors to replicate the intervention. When counselors apply the independent variable (or multiple independent variables), they must use the intervention(s) within each session until a stable pattern in the target is seen. When a stable pattern in the target is observed, then the counselor can apply the next independent variable. For example, the play therapist may decide to employ encouragement (a very specifically defined intervention in Adlerian theory). When it is observed that the child is acting age-appropriately and self-reliantly in the play therapy room as a result of the encouragement, the therapist may attempt to help the child generalize this new behavior in situations at home as well. The therapist may choose to use a specific Adlerian intervention "spitting in the soup" (which is a mild confrontation that helps clients make sense of their behavior). The counselor will measure whether the target is achieved in the home through a systematic means of observation that involves the parents.

Visual inspection of graphed data to determine patterns (trends) in data has been the traditional method of evaluating outcomes using single-case research designs. The data are used as the means to demonstrate causality and generalizability and to make treatment decisions. Presently, a variety of techniques have been suggested for the analysis of data resulting from single-case research designs, but there is no general consensus regarding the appropriate statistical approach. Lundervold and Belwood (2000) cite several sources for a more in-depth examination of single-case research designs.

Population and Sampling
Considerations in Program Assessment and Evaluation

In program assessment and evaluation we need to decide *who* to study—more specifically, who will receive the service (e.g., needs assessment) or who will participate in a particular activity (e.g., focus group). Hadley and Mitchell (1995) refer to such individuals as the targets, the persons to receive or participate in services.

If the program assessment and evaluation methodology is going to be quantitative, then the researcher will follow sampling methods previously described in this chapter. Researchers will need to make sure that the sample of persons or programs represents the population of persons or programs being assessed. Having a large representative sample is important so that researchers can generalize their findings about the sample to the population.

If researchers use qualitative methodology for their program assessment and evaluation, it is possible that the researchers may use very small samples. In this process the researcher does an in-depth inquiry with subjects who are often purposely selected (based on the phenomenon to be studied). As described in Chapter 2, in qualitative research the results cannot be generalized to the general public.

Population and Sampling
Considerations in Grant Proposals

In Chapter 5 we discussed the importance of including well-written objectives in the proposal narrative. It is important that you focus the objectives on the population that the grant will serve. You will need to clearly delineate the recipients of the grant. Often the population includes the consumers of the organization or program to be funded (such as parents of children receiving services at a children's agency). However, staff or volunteers of an organization or program may be the focus of the grant. For example, the purpose of the grant may be to expand professional development activities for such personnel. In describing the population to be served by the grant, besides detailing who will be served, you will need to specify if the entire population, or what percentage of it, will be served.

A C T I V I T Y

6.1

Selecting a Population and Sample

(We designed this activity to guide you in the development of a research proposal. Please adapt it to fit your situation if you are doing a program assessment and evaluation or a grant proposal.)

1. First, describe the population with which you plan to work (e.g., senior high-school students in the New England states).

2. Second, describe your accessible population (e.g., senior high-school students from a public high school in Vermont that has a graduating class of 300 and a private high school in Maine with a graduating class of 150).
3. Third, describe your method of sampling (e.g., proportional stratified random sampling so that the resulting sample will proportionally represent the two schools).
4. Fourth, describe your resulting sample (e.g., 90 senior high-school students from the New England states, 60 of whom are from a public high school in Vermont and 30 of whom are from a private high school in Maine. Of those from the school in Vermont, 30 are randomly assigned to the experimental group, and the remaining 30 are randomly assigned to the control group. Of the 30 students from the school in Maine, 15 are randomly assigned to the experimental group, and 15 are randomly assigned to the control group).
5. Examine again what you have written and decide if you want to make any adjustments based on the cultural considerations described in the chapter.

A C T I V I T Y

Choosing a Research Design

6.2

(We designed this activity to guide you in the development of a research proposal. Please adapt it to fit your situation if you are doing a program assessment and evaluation or a grant proposal.)

After each response, indicate which design in Figure 6.4 matches your criteria:

1. Will you use a control group?   1 2 3 4 5 6 7 8 9 10 11 12
   Circle one: yes no
2. Will your subjects be randomly   1 2 3 4 5 6 7 8 9 10 11 12
   assigned?
   Circle one: yes no
3. Will you use a pretest?   1 2 3 4 5 6 7 8 9 10 11 12
4. Will you be manipulating only   1 2 3 4 5 6 7 8 9 10 11 12
   one independent variable?
5. Will you be manipulating more   1 2 3 4 5 6 7 8 9 10 11 12
   than one independent variable?
6. Which designs appear to best   1 2 3 4 5 6 7 8 9 10 11 12
   control threats to internal validity?
7. Which designs appear to best   1 2 3 4 5 6 7 8 9 10 11 12
   control threats to external
   validity?
8. Other_____   1 2 3 4 5 6 7 8 9 10 11 12

P R O C E S S G O A L	Research Proposal

Sampling and Research Design

Define a process goal for selecting the method of sampling and research design for the study. Some suggestions:

> This week I will review Chapter 3 of the sample proposal and pay particular attention to the sections that describe the population and method of sampling.

> This week I will review Chapter 3 of the sample proposal and pay particular attention to the sections that describe the research design.

> This week I will draft the section of my Chapter 3 research proposal related to research design.

Write your own process goal to help you finalize your method of sampling.

P R O C E S S G O A L	Program Assessment and Evaluation

Population and Sampling

Define a process goal for selecting the method of sampling for the program assessment and evaluation. Some suggestions:

> This week I will review the purpose and methodology that I decided upon (at the end of Chapter 5 of the book) for my program assessment and evaluation.

> This week I will decide whom my program assessment and evaluation will serve.

> This week I will draft the section of my program assessment and proposal related to population and sampling.

Write your own process goal to help you finalize your method of sampling.

P R O C E S S G O A L	Grant Proposal

Population

Define a process goal for writing about populations. Some suggestions:

> This week I will review the objectives that I wrote (at the end of Chapter 5 of the book) for my grant proposal.

> This week I will decide whom my grant proposal will serve.

This week I will draft the section of my grant proposal related to population.

Write your own process goal to help you finalize the population served by the grant.

Summary

An important aspect of research planning and design is the process of sampling. In this chapter we attempted to provide a rationale for sampling and to illustrate the various types. We provided you with steps to use in the sampling process. The selection of the research design dictates to a great extent the specific procedures of a study. We gave you an overview of research designs as well as a summary of selected ones from Campbell and Stanley. The single-case experimental design is offered to you as being useful in evaluating counseling practice and in conducting clinically relevant research in practice settings. The practice exercises and research guidelines involve the selection of sampling type and research design.

Key Terms

accessible population
baseline phase
biased sample
blocking
clusters
cluster random sampling
counterbalanced design
equivalent time-samples
   design
factorial designs
multiple time-series
   design (or control group
   time series design)
nonequivalent control
   group design
one-group pretest-
   posttest design

one-shot case study
parameters
population
posttest-only control
   group design
pre-experimental
pretest-posttest control
   group design
proportional stratified
   random sampling
purposive sampling
quasi-experimental
random assignment
sample
simple random sampling
single-case experimental
   design

single-variable designs
Solomon four-group
   design
static-group comparison
strata
stratified random
   sampling
stratify
systematic random
   sampling
target population
time-series design
treatment phase
true experimental

7

Descriptive Statistics: Describing Single Distributions

Counselors and student affairs professionals who are unfamiliar with *statistical procedures* may have difficulty in evaluating the abilities and achievement of their students and clients, conducting program assessments, reviewing research in their areas of specialization, and acquiring up-to-date information. Knowledge of some basic statistical procedures is essential for individuals proposing to carry out research or assessment so that they can analyze and interpret their data and communicate their findings to others. Since it is imperative that counselors and student affairs professionals keep abreast of research and make use of research findings, you need to be familiar with statistical procedures in order to understand and evaluate research studies conducted by others. The proper administration and interpretation of assessments used in schools, universities, and agencies also require some understanding of statistical procedures. This chapter introduces you to statistical procedures used when conducting quantitative research. These same tools may also be helpful in program assessment and grant proposal writing.

Statistical procedures are basically methods of handling quantitative information in such a way as to make that information meaningful. These procedures have two principal advantages for researchers. First, they enable us to describe and summarize our observations. Such techniques are called **descriptive statistics.** Second, they help us determine how reliably we can infer that those phenomena observed in a limited group, a **sample,** will also occur in the unobserved larger population of concern, from which the sample was drawn. In other words, how well we can employ inductive reasoning to infer that what we observe in the part will be observed in the whole. For problems of this nature we will need to employ **inferential statistics.** This chapter will focus on descriptive statistics that are used when describing **single distributions.**

Our Approach to Statistics:
Hand Computation and Technology

Since the introduction of commercial statistical packages such as SPSS (Statistical Package for Social Sciences), computerized programs are readily available to help students and researchers "crunch data." Although we find these programs invaluable for analyzing data, we believe that students should first acquire a basic theoretical understanding of the statistical procedures they are using before entering data into "the black box." We have found that students gain this understanding by first analyzing data through hand computation. Later when they run statistical analyses, for example a t-test, they will realize the function of the analysis (in this case, the comparison of the means of two groups). Therefore, as we cover statistical procedures in the book, we will first walk you through the steps for hand computation in the hope that it will provide you with a general understanding of the procedures. We will then provide an example of a computer printout so that you will become familiar with analyzing the results from a computer analysis. Because numerous statistical packages are available, it is beyond the scope of this book to walk you through data entry and the steps in performing statistical analysis on the computer. We encourage you (in consultation with your professor) to familiarize yourself with a program to which you have access. It is our hope that, after you do the problems by hand, you will then carry them out on the computer. Even if you use a different program than the SPSS version on which our sample printouts are based, you should become familiar with reading and understanding the printouts through your increased knowledge of statistical concepts.

Single Distribution

An example of a *single distribution* is the list of salaries of 10 school counselors in a moderately sized school district. This list is the **data set. Data** are the count or observations of characteristics or events. How would we make sense out of this data if they were merely listed in no particular way, as shown next?

$33,000	$44,000	$33,000	$50,000	$55,000
$38,000	$38,000	$48,000	$60,000	$38,000

One way to do this would be to line up the salaries from largest to smallest, as follows:

$60,000

$55,000

$50,000

$48,000

$40,000

$38,000

$38,000

$38,000

$33,000

$33,000

By lining up the salaries, we begin to see some order in them. At a glance we can see the highest salary as well as the lowest. We can also notice which salaries are duplicated. Therefore, to provide an even more organized presentation, it would be better to use a **frequency distribution,** where each salary is listed only once and the number of times it occurs in the distribution is written next to the salary. Table 7.1 shows these salaries in a frequency distribution.

By using a frequency distribution, we can more readily make observations about the distribution. For example, we notice that half of salaries fall under $40,000, and the six lowest salaries are closely clustered. We may further be interested in grouping the salaries into **intervals.** Note that the intervals must be equal in size, as shown in Table 7.2.

Table 7.1   Frequencies for a Distribution of 10 School Counselors' Salaries

Salary	Frequency (f)
$60,000	1
$55,000	1
$50,000	1
$48,000	1
$40,000	1
$38,000	3
$33,000	2
	$N = 10$

Table 7.2   Frequencies of Intervals for a Distribution of 10 School Counselors' Salaries

Salary Interval	Frequency (f)
$55,001–$60,000	1
$50,001–$55,000	1
$45,001–$50,000	2
$40,001–$45,000	0
$35,001–$40,000	3
$30,001–$35,000	3
	$N = 10$

In some instances, we are interested in the number of scores in a distribution below particular values. This information is shown in a **cumulative frequency** distribution. This is prepared by adding successively from the bottom of the distribution the number of cases (f) in each interval. Thus, the cumulative frequency (cf) of any interval is the total number of scores in the distribution which are lower in value than the upper real limit of that interval. In other words, the cf of an interval indicates the number of scores up to and including that interval. Using the school counselors' salaries, the cumulative frequencies appear below.

At times it is useful to indicate the percent of scores that fall below certain values. To do this, cumulative frequencies are converted into **cumulative percents** by dividing each cf by the N, the total number, and multiplying by 100 (cf/N x 100). The last column in Table 7.4 shows the cumulative percents.

In a distribution of only 10 salaries it is not too difficult to arrange the salaries in this manner; however, this procedure would be very unwieldy if the number of counselors were much higher. You may never have the need to set up a frequency distribution by hand since all statistical packages readily provide you with this information.

Table 7.3   Cumulative Frequencies for a Distribution of 10 School Counselors' Salaries

Salary Interval	Frequency (f)	Cumm. Frequency (CF)
$55,001–$60,000	1	10
$50,001–$55,000	1	9
$45,001–$50,000	2	8
$40,001–$45,000	0	6
$35,001–$40,000	3	6
$30,001–$35,000	3	3
	$N = 10$	

Table 7.4 Cumulative Percentages for a Distribution of 10 School Counselors' Salaries

Salary Interval	Frequency (*f*)	Cumm. Freq. (*CF*)	Cumm. Percent.
$55,001–$60,000	1	10	100
$50,001–$55,000	1	9	90
$45,001–$50,000	2	8	80
$40,001–$45,000	0	6	60
$35,001–$40,000	3	6	60
$30,001–$35,000	3	3	30
		$N = 10$	

Figure 7.1 presents this data in a data file in SPSS. Statistical programs organize data files in rows and columns. Although we only list the one variable of concern here (salary), for each case (identified by ID), this format allows us to add additional variables (such as sex, years of experience, etc.) as needed. Figure 7.2 provides a list of frequencies.

id	salary
1.00	60000.00
2.00	55000.00
3.00	50000.00
4.00	48000.00
5.00	40000.00
6.00	38000.00
7.00	38000.00
8.00	38000.00
9.00	33000.00
10.00	33000.00

Figure 7.1 Frequency Data Set: School Counselors' Salaries

		Frequency
Valid	33000.00	2
	38000.00	3
	40000.00	1
	48000.00	1
	50000.00	1
	55000.00	1
	60000.00	1
	Total	10

Figure 7.2 Cumulative Frequency Data Set: School Counselors' Salaries

In addition to presenting data in a table, the information can also be presented in a **graph.** Graphs concisely provide a visual representation of the data. Graphs often used in the fields of counseling and student affairs include bar graphs (referred to as histograms when describing interval or ratio scale data), circle (or pie graphs), line graphs (e.g., frequency polygons) and scatter graphs (scattergrams). With the exception of circle graphs, the scores or categories are usually recorded on the graph's **abscissa** (horizontal axis), while the frequencies are recorded on its **ordinate** (vertical axis). The type of variable and the scale of measurement determine the type of graph. The appropriate type of graph to use with each scale or measurement follows the scale descriptions. The *Publication Manual of the American Psychological Association* (2001) describes a more extensive explanation of the graphs.

[handwritten margin note: ordinate / abscissa]

Scales of Measurement

Variables can be categorized in several ways. For example a variable can be considered either *continuous* or *discrete*. A continuous variable can theoretically have an infinite number of values (e.g., time), while a **discrete variable** will have a finite number of values (e.g., number of students at a university). Variables can also be distinguished by the way they are counted or measured. The characteristics of the variable determine how you will count or measure the variable. There are four **scales of measurement** by which we measure variables: (1) nominal, (2) ordinal, (3) interval, and (4) ratio. At each **level of measurement** (used interchangeably with scale of measurement) assumptions about the data may be measured, and specific mathematical operations can be applied. Scale of measurement plays a significant role in determining the type of statistical test to use in data analysis, which will be discussed in Chapter 10.

[handwritten margin note: nominal / ordinal / interval / ratio]

Nominal Scale. **Nominal scale** is the simplest type of measurement. The numbers assigned to each condition of the variable serve as names or labels. Take for example the following:

Concentration in the Counseling Program:

1. School
2. Community
3. Mental Health
4. College
5. Student Affairs

[handwritten margin note: nominal scale — counting the frequencies in each category]

In this case a student majoring in school counseling would be assigned a "1," while a student affairs student would be labeled "5." The only mathematical operation permitted on the nominal scale is counting of frequencies in each category. **Bar graphs** and **circle graphs** are examples of the types of graphs used when the data represent a nominal scale.

Ordinal Scale. **Ordinal scale** divides observations into categories and provides measurement by order or rank. The classic example of ordinal measurement is the top "team" found in football and basketball, or "hit" rankings in the recording industry. Consider the following rankings for the top college football teams for a hypothetical week.

1. Miami
2. Texas
3. Ohio State

4. Michigan

5. Florida State

6. Nebraska

7. Alabama

8. LSU

9. Penn State

10. Arizona State

Ordinal ranks do not imply a value between ranks. Miami is not five times better, as a football team, than Florida State. As a matter of fact, there may be little difference between all "top 10" teams, as can be seen when a ninth ranked team "knocks off" a second ranked team. Ordinal measurement is not sensitive to differences within ranks. There may also be extreme differences between the ranks. Namely, if there were only 10 universities in the country fielding football teams and four high schools in the country that schedule football as a major sport, then it is possible that the number 1 ranked team may be much more than 10 times better than the number 10 team. Again, ordinal measurement is not sensitive to these differences (Bartos, 1992).

The **Likert-type scale** on a questionnaire (e.g., 1 = strongly agree...5 = strongly disagree) is an example of ordinal measurement. It would be reasonable for a student affairs professional to conclude that a student who answers "1" to the statement, "The University food service provides quality meals," has a more favorable attitude toward the food services department than a student who indicates a "5." The mathematical property of "greater than and lesser than" can be applied to this scale. Bar graphs and circle graphs are appropriate to use with ordinal scale data.

Interval Scale. Interval measurement is a standardized scale measurement having the properties of order and equal intervals. With interval measurement, there is no **perfect, or absolute, zero** (meaning total absence of a quality being measured). A common example from the scientific field is temperature measured on a Fahrenheit or celsius scale. In the area of counseling and student affairs, examples include most standardized assessments such as achievement tests, IQ tests, personality inventories, and environment scales (Association for Advanced Training, 1996). It is possible to say that the interval between 45 and 50 on a personality inventory is the same as the interval of 50 and 55. It should be noted, however, that "Although most authorities treat scores on IQ tests and other standardized tests as interval data, some believe that the intervals between scales are not equal throughout the range of scores and, therefore, regard these scores as representing ordinal rather than interval" (Association for Advanced Training, 1988, p. 4). For example, a student with a personality score of 90 has a qualitatively greater response on the scale than a student with a score of 45. However, it cannot be said that the student with the score of 90 has twice the personality as the student with a score of 45. Also, is it possible to identify a perfect absence of personality? (Apparently some students believe so. Occasionally in an introductory psychology class students indicate "false" to the question "Everyone has personality"!) The property of equal intervals allows researchers to perform addition and subtraction on the data. **Histograms** and **line graphs** (e.g., **frequency polygons**) are used with interval data.

Ratio Scale. Ratio scale measurement incorporates all of the characteristics of nominal, ordinal, and interval measurement. In addition, ratio measurement incorporates a perfect, or absolute, zero. Examples of a ratio scale include temperature when measured in Kelvin scale and number of correct items on a test. In the counseling field a school counselor might observe a student during two half-hour periods (one in the morning and one in the afternoon) in order to record time on task. If the student were to spend 20 minutes on task during the first observation period but only 10 minutes on task during the second observation period, then the observer could report that the student spent twice as much time on task in the morning. It is possible in this case to report zero time spent on task if the student was distracted during the entire observation period. An absolute zero point permits the mathematical operations of multiplication and division. Also, it allows the researcher to more precisely compare how much more or less of a characteristic one person possesses than another. Histograms and line graphs (e.g., frequency polygons) are used with ratio data.

A C T I V I T Y

Scales of Measurement

7.1

Identify the following with the correct scales of measurement:
a. nominal   b. ordinal   c. interval   d. ratio

1. _c_ temperature in degrees F
2. _a_ number on a player's jersey
3. _b_ level in college (freshman, sophomore, etc.)
4. _b_ class rank
5. _d_ number of observations per minute

Scales of Measurement and Statistics

It is possible to perform arithmetic calculations upon interval and ratio measurements. As a result, it is necessary to have one type of statistical procedure for nominal and ordinal measures and another type of statistical procedure for interval and ratio measures. The techniques used for nominal and ordinal measures are called *nonparametric* **nonparametric procedures.** The techniques used for interval and ratio measures are called **parametric procedures.** One key element in good research involves *Parametric* matching the appropriate statistical method to the research design you choose. Important in this consideration is the determination of the scale of measurement, paired with an understanding of the statistical limitations imposed by the type of measurement scale.

Central Tendency and the Normal Curve

As discussed in Chapter 1, people often use statistics in their everyday conversation. We often use one **index** to summarize a single distribution. For example, we may say that there are 1.5 children in a typical American family. This is a convenient way of summarizing data that represents a whole set of measures. Another example is finding a single score that gives an indication of the SAT scores by this year's group of entering freshmen as compared to last year's, for a college admission counselor's comparative purposes. In statistics three indices are available for such use. They are called measures **of central tendency** or **averages.** We will examine how these measures of central tendency relate to the normal curve.

According to Cherry (2000), the **normal curve,** which serves as the basis for sampling and inferential statistics was discovered accidentally in the 1800s by Belgian scientist Adolphe Quetelet. While plotting the chest measurements of Scottish soldiers, he noted that their measurements clustered around a central value with some variability. The variability assumed a symmetrical bell-shaped curve. When values on a variable are **normally distributed,** we can make certain assumptions about the number of cases falling between specific points on the distribution. A normal curve is referred to as **mesokurtic.** The relative peakedness of a distribution is referred to as **kurtosis.** A **leptokurtic** distribution is one that is more peaked than the normal distribution. You would probably get this type of curve if you were to graph the heights of the players on a college basketball team. A **platykurtic** distribution is one that is less peaked than the normal distribution. Students' pretest scores on a statistics tests would probably show a wide range of scores and represent this shape. Since plat rhymes with flat, it is an easy way to remember that platykurtic refers to the less peaked distribution, while leptokurtic refers to the more peaked one. Distributions can also be asymmetrical as explained in the discussion on skew later in the chapter.

Measures of Central Tendency

Most individuals are more familiar with the term *average* than *central tendency.* To most laypersons the term *average* means the sum of the scores divided by the number of scores. To a statistician the average can be this measure, known as the **mean,** or one of the other two measures of central tendency, known as the mode and the median. Each of these three can serve as an index to represent a group as a whole.

The Mode. The **mode** is that value in a distribution that occurs most frequently. As a way to remember this, you can remind yourself of its meaning in French. If you are like most students, you might be reminding yourself that *à la mode* has something to do with ice cream. But then you will probably ask yourself what ice cream has to do with statistics? Actually, "à la mode" means "in fashion." The value that occurs most frequently is the one that is most fashionable! In all seriousness, however, the mode is the most simple to find of the three measures of central tendency since it is determined by inspection rather than by computation. Looking back at the school counselors' salaries, one can readily see that the mode is $38,000 because it is the most frequent salary.

Sometimes there is more than one mode in a distribution. For example, if the school district hired an 11th counselor and that newly hired counselor earned $33,000, as do the other two at the bottom of the list, we would have two modes: $33,000 and $38,000. The distribution would be **bimodal.** A distribution could also have no mode. This would occur if no value appears more than once. An example of this would be if each of the counselors in the school district had a different salary.

The mode is not often a useful indicator of central tendency in a distribution, for two reasons. In the first place, it is unstable. For example, two random samples drawn from the same population may have quite different modes. In the second place, as discussed above, a distribution may have more than one mode. In published research the mode is seldom reported as an indicator of central tendency. Its use is largely limited to inspectional purposes. A mode may be reported for any of the scales of measurement, but it is the only measure of central tendency that may legitimately be used with nominal scales.

The Median. The **median** is defined as that point in a distribution of measures below which 50% of the cases lie (which means that the other 50% will be above this point). For example, given the following distribution of nine scores,

14   16   16   17   18   19   19   21   22

we find the score, that 18 exactly separates the distribution in half. Thus, the median of this distribution is 18. Note that to find this value, we first placed the nine scores of the distribution in rank order (that is from the lowest to the highest), and then found the score that exactly separates the distribution.

Mathematically we can compute the median for a distribution with an odd number of values by using the following equation:

$$Md = \frac{N+1}{2}$$ (Equation 7.1)

Where N = number of cases

The result is not the value of the median but the position in the distribution that is the median. Again, we must first rank order the scores before computing the median. In this case $(N + 1) \div 2 = (9 + 1) \div 2 = 5$. Thus, the median is in the fifth position. We again find that 18 is in the fifth position.

Let us consider the above distribution with an additional score of 19.

14   16   16   17   18   19   19   19   21   22

We now have a distribution with an even number of scores. Given this distribution of scores, the point below which 50% of the cases fall is halfway between 18 and 19. Thus the median of this distribution is 18.5. Again, we placed the ten scores of the distribution in rank order, and then found the point below which one-half of the scores lie. This point, 18.5, which exactly separates the two values 18 and 19, is called in statistical terminology the **upper limit** of the score 18 and the **lower limit** of the score 19. In computing the median, each score is thought of as representing a range, or interval, from halfway between that score and the next lowest score up to halfway between that score and the next highest score. Thus, in the example, 18 is thought of as representing an interval from 17.5 to 18.5 while 19 represents an interval from 18.5 to 19.5.

Mathematically we can compute the median for a distribution with an even number of values by using the following equation:

$$Md = \text{halfway between } \frac{N}{2} \text{ and } \frac{N+2}{2}$$

(Equation 7.2)

Where N = number of cases

The result again tells us the position in the distribution that is the median; therefore, we must first rank order the scores before computing the median. In this case the position of the median is going to be halfway between $\frac{N}{2}$ and $\frac{N+2}{2}$. Thus, the median is halfway between the fifth position and the sixth position (halfway between 18 and 19, or 18.5).

Consider the list of counselors' salaries again. What is the median salary?

$60,000
$55,000
$50,000
$48,000
$40,000
$38,000
$38,000
$38,000
$33,000
$33,000 (answer: $39,000)

As suggested in the scenario above, let us consider that an additional school counselor is hired at the entry level of $33,000. What is the median salary now? (Answer: $38,000.)

The Mean. The most widely used measure of central tendency is the *mean*, which is popularly known as the average or the **arithmetic average.** It is the sum of all the values in a distribution divided by the number of cases. In terms of an equation it is:

$$\overline{X} = \frac{\Sigma X}{N}$$

(Equation 7.3)

Where

$\overline{X}$ = the mean
Σ = the sum of
X = each of the values in the distribution
N = number of cases

Using the original list of 10 school counselors' salaries, what is the mean salary? (Answer: $43,300.)

Note: $\overline{X}$ (X bar) is used when calculating a mean for a sample. μ (pronounced mu) is used when figuring the population mean.

Students and consumers need to be cautious when they hear the term average used. As we can see in the distribution of 10 school counselors' salaries, the average can be reported very differently. In response to community members complaining about the high salaries of school counselors, the superintendent might report that, on average school counselors only make $38,000. However, when trying to recruit the best school-counseling candidates, the same superintendent might advertise that, on average, school counselors in the district earn $43,300. As you can see, in the first example the superintendent uses the mode since it suits the situation, while in the second situation the superintendent quotes the mean.

Of the measures of central tendency, the mean is the most sensitive to extreme scores. The salaries of $60,000 and $55,000 affected the mean salary in this example.

Shapes of Distributions

As discussed earlier, distributions of scores may be symmetrical or asymmetrical. We find that when a distribution of measures is symmetrical, the values of the mean and median coincide. If a distribution of measures is symmetrical, the values of the mean and the median coincide. If such a distribution has a single mode, rather than two or more modes, the three indices of central tendency will coincide, as shown in Figure 7.3.

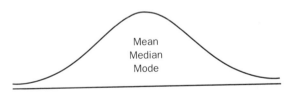

Mean
Median
Mode

Figure 7.3 Central Tendency and a Symmetrical Distribution

If a distribution is not symmetrical, it is described as being **skewed**. In skewed distributions, the values of the measures of central tendency differ. In such distributions the value of the mean, because it is influenced by the size of extreme scores, is pulled toward the end of the distribution in which the extreme scores lie, as shown in Figures 7.4 and 7.5. Extreme values have less of an effect on the median since this index is influenced not by the size of scores, but by their frequency. Extreme values have no impact on the mode since this index, because of its nature, has no relation to either of the ends of the distribution. When the distribution is skewed toward the lower end, or negatively skewed, the mean is always smaller than the median and the median is usually smaller than the mode (Figure 7.4). When a distribution is skewed toward the higher end, or positively skewed, the mean is always greater than the median and the median is usually greater than the mode (Figure 7.5). In cases where the distribution is asymmetrical, or skewed, the median or mode might be better representations.

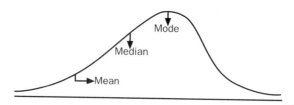

Figure 7.4 A Negatively Skewed Distribution

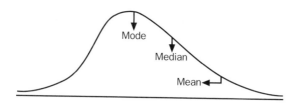

Figure 7.5 A Positively Skewed Distribution

The skew of a distribution can be visually identified by the flat end (or tail) of the distribution. The extreme scores of the distribution are usually located in the tail of the distribution. For instance, if an entire class of students (except for two) found a test to be quite easy, their scores would cluster at the positive end of a distribution (as shown in Figure 7.4). The extreme scores of the two students who had difficulty are found in the tail of the distribution (in this case in the negative end). Therefore, we can say that the distribution is negatively skewed. An easy way to remember this is to state, "The tail tells the tale."

If you have a basic knowledge of the relationship of the mean and median, you can identify the skew of a distribution by comparing the mean and the median without necessarily constructing a visual presentation. At other times graphs, such as the ones described below, are helpful in understanding the shape of the distribution.

Graphs

The *Publication Manual of the American Psychological Association* (2001) describes graphs as figures that show relations—comparisons and distributions—in a set of data. Information is presented on horizontal and vertical axes in an orderly fashion (e.g., small to large) and consistently (e.g., in comparable units of measurement).

Bar graphs are useful for frequency distributions and also for comparing subsamples of a quantitative variable. The following bar graph (Figure 7.6) shows the number of students enrolled in the counseling program described above.

Circle (or pie) graphs are used to show percentages and proportions. They usually represent the frequency distribution of a nominal variable, but can be used for ordinal, interval, or ratio variables for which values have been classified into categories. The

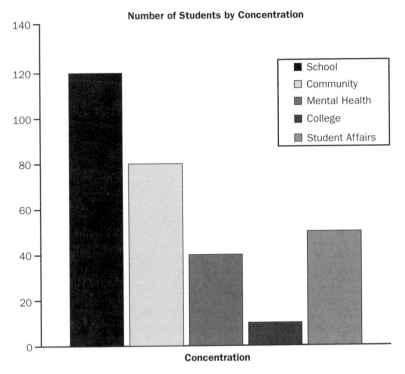

Figure 7.6 A Bar Graph

proportion of students in various concentrations in the counseling program described above is shown in the circle graph in Figure 7.7.

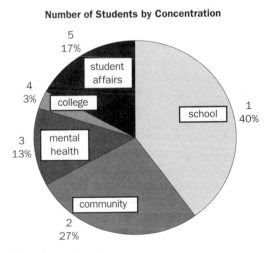

Figure 7.7 A Circle Graph

quantitative

Line graphs are used to show the relationship between two quantitative variables. Both variables need to be continuous, or if discrete, have many possible values. Grid marks on each axis indicate units of measurement. The line graph is constructed by connecting both data points; therefore, all values along the line are meaningful for both variables. A line graph would not be appropriate for showing the information regarding proportion of students in various concentrations in the counseling program (diagramed above) since the students' concentration is nominal data rather than continuous (interval) data. Figure 7.8 is an example of a line graph.

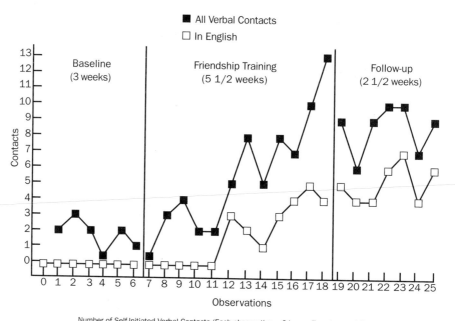

Number of Self-Initiated Verbal Contacts (Each observation = 2 hours; Tuesdays and Thursdays)

Figure 7.8 A Line Graph. *Source:* From "Enhancing Cultural Adaptation Through Friendship Training: A Single-Case Study," by Yi-Ching Liu and Stanley B. Baker, 1993, *Elementary School Guidance and Counseling, 28,* p.97. Copyright ©1993. Reprinted with permission of American School Counselors Association.

Scatter graphs (also referred to as **scattergrams**) consist of single dots plotted to represent the values of single events on the two variable scales on the horizontal, or x, axis (also known as the abscissa) and the vertical, or y, axis (also called the ordinate). These are used for depicting more than one distribution such as correlation coefficient analyses. Figures 7.9 and 7.10 are examples of scattergrams.

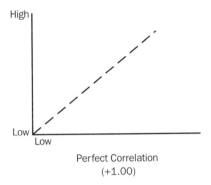

Figure 7.9 Perfect Positive Correlation

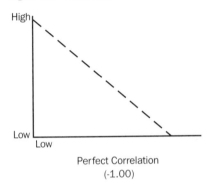

Figure 7.10 Perfect Negative Correlation

A   C   T   I   V   I   T   Y

Central Tendency

7.2

The following activities will help you examine the above concepts. Listed below are the scores that students received on an exam.

Score	f
10	1
9	1
8	1
7	1
6	2
5	4
4	2
3	1
2	1
1	1
0	1

continues

continued

Graph the scores. Which type of graph is the most appropriate?
What is the mean?
What is the median?
What is the mode?

7.3

The Mean and Extreme Scores

In the previous activities you may have assumed that 10 was a perfect score on the exam. Let us say that actually 100 was a perfect score and that in addition to the above scores, one student got a perfect 100. The number of students taking the exam is now 17. Now figure the following:

Mean

Median

Mode

What will happen to the graph? Explain.

degree of dispersion

Measures of Variability

Although indices of central tendency allow us to describe data in terms of average value or typical measure, they do not give us the total picture of a distribution. The mean values of three distributions may be identical, but the degree of dispersion, or **variability,** of their scores might be quite different. In one distribution the scores might cluster around the central value, in another they might be scattered, and in still another there may be no variability. As an illustration, consider the following distributions of scores:

$$\text{(A) } 24, 24, 25, 25, 25, 26, 26 \quad X = \frac{175}{7} = 25$$

$$\text{(B) } 16, 19, 22, 25, 28, 30, 35 \quad X = \frac{175}{7} = 25$$

$$\text{(C) } 25, 25, 25, 25, 25, 25, 25 \quad X = \frac{175}{7} = 25$$

The value of the mean in all three of these distributions is 25, but the degree of scattering of the scores differs considerably. While the scores in distribution (C) do not vary at all, the scores in distribution (A) are obviously much more homogeneous than those in distribution (B). There is clearly a need for an index that can describe distributions in terms of variation of scores. Measures of variability, then, describe in a single number the degree to which scores vary around the central tendency. They describe the spread of the distribution. In statistics, several indices are available for this purpose. The most commonly used are *range*, *variance*, and *standard deviation*.

Range. The simplest of all indices of variability is the **range.** It is the distance between the highest and lowest scores in a distribution and is found by subtracting the smallest value from the highest. For example, the range of distribution (A) above is 2, the range of distribution (B) is 19, and the range for distribution (C) is 0.

The range is an unreliable index of variability in that it is based on only two scores, the highest and the lowest. It is not a stable indicator of the nature of the spread of the measures around the central value. For this reason the use of range is mainly limited to inspection. In some research reports, reference is made to the range of distributions, but such references are usually used in conjunction with other measures of variability, such as standard deviation.

Variance and Standard Deviation. Variance and **standard deviation** are very useful measures of variability. They use the mean as the point of reference and take into account the size and location of each score.

The basic ingredient of both statistics is the **deviation score.** This score (symbolized by x) is the difference between a raw score and the mean. Symbolically this is shown as $x = X - \bar{X}$. Raw scores below the mean will have negative deviation scores, and raw scores above the mean will have positive deviation scores. By definition, the sum of the deviation scores of a distribution is always zero.

It is for this reason that we must square each of the deviation scores in order to use the deviation scores to generate an index of variability. Since the squares of both negative and positive numbers are positive, the sum of the squared deviation scores will be greater than zero. The sum of these squares can be employed to indicate the variability of the scores in a distribution. The mean of the squared deviation scores, called the *variance*, is sometimes used as an index of variability. The definition of variance in mathematical form is

$$\sigma^2 = \frac{\Sigma\left(X - \bar{X}\right)^2}{N} \text{ or } \sigma^2 = \frac{\Sigma(x)^2}{N} \qquad \text{(Equation 7.4)}$$

σ^2 = variance of the population Σ = sum of x = the deviation of each score from the mean $(X - \bar{X})$ N = the number of cases

The following definition of variance in mathematical form is used for the sample of the population

σ² = of the population
s² = of the sample

$$s^2 = \frac{\Sigma(X - \overline{X})^2}{N - 1} \text{ or } s^2 = \frac{\Sigma(x)^2}{N - 1}$$

(Equation 7.5)

s^2 = variance of the sample of the population	Σ = sum of	x = the deviation of each score from the mean $(X - \overline{X})$	N = the number of cases

Note: When calculating a sample variance, the denominator $N - 1$ is used since a sample variance tends to underestimate the population variance.

Let us look at the distribution of intelligence quotients for five children.

(I.Q.s)

X	$x = X - \overline{X}$	x^2
136	0	0
148	+12	144
138	+2	4
134	− 2	4
124	−12	144
680 = ΣX	$\overline{X}$ =136	296 = Σx^2

$$s^2 = \frac{296}{4} \qquad s^2 = 74$$

Column (1) shows the distribution of the intelligence quotients of the five students. The mean of this distribution is 136. Column (2) presents the deviations for each of the quotients. For example, the deviation of the intelligence quotient 136 from the mean is 0, the deviation of the intelligence quotient 148 from the mean is +12, and so forth. Column (3) shows the squares of each of these deviation scores. The sum of these squared deviation intelligence quotients is 296. Putting this value in the formula and dividing by 4, the number of cases minus one (since we are using a sample of the population), we arrive at 74, which is the mean of the squared deviation scores.

Since each of the deviation scores is squared, the variance is expressed in units that are squares of the original units of measure. For example, we find that the variance of the intelligence quotients of these children is 74 points. This tells us that these children are more heterogeneous in intelligence than students with a variance of 4 points and more homogeneous than students with a variance of 100 points.

A variance of 74 points is hard to conceive when the students' intelligence quotients were clustered rather closely. This is due to the squaring of the deviation scores. In order to make this number more meaningful, most counselors prefer to summarize the data in the same unit of measurement as the original data. *Standard deviation* (σ for population and s for the sample of the population), the square root of variance, provides such an index. By definition, the standard deviation is the square root of the mean of the squared deviation scores. By taking the square root of the mean of the squared deviation scores, the numbers are transformed back into the same unit of measurement as the original data. Rewriting this definition using symbols, we obtain

$$\sigma = \sqrt{\frac{\Sigma(X - \overline{X})^2}{N}}$$ (Equation 7.6)

σ = standard deviation for population

$$s = \sqrt{\frac{\Sigma(X - \overline{X})^2}{N - 1}}$$ (Equation 7.7)

s = standard deviation for sample of population

The square root of the mean of the squared deviation scores is 8.60, which is the standard deviation of this distribution.

A C T I V I T Y

Variance and Standard Deviation

7.4

Compute the variance and standard deviation using the following scores. First compute them as if the distribution of scores were a population. Then compute them as if the distribution were a sample of a population.

Scores	Deviation $x = X - \overline{X}$	Deviation squared x^2
7		
6		
6		
5		
5		
5		
5		
4		
4		
3		

The foregoing procedure is convenient when the mean of the distribution is a round number, but it is not in most cases. Therefore, the following formula has been developed to eliminate the tedious task of working with fractional deviation scores. This formula gives the same result with much less labor.

$$s = \sqrt{\frac{\Sigma X^2 - \frac{(\Sigma X)^2}{N}}{N - 1}} = 1.15$$ (Equation 7.8)

Both formulas arrive at the same answer. In this equation the distribution of scores was summed (ΣX) for a total of 50. Then each score was squared. The distribution of squared scores was then summed (ΣX^2) for a total of 262. When these numbers were plugged into the formula it looked like

$$\sqrt{\frac{262 - \frac{2500}{10}}{9}} = \sqrt{\frac{262-250}{9}} = \sqrt{\frac{12}{9}} = \sqrt{1.33} = 1.15$$

The standard deviation belongs to the same statistical family as the mean; that is, like the mean, it is an interval or ratio statistic, and its computation is based on the size of individual scores in the distribution. It is by far the most frequently used measure of variability and is used in conjunction with the mean.

A C T I V I T Y

7.5

The Effect of Constants on Central Tendency and Variability

Using the data in Activity 7.4 compute the mode, median, mean, and standard deviation when a constant of 5 is added to each score.

Scores (C)

7
6
6
5
5
5
5
4
4
3
mode
median
mean
standard deviation

Mathematical Operations on Measures of Central Tendency and Variability

As the above activity illustrates, when a constant is added to every score in a distribution the measures of central tendency are affected, while the measures of **variability** are not. However, when each score in a distribution is multiplied by or divided by a constant, the **measures of central tendency** and variability are both affected.

Standard Scores

If you were to get a 20 on a test and excitedly shared the news with your friends, they might initially think that you had lowered your personal expectations! This would be the case, that is, if the test were based on a possible score of 100. However, your elation would certainly be appropriate if the test had only 20 possible points! A **raw score** (such as the 20 points) is the number of correct answers (in the case of an achievement or ability test) or the number of keyed responses in an interest or personality scale. By itself the raw score has little meaning since we have nothing to compare the data with. **Normative data,** which provides an interpretation of an examinee's test performance relative to a standard to which one can compare the data, is necessary. As long as the norms of a test are based on a standardized or **normative sample** (representative sample of people) raw scores from any subsequent examinees can be compared to the normative group.

Likewise, we can only make a comparison between the relative positions of an individual on two different tests if the two tests have the same means and standard deviations. This seldom happens in practice. To overcome this difficulty we can translate measures into **standard scores,** transformed scores that describe an examinee's test performance in terms of standard deviation from the mean achieved by the normative sample.

Z-scores. A widely used standard score that plays an important role in statistical analysis is the **z-score,** which is defined as the distance of a score from the mean, as measured by standard deviation units. The z-score assumes a normal distribution having a mean of zero and a standard deviation of 1. Z-scores are usually expressed in a range from –3 to +3. The formula for finding a z-score is

$$z = \frac{X - \overline{X}}{\sigma} \qquad\qquad \text{(Equation 7.9)}$$

Applying this formula, a score exactly one standard deviation above the mean becomes a z of +1, a score exactly one standard deviation below the mean becomes a z of –1, and so on. A score with the same numerical value as the mean will have a z-score of zero. For illustration, suppose a student's score on a psychology test is 72, where the mean of the distribution is 78, and the standard deviation equals 12. Suppose also that the same student has a score of 48 on a statistics test, where the mean is 51, and the standard deviation is 6. If we substitute these figures for the appropriate symbols in Equation 7.9, we can derive a z-score for each test.

Psychology Statistics

$$z = \frac{72 - 78}{12} = -0.50 \qquad z = \frac{48 - 51}{6} = -0.50$$

Both of these standard scores belong to the z-distribution, where by definition the mean is zero and the standard deviation is one; therefore, they are directly comparable.

It is apparent in this example that the score of 72 on the psychology test and the score of 48 on the statistics test are equivalent. That is, both scores are indicative of the same relative level of performance. In other words, the standing of the student who has obtained these scores is the same in both tests when compared with the performance of the other students. It would be very difficult to make such a comparison without employing the z-score technique.

Let us look at another example: Suppose a student who has taken these same tests has obtained a score of 81 on the psychology test and a score of 53 on the statistics test. As before, it is difficult to compare these raw scores to show on which test this student has done better. Converting the scores to z-scores makes the comparison easy. Using Equation 7.9, we find the values of the z to be:

Psychology   Statistics

$$z = \frac{81 - 78}{12} = +0.25 \qquad z = \frac{53 - 51}{6} = +0.33$$

This rather surprising result shows that the score of 53 on the statistics test actually indicates a slightly better relative performance than the score of 81 on the psychology test. Compared with the other students, this student has done somewhat better in statistics than in psychology.

A disadvantage of z-scores is that we have to deal with negative values and decimal fractions. To overcome these difficulties we can convert z-scores to **T-scores** when comparisons between the scores in various distributions are to be made.

T-scores. The T-distribution has by definition a mean of 50 and a standard deviation of 10. To transform z-scores to T-scores we multiply the z-value by 10 and add 50. The T-score formula is:

$$T = z(10) + 50 \qquad\qquad \text{(Equation 7.10)}$$

The student who had a z-score of .25 on the psychology test has a T-score of 52.50. $T = .25(10) + 50$, which is $2.5 + 50$.

A C T I V I T Y

7.6

T-scores

What is the T-score for the student who had a z-score of .33 on the statistics test?

$$T = .33 (10) + 50 = $$ 53.3

GRE and SAT scores. Several standardized educational exams use a mean͙ a standard deviation of 100. It is important to note that sometimes these means͙ dard deviations apply to subtests rather than the entire test. Examples of these ͙ Graduate Record Exam (GRE) and the Scholastic Assessment Test (SAT). A score of͙ would be one standard deviation above the mean while a 300 would be two standar͙ deviations below the mean.

IQ scores. IQ scores are a commonly used standard score with the mean set at 100. Different tests, though, have set different standard deviations (e.g., Wechsler is 15, while the Stanford-Binet is 16). An IQ score of 130 is two standard deviations above the mean. If an IQ score of 130 sounds familiar, it is probably because many gifted and talented programs use that score as one of the criteria for admittance. One standard deviation below the mean is 85, two standard deviations below the mean is 70, and three standard deviations below the mean is 55. These IQ scores are also meaningful in terms of educational placements.

Stanine. One commonly used type of normalized standard score is the **stanine** (abbreviation of standard nine) developed by the United States Air Force during World War II. Stanines have a mean of 5, a standard deviation of approximately 2, and range from 1 to 9. Raw scores can be easily converted to stanines. The lowest 4% of scores receive a stanine of 1, the next 7% receive a 2 and so forth (see normal curve chart, Figure 7.9).

Percentiles

Most of you are probably familiar with **percentiles.** You all probably remember as students in elementary, middle, and high school getting back standardized test scores. They were often reported in percentiles. A percentile refers to the proportion of people in the norm group whose scores fell below a particular test score. If 20% of the people in the original sample scored below 15, then the score of 15 is said to be at the 20th percentile. If you got a score that placed you at the 80th percentile, you are said to have done better than 80% of those in the norm group.

The derivation of percentiles is based on the calculation of cumulative frequency distribution, where for each score point we calculate the percentage of persons whose scores fall at or below that score point. The 50th percentile corresponds with the median. Two other useful points are known as the **first quartile** (the 25th percentile) and the **third quartile** (the 75th percentile).

In interpreting percentile scores, the higher the percentile is, the higher the person's score is relative to other people. The converse is also true. One disadvantage of using percentiles is that the distance between percentile scores can be misleading, as shown on the normal curve chart shown in Figure 7.11.

The Normal Curve as It Relates to the Distribution of Measures

As previously mentioned, **the normal curve** is a symmetrical distribution of measures with the same number of cases at specified distances below the mean as above the mean. Its mean is the point below which exactly 50% of the cases fall and above which the other

50% of the cases are located. The median and the mode in such a distribution are identical values and coincide with the mean. In a normal curve most of the cases concentrate near the mean. The frequency of cases decreases as we proceed away from the mean in either direction. Approximately 34% of the cases in a normal distribution fall between the mean and one standard deviation above or below the mean. The area between one and two standard deviations from the mean on either side of the distribution contains about 14% of the cases. Only about 2% of the cases fall between two and three standard deviations from the mean, and only about 0.1% of the cases fall above or below three standard deviations from the mean.

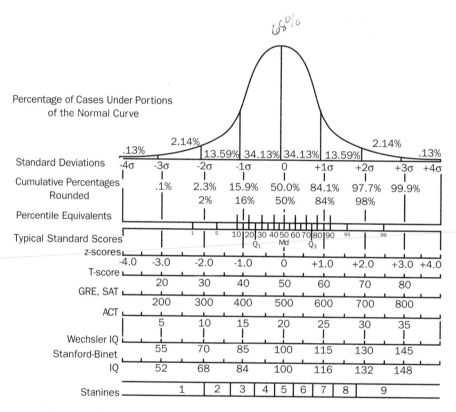

Figure 7.11 The Normal Curve

It is possible to determine the percentage of the cases below and above each z-score in the normal distribution by consulting the normal curve chart above which gives the areas of the normal curve. The chart provides the area under the curve between each z-score. This normal curve chart also provides other standard scores. If you know one standard score (i.e., the T-score) you can easily transform it to another standard score (i.e., stanine) by locating the score you do know on the chart and looking vertically to the appropriate row. For example, you want to know what stanine corresponds to a T-score of 60. First you locate the T-score of 60 and line it up with the equivalent stanine, which is 7. You can just as easily transform the T-score to an approximate z-score, or any of the others shown, through this visual method.

Standard Scores on Tests

7.7

The results of a test indicate that the mean is 50 and the standard deviation is 5. What is the z-score for the following students?

Sam has a score of 60. +2

Lynn has a score of 55. + 1

Bob has a score of 40. − 2

Hints: If any of your answers are outside of the −3 to +3 range, you will want to recheck them.

Using either an equation or the normal curve chart, convert each of their z-scores to T-scores, SAT-type scores, and stanines.

Student	z-score	T-score	SAT-type score	stanine
Sam	+2	70	700	9
Lynn	+1	60	600	7
Bob	−2	30	300	1

Comparing Standard Scores

7.8

Pretend that you are an admissions counselor at a community college and that there is one more opening in the current Culinary Arts curriculum. Since the five students from whom you are to choose are very similar in all areas, you have been instructed to select the one student who shows highest scores in culinary arts. Whom would you select and why?

Student	Exam	Score
Chris	Culinary Arts Success Exam	Stanine = 3.5
Terry	Foods Assessment Test	$z = 1.5$
Bobby	Nutrition Battery of Tests	Percentile = 88
Mickey	Foods Aptitude Test	Raw Score = 95
Brandon	Culinary Placement Exam	T score = 33

Worksheet 7.1   Descriptive Statistics

Name _____

1. A teacher gave a test resulting in the following scores. Compute the following.
Note: Always round the mean to the nearest whole number. Round off all other
answers to two decimal points.

Scores

77	68	61	57
75	66	60	56
71	66	60	56
70	65	59	55

Find the mean.
Find the median.
Find the s^2.
Find the s.
The score of 66 falls at what percentile?
What is the z-score for the raw score 56?
What is the t-score for the raw score 59?
What is the t-score for the raw score 68?
What is the stanine for the raw score 75?

2. Find the following for the distribution of scores listed below:

Scores

89	80	71
87	80	70
83	76	70
82	74	68
		67

Find the mean.
Find the median.
Find the s^2.
Find the s.
The score of 87 falls at what percentile?
What is the z-score for the raw score 80?
What is the z-score for the raw score 68?
What is the t-score for the raw score 68?
What is the stanine for the raw score 67?

P R O C E S S G O A L	Research Proposal

Finalizing Those Components That Rely on Literature

Define a process goal for finalizing those components that rely on literature. Some suggestions:

> I will check that I have correctly reported descriptive statistics in the development of the significance of the study section in Chapter 1.

> I will check that I have correctly reported descriptive statistics in my review of the literature.

> For the next 5 weeks I will spend one evening a week pulling together Chapters 1 and 2.

> For the next 5 weeks I will add the information from one new source each week.

> Each week I will do one of the following activities in order to complete Chapters 1 and 2:

>> Check my in-text citations to see that they comply with APA style.

>> Check my reference page to see that all citations in the text match those on the reference page.

Write your own process goal to help you complete your Chapter 2.

P R O C E S S G O A L	Program Assessment

Finalizing Those Components That Rely on Literature

Define a process goal for finalizing the program assessment components that rely on literature. Some suggestions:

> I will check over my program description for instances where I have reported descriptive statistics to ensure that I reported them correctly.

> For the next 2 weeks I will spend one evening a week reviewing the program description I have written and make necessary additions.

> Each week I will do one of the following activities in order to ensure that the parts of my program assessment that rely on literature are complete and correct:

>> Check my citations to see that they comply with APA style.

>> Check my reference page to see that all citations in the program assessment match those on the reference page.

Write your own process goal to help you complete your program assessment up to this point.

P R O C E S S G O A L	Grant Proposal

Finalizing Those Components That Rely on Literature

Define a process goal for finalizing the grant proposal assessment components that rely on literature. Some suggestions:

> I will check over my grant proposal for instances where I have reported descriptive statistics to ensure that I reported them correctly.

> For the next 2 weeks I will spend one evening a week reviewing the grant proposal components that rely on literature and make necessary additions.

> Each week I will do one of the following activities in order to ensure that the parts of my grant proposal that rely on literature are complete and correct:

>> Check my citations to see that they comply with APA style.

>> Check my reference page to see that all citations in the grant proposal match those on the reference page.

Write your own process goal to help you complete your grant proposal up to this point.

Summary

In this chapter we attempted to demystify statistical procedures by helping you realize that descriptive statistical procedures assist in organizing and understanding data. We provided statistics that are used to describe single distributions beginning with an introduction of the four scales of measurement. While measures of central tendency (mean, median, and mode) provide an index of the average of the distribution, the variance is an index of the spread of the distribution. We presented standard scores as a useful means to understand students' performance on a test and to make a comparison between the relative positions of individuals on different tests.

Key Terms

abscissa
arithmetic average
averages
bar graphs
bimodal
central tendency
circle graphs
cumulative frequencies
cumulative percent
data
data set
descriptive statistics
deviation score
discrete variable
first quartile
frequency distribution
frequency polygons
graphs
GRE scores
histogram
index
inferential statistics
interval measurement
interval scale

intervals
IQ score
kurtosis
leptokurtic
level of measurement
Likert-type scale
line graphs
lower limit
mean
measures of central
    tendency
median
mesokurtic
mode
nominal scale
nonparametric
    procedures
normal curve
normally distributed
normative data
normative sample
ordinal scale
ordinate
parametric procedures

percentiles
perfect (or absolute) zero
platykurtic
range
ratio scale
raw score
SAT scores
sample
scales of measurement
scatter graphs
scattergrams
single distributions
skewed
standard deviation
standard scores
stanine
statistical procedures
the normal curve
third quartile
T–scores
upper limit
variability
variance
z–score

8

Descriptive Statistics: Describing Multiple Distributions

Our discussion of statistical techniques so far has described single distributions of scores. We will now discuss a method of indicating the relationship between pairs of scores.

Correlational Procedures

Statistical techniques for determining relationships between pairs of scores are known as **correlational procedures.** Typically measurements on two variables are available for each member of a group, and one determines if a relationship exists between these paired measurements. The relationship is concisely described by the statistical indices known as **correlation coefficients.** These coefficients show the extent to which change in one variable is associated with change in another variable. For example, we know that achievement and intelligence are related, and so we would expect students with high IQs to earn above-average scores on achievement tests. A simple way of showing this relationship is to plot the intelligence test scores and achievement test scores of a number of individuals in a two-dimensional array called a **scattergram.** Scores of one variable are plotted on the horizontal axis, with the lowest number on the left and the highest on the right. Scores on the other variable are plotted on the vertical axis, with the lowest number at the bottom and the highest at the top. A single point in the scattergram then indicates the position of each individual on the two tests. The achievement test scores of 14 tenth graders are plotted against their intelligence test scores in Figure 8.1. An examination of this figure reveals that there is a tendency for achievement scores to be high when the intelligence test scores are high.

Plotting a scattergram enables us to see both the **direction** and the **strength of a relationship.** *Direction* refers to whether the relationship is positive or negative. In Figure 8.1 the dots form a pattern going from lower left to upper right, because low scores on one variable (intelligence) are associated with low scores on the other variable (achievement), and high scores on one variable are associated with high scores on the other. (By convention, scores of the independent variable [X] are plotted along the horizontal axis, and scores of the dependent variable [Y] are plotted on the vertical axis.) We call such a relationship between variables a **positive relationship** because high scores are associated with high scores and low scores with low scores.

The relationship between two variables is not always positive. Some variables are negatively related. For example, there is a **negative relationship** between number of children in a classroom and the amount of attention the teacher can give to each student. With a negative relationship, high scores on one variable are associated with low scores on the other variable, and the dots on the scattergram go from upper left to lower right. A negative relationship is also referred to as an **inverse relationship.**

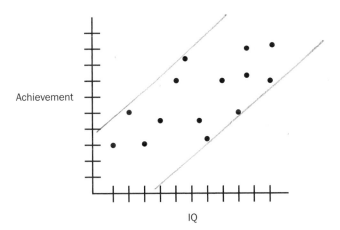

Figure 8.1 Scattergram of the Relationship Between Intelligence and Achievement

Correlation Coefficient

Statistical indices are used to indicate both the direction (negative or positive) and the strength of a relationship between variables. These indices are called *correlation coefficients.* Calculation of a correlation coefficient between two variables results in a value that ranges

−1.0 to +1.0
perfect to perfect,
neg   positive

and zero −
no trends
present

from −1.00 to +1.00. The sign (− or +) of the correlation indicates whether the correlation is negative or positive. A correlation coefficient of −1.00 indicates a perfect negative relationship, a value of +1.00 implies a perfect positive relationship, and the midpoint of this range, zero, indicates no relationship at all. A perfect positive correlation (as illustrated in Figure 7.9) results when each individual's score on one variable is identical in size and sign to the score on the other variable. A perfect negative correlation (as illustrated in Figure 7.10), on the other hand, results when each individual's scores are the same in size but opposite in sign. A zero correlation (Figure 8.2) results when no such trends are present, when positions on one variable are not associated with positions on the other (Bartos, 1992).

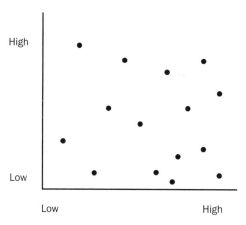

Figure 8.2 Zero Correlation

The strength of the relationship is indicated by the absolute value of the correlation coefficient. The absolute value indicates the distance of the index from zero. For example, the absolute value of +.70 is written |+.70| and equals .70. On the other hand, the absolute value of −.80 is written |−.80| and equals .80. As noted and diagramed in Figure 8.3, −.80 is further from zero than +.70 and thus -.80 is a stronger relationship.

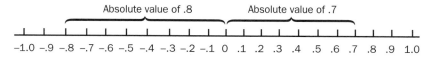

Figure 8.3 Absolute Value

A scattergram of scores also reveals the strength of the relationship between variables. If the dots in the scattergram form a straight line, the correlation is perfect (either +1.0 or −1.0). If the dots in the scattergram form a narrow band, so that when a straight line is drawn through the band the dots will be near the line, a strong relationship exists between the variables. Widely scattered dots, however, indicate a relatively weak relationship between the variables. The greater the deviation of the scores from a straight line, the nearer to zero is the coefficient of correlation.

Correlation coefficients in educational and psychological measures, because of the complexity of these phenomena, seldom reach the maximum points of +1.00 and −1.00. For these measures, any coefficient that is more than .90 plus or minus is usually considered to be very high.

In interpreting the coefficient of correlation, one should keep the following points in mind.

1. *Correlation does not necessarily indicate causation.* When two variables are found to be correlated, this indicates that relative positions in one variable are *associated* with relative positions in the other variable. It does not necessarily mean that changes in one variable are *caused* by changes in the other variable. In our example we found a correlation of +.82 between scores in a test on descriptive statistics and another test on inferential statistics. This correlation coefficient tells us that a person with an above-average score on one test will probably obtain an above-average score on the other test. We cannot say that a high performance on one test *causes* a high performance on the other. Scores on both tests may be the result of other causes such as the numerical aptitude of the persons who take these tests (Bartos, 1992).

2. *The size of correlation is in part a function of the variability of the two distributions to be correlated.* Restricting the range of the scores to be correlated reduces the observed degree of relationship between two variables. For example, it has been observed that success in playing basketball is related to height; that is to say, the taller an individual is, the more probable it is that person will do well in this sport. This statement is true about the population at large, where heights range widely. However, within a basketball team whose members are all tall, there may be little or no correlation between height and success since the range of heights is restricted (Bartos, 1992). We say that the restriction of range **attenuates** (reduces) the size of the correlation coefficients. This is referred to as **attenuation due to restriction of range.** The effect is explained by the strength of the relationship (which is indicated by how tightly the points in the scattergram surround a line). Scattergrams that look like cigars have higher correlations than scattergrams resembling a square. Let us assume that the two plotted variables in Figure 8.4 have a correlation of .85. If we restrict our observations to X values of 120 or more, we observe those limited points in the upper-right corner box. We can estimate that the correlation coefficient for these values will be only about .30, which is a significant attenuation in the observed correlation due to the restriction in range. In a college that accepts students with a wide range of scores on an aptitude test, we would expect a correlation between the test scores and college grades. In a college that accepts only students with very high scholastic aptitude scores, we would expect very little correlation between the test scores and grades because of the restricted range of test scores in this situation.

3. *Avoid interpreting the coefficients of correlation in an absolute sense.* In interpreting the degree of correlation, keep in mind the purpose for which it is being used. For example, a coefficient of correlation equal to +.50 might be satisfactory when predicting the future performance of a group of individuals, but it might not be wise to use this coefficient of correlation for predicting the performance of one person in a future task. This is, the coefficient of +.50 is not an absolute value with the same implication in both cases (Bartos, 1992).

4. *Correlation coefficient should not be interpreted in terms of percentage of perfect correlation.* Since correlation coefficients are expressed as fractions, individuals who are not trained in statistics sometimes interpret correlation coefficients as a percentage of perfect correlation. An *r* of .80 does not indicate 80% of a perfect relationship between two variables. This interpretation is erroneous since, an *r* of .80, for example, does not express a relationship that is twice as great as an *r* of .40 (Bartos, 1992).

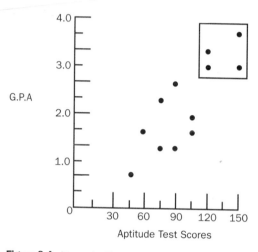

Figure 8.4 Attenuation Due to Restriction of Range

Coefficient of Determination

A way of determining the degree to which researchers can predict one variable from the other is to calculate an index called the **coefficient of determination** (also known as the **percent of predictability**). The coefficient of determination is the square of the correlation coefficient. It gives the percentage of variance in one variable that is associated with the variance in the other. For example, if we find a correlation of +.80 between graduate school G.P.A. and undergraduate G.P.A., 64% ($.80^2$) of the variance in graduate school G.P.A. is associated with variance in undergraduate G.P.A. We can replace the words "is associated with" by "is explained by" or "is determined by." In this example, 64% of the variance in graduate school G.P.A. is explained by undergraduate G.P.A. We can determine the percentage that is not explained by subtracting the explained percentage from 1.0. For example, $1.0 - .64 = .36$. The remaining 36% is attributed to other factors such as motivation, study habits, course load, etc. We caution you that this does not imply that *Y* is caused by *X*. It merely indicates that *X* and *Y* share a certain portion of variability.

Using Correlations in Prediction

While measures of relationship can be used to describe relationships between variables (presently available), **regression analysis** uses the relationship between variables for the purpose of prediction. In other words, when correlational analysis indicates some degree of relationship between two variables, we can use the information about one of them to make predictions about the other. An example of regression analysis is using scores on the Graduate Record Exam (GRE) to predict success in graduate school. In this case, GRE scores are the **predictor variable** and G.P.A. in graduate school is the **criterion,** the variable to be predicted. The accuracy of such prediction is a function of the degree of the relationship between the variables being investigated, that is, the strength of the correlation between them. A higher correlation in either a positive or negative direction, will result in more accurate predictions. A coefficient of correlation near unity, either −1.00 or +1.00, indicates a high degree of relationship. Such high relationships enable one to make accurate predictions about one variable on the basis of information about the other. A negative correlation coefficient is just as good for prediction as a positive correlation.

Scattergrams are used in regression analysis. In such scattergrams, the predictor variable (known as variable X) is shown on the horizontal axis and the criterion (known as the Y variable) is shown on the vertical axis.

In regression a "line of best fit" or regression line is fitted to the points of the scattergram. A straight line that best summarizes the relationship between the two variables and can be described by an equation. For our purposes, we will not describe the equation. It is useful to know, though, that by plugging the predictor variable into the equation, we can estimate a person's score on the criterion variable.

A critical aspect of the use of regression analysis involves the possibility of error in prediction. Although the regression line attempts to minimize error in prediction, it cannot eliminate error altogether unless $r = 1.00$ (which is extremely rare). This potential for error is taken into account, and a statistic called the **standard error of measurement** (discussed in Chapter 9) is computed and used in the process.

Multiple regression can be used to predict a criterion score from two or more predictor or independent variables. An example would be if a graduate program used several variables, such as undergraduate G.P.A., GRE scores, ratings on recommendations, and scores on interviews, to predict success in graduate school. Another example is insurance companies that establish rates based on multiple predictor variables, such as age, sex, and the driving record of the customer.

A C T I V I T Y

Relationships Between Variables

8.1

1. List some examples of positive relationships.
2. List some examples of negative relationships.
3. Which of the following could be possible correlation coefficients?

   +.90   0   −.55   +1.1   −.33
4. Which of the following is the strongest relationship?

   +.60   −.20   −.60   −.70   0
5. What are some other examples of regression analysis?
6. What are some other examples of multiple regression analysis?

continues

continued

7. The correlation between graduate school G.P.A. and scores on the GRE is .70. (a) What is the coefficient of determination? (b) State in your own words what the coefficient of determination tells us in this example. (c) What percentage of the variance in graduate school G.P.A. can be attributed to other factors? (d) What might some of those other factors be?

Procedures for Generating the Correlation Coefficient

Pearson Product-Moment Correlation

The Pearson Product Moment Coefficient of Correlation is the statistical index used for finding the relationship between two sets of linearly distributed interval data such as the scores on a pretest and a posttest. Formula 8.1 and the accompanying problem give some indication as to its applicability in determining relationship.

$$r = \frac{\Sigma^{xy} - \dfrac{(\Sigma^{x})(\Sigma^{y})}{n}}{\sqrt{\left(\Sigma^{x^2} - \dfrac{(\Sigma^{x})^2}{n}\right)\left(\Sigma^{y^2} - \dfrac{(\Sigma^{y})^2}{n}\right)}} \qquad \text{(Formula 8.1)}$$

Let us suppose that we want to use the Pearson Product Moment Coefficient of Correlation to find the correlation between students' performance on Test 1 and Test 2.

Student	Test 1	Test 2
A	8	3
B	2	1
C	8	6
D	5	3
E	15	14
F	11	12
G	13	9
H	6	4
I	4	4
J	6	5

In Table 8.1 we show the calculated values that need to be substituted in the formula. The steps in calculating the formula follow.

Table 8.1

Subject	Test 1 X	Test 2 Y	X^2	Y^2	XY
A	8	3	64	9	24
B	2	1	4	1	2
C	8	6	64	36	48
D	5	3	25	9	15
E	15	14	225	196	210
F	11	12	121	144	132
G	13	9	169	81	117
H	6	4	36	16	24
I	4	4	16	16	16
J	6	5	36	25	30
	78	61	760	533	618

$$r_{xy} = \frac{618 - \dfrac{(78)(61)}{10}}{\sqrt{\left(760 - \dfrac{(78)^2}{10}\right)\left(533 - \dfrac{(61)^2}{10}\right)}}$$

$$= \frac{618 - 475.8}{\sqrt{(760 - 608.4)(533 - 372.1)}}$$

$$= \frac{142.2}{\sqrt{(151.6)(160.9)}}$$

$$= \frac{142.2}{\sqrt{24392.44}}$$

$$= \frac{142.2}{156.2}$$

$$= 0.91$$

The Rank Correlation Coefficient

In research we sometimes wish to find the coefficient of correlation between two sets of measures that are rank-ordered, that is, ordinal rather than interval data. For example, we might want to correlate the ranks assigned by two teachers to a group of students with respect to originality. The index employed in such cases is the Spearman rho (rank) correlation coefficient (p), which is calculated by means of Formula 8.2.

$$\rho = 1 - \frac{6 \Sigma D^2}{N(N^2 - 1)}$$ *(sum of D^2)*

(Formula 8.2)

number of cases

For illustration, consider Table 8.2, which shows the ranking of 11 students by two teachers. Columns 2 and 3 of Table 8.2 present the rankings of Teacher one and Teacher two, respectively. Column 4 shows the differences between these ranks. For example, the difference between the ranking of student A by these teachers is –3, of student B is –1, and so forth. The sum of the values in this column is always zero. Column 5 gives the

Table 8.2

Column 1 Student	2 First Teacher's Rank	3 Second Teacher's Rank	4 Difference D	5 D^2
A	1	4	–3	9
B	2	3	–1	1
C	3	1	2	4
D	4	2	2	4
E	5	5	0	0
F	6	6	0	0
G	7	8	–1	1
H	8	9	–1	1
I	9	7	2	4
J	10	11	–1	1
K	11	10	1	1
			0	26

sum of squared diff. D^2

square of these differences. The sum of D2 value is 26 and the number of cases is 11. When these values are substituted into the formula, the computation gives a Spearman rank correlation of +.88.

$$p = 1 - \frac{(6)(26)}{11(121-1)}$$

$$p = +.88$$

The Spearman rho rank correlation coefficient is part of the same statistical family as the median. It is an ordinal statistic designed for use with ordinal data. Like the Pearson Product Moment Coefficient of Correlation, it ranges from −1 to +1. When each individual has the same rank on both variables, the rank correlation will be +1.00, and when their ranks on one variable are exactly the opposite of their ranks on the other variable, rho will be −1.00. If there is no relationship at all between the rankings, the rank correlation coefficient will be zero.

Use of Quantitative Data in the Research Proposal

As described in Chapters 7 and 8, descriptive statistics are used to organize and describe quantitative data in order to understand research literature related to research questions. The primary descriptive statistics we use include measures of central tendency, variability, relative position (such as standard scores), and relationships. Although descriptive statistics provide a means by which to summarize data, they do not offer conclusions about research questions. Inferential statistics, which are concerned with comparing results with chance expectation, are discussed in Chapter 10.

Use of Quantitative Data in Program Assessment and Evaluation

In Chapter 5 we stated that what method is most appropriate for program assessment and evaluation depends on the purpose of the assessment. If a quantitative method is deemed most appropriate, then the researcher needs to develop a plan for data collection. In fact, the plan should include a two-pronged approach. In the first phase the researcher should propose how data will be collected during the implementation of the program. The second phase should cover the way data is collected to show the progress of the program. Phase one is discussed in this chapter, while phase two is presented in Chapter 9.

Heppner et al. (1999) suggest that the researcher develop a matrix for each question or problem that will be examined. The creation of such a matrix helps to focus the

Table 8.3 An Example of a Question in an Evaluation Planning Matrix

Evaluation Questions	Sources of Information	Needed Resources	Data Collection Methodology	Time Line	Data Analyses
How many students attended the educational fair?	Educational fair attendees (e.g., name, address, phone, school, etc.)	A notebook with headings registration desk will ask each student to sign in.	A counselor seated at the of the fair	The entire duration	Descriptive statistics

research. "For each evaluation question, five categories are examined: (a) sources of information, (b) needed resources, (c) data collection methodology, (d) time line, and (e) data analyses" (p. 498). For example, let us suppose that a group of high school counselors in a rural area decides to establish an educational fair that will include representatives from at least 20 postsecondary technical schools and will serve at least 75 students. One simple but important question the counselors will want to examine is "How many students attended the educational fair?" The matrix as proposed by Heppner et al., which is related to this question, is found in Table 8.3.

Use of Quantitative Data in the Grant Proposal

In Chapter 5 we said that stating goals and objectives is a significant aspect in the development of the grant proposal. In the next section, the Plan of Operation, the researcher explains how the goals and objectives will be carried out. This part of the proposal is considered to be central to the proposal itself and is often called the methodology or implementation plan. In this section that the researcher describes how data will be collected.

Initially in this section the researcher gives an overall description of the strategies involved in the project. This includes a detailed account of what will be accomplished through implementation of the project (e.g., research, training, a product). The researcher needs to explain how the strategies evolved and the sources from which they were developed. The researcher will want to provide a time line for carrying out the project and to describe the data collection method, including how the data will be reported and used. Finally any innovative aspects of the project need to be described along with the potential impact of the project.

Another aspect of the grant proposal that uses quantitative data is the budget section. Like the Plan of Operation, the budget serves as a core component since everything else is built around it. Funding sources evaluate a budget by considering its adequacy in terms of the project goals and the cost-effectiveness of the project, based on the information provided. Although most grant proposals provide formats for outlining the budget, they all ask for such common elements as personnel, fringe benefits, travel expenses, equipment, supplies, and contractual agreements for subcontracting services.

Worksheet 8.1   Descriptive Statistics

1. Find the Spearman rho rank correlation coefficient of the two sets of numbers below using Formula 8.2. Also find the percent of predictability.

	X	Y	Plot these scores on a scattergram:
A.	19	93	
B.	17	87	
C.	17	92	
D.	14	73	
E.	12	86	
F.	11	83	
G.	11	83	
H.	10	81	
I.	9	80	
J.	4	80	

2. A statistics teacher decided to give two types of final exams, one an objective test and the other an essay test. He wanted to see if there was any relationship between the two scores. What would you conclude from the data presented after finding the Spearman rho rank correlation coefficient for the numbers below?

	X (Objective Test)	Y (Essay Test)
A.	98	96
B.	96	93
C.	95	91
D.	94	87
E.	92	87
F.	90	88
G.	88	84
H.	83	82
I.	81	82
J.	80	81
K.	76	79
L.	71	68

Correlations

1.

Spearman's rho X		X	Y
	Correlation Coefficient	1.000	.736*
	Sig. (2-tailed)	.	.015
	N		10	10
Y	Correlation Coefficient	.736*	1.000
	Sig. (2-tailed)	.015	.
	N	10	10

*.Correlation is significant at the .05 level (2-tailed).

Correlations

2.

Spearman's rho X		X	Y
	Correlation Coefficient	1.000	.975**
	Sig. (2-tailed)	.	.000
	N	12	12
Y	Correlation Coefficient	.975**	1.000
	Sig. (2-tailed)	.000	.
	N	12	12

**.Correlation is significant at the .01 level (2-tailed).

Figure 8.5 Computer Printouts for Worksheet 8.1

Note: The results on the computer printouts differ from the hand computations because of rounding.

P R O C E S S G O A L	Research Proposal

Using Quantitative Data

Define a process goal for using quantitative data. Some suggestions:

> I will review the dependent variables in my proposed study and identify what data needs to be described (e.g., achievement test scores, pregnancy rates, etc.). Note: If I decide I want to select a standardized test, I realize they will be discussed further in Chapter 9.

> I will write the data collection section of Chapter 3, using the sample proposal as a guide.

Write your own process goal to help you finalize your data collection section.

P R O C E S S G O A L	Program Assessment and Evaluation

Using Quantitative Data

Define a process goal for using quantitative data. Some suggestions:

> I will determine what data needs to be collected in the implementation phase of the program.

> I will design a matrix for each question or problem to be examined in the assessment, which will include the following categories: (a) sources of information, (b) needed resources, (c) data collection methodology, (d) time line, and (e) data analyses.

Write your own process goal to help you finalize your data collection section.

P R O C E S S G O A L	Grant Proposal

Using Quantitative Data

Define a process goal for using quantitative data. Some suggestions:

> I will draft a Plan of Operation, which will include: (a) an overall description of the strategies involved in the project, including a detailed account of what will be accomplished and how the strategies evolved; (b) a time; (c) the data collection method, including how the data will be reported and used; and (d) any innovative aspects of the project along with the potential impact of the project.

> I will develop a budget including the following line items: personnel, fringe benefits, travel expenses, equipment, supplies, and contractual agreements for subcontracting services.

Write your own process goal to help you finalize your data collection section.

Summary

In this chapter we discussed multiple distributions and methods of indicating the relationship between multiple distributions. Specifically, we discussed the correlation coefficient, which indicates the strength of a relationship and whether or not the variables in the distributions are positively or negatively related. We stressed that a correlation merely indicates how one distribution of scores is associated with another and that it does not imply causality. The coefficient of determination (or percent of predictability), the square of the correlation coefficient, indicates the percentage of variance in one variable that is associated with the variance in the other. When correlational analysis indicates some degree of relationship between two variables, we can use the information about one of them to make predictions about the other. We refer to this concept as regression analysis. Although researchers use many methods for measuring correlation, we introduced the Pearson Product-Moment Correlation as one used with interval data and the Spearman Rho to find the correlation between two sets of measures that are rank ordered. We included practice activities for hand calculation as well as computer analysis.

Key Terms

attenuate	criterion	predictor variable
attenuation due to restriction of range	direction	regression analysis
	inverse relationship	scattergram
coefficient of determination	multiple regression	standard error of measurement
	negative relationship	
correlational procedures	percent of predictability	strength of the relationship
correlation coefficients	positive relationship	

9

Reliability

Let us suppose you have affectionately nicknamed your twelve-year-old car "ol' reliable."

How would you probably describe "ol' reliable"? More than likely "ol' reliable" is not much to

look at these days, but it dependably gets you where you need to go. Likewise in research,

when we measure the dependent variables, we need the instruments to be *reliable*.

The **reliability** of a measuring instrument refers to the degree of consistency with which

it measures whatever it is measuring. This quality is essential in any kind of measurement. A

post office will readily take action to repair a scale if the scale sometimes underestimates and

other times overestimates the weight of packages. Counselors and college student affairs pro-

fessionals are equally concerned about the consistency of their measuring devices when

they attempt to measure such complex traits as intelligence, achievement, motivation, or

anxiety. They would not consider an intelligence test worthwhile if it yielded markedly differ-

ent results each time it was used on the same subject. People who use such measuring instru-

ments must identify and utilize techniques that will help them to determine the consistency and reliability of their measuring instruments. In counseling and student affairs, we are concerned about two dimensions of reliability, dependability over time and consistency among items (**internal consistency**).

Theory of Reliability

Since *reliability* refers to the accuracy of a measurement, a reliable measure is one that is free from error and provides consistent results. The reliability of a measurement is understood in terms of the relationships among the following elements:

X = the measurement obtained by the subject

T = the "true" amount of the attribute that the subject possesses

E = the presence of random error

We can summarize this relationship as $X = T + E$: The obtained measurement equals the true amount of the attribute plus random error. The more reliable the measure, the more the obtained measure (X) reflects truth (T). Likewise, the less reliable the measure, the more the obtained measure reflects error (E). Let us suppose that an examinee takes a mathematical aptitude exam on two distinct occasions and obtains two different scores. Since it is assumed that mathematical aptitude is stable over time, the inconsistency in scores is likely due to error. The **random error** may be due to the subject's variable feelings or ability to concentrate. It is important to point out that the reliability does not indicate what attribute is actually being measured (referred to as validity); reliability merely provides the degree of consistency with which the attribute is being measured (Bartos, 1992).

As a way of distinguishing the reliability of an instrument from its validity, it is useful to identify **random errors of measurement** and **systematic errors of measurement.** *Random error* refers to error that is the result of pure chance. Random errors of measurement may inflate or depress any subject's score in an unpredictable manner. For example, a physical education teacher may measure students' physical fitness level by a baseball throw. The teacher instructs students to throw a baseball as far as they can and then measures the distance of the throw. Although the object of the test is to get a score typical of a subject's performance, certainly if the teacher has a single subject throw a baseball on several occasions, the teacher would find that the student does not throw it the same distance each time.

Assume that the teacher has each student make a throw on two consecutive days. In comparing the two scores (distance thrown) for each student, the teacher would find that they are almost never exactly the same. Most of the differences would be small, but some would be moderately large and a few, quite large. The results are inconsistent from one day's throw to the next. One throw is not completely reliable as a measure of a student's throwing ability.

Three types of chance or random influences lead to inconsistency between scores achieved on the two days:

1. The student may actually change from one day to the next. On one day he or she may feel better than on the other. On one day the student may be more motivated or less fatigued. Perhaps the student's father, hearing about the task, begins coaching the child in throwing a baseball.

2. The task itself may change for the two measurements. For example, the ball used one day may be firm, whereas on the second day it may be wet and soggy. Perhaps on one day the examiner permits the students to take a running start up to the throwing line, whereas on the second day the examiner permits them only a couple of steps. These changes may affect some students more than others.

3. The limited sample of behavior results in an unstable score. A small sample of behavior is subject to many kinds of chance influences. Maybe there is a gust of wind as the ball is thrown. Maybe the student loses his or her balance when starting to throw the ball, or maybe the student's fingers slip while gripping the ball.

Reliability is concerned with the effect of such random errors of measurement on the consistency of scores. (The initial "r" in both reliability and random error is an easy way to remember that reliability is related to random error).

On the other hand, some errors involved in measurement are predictable or systematic. Using the example of the baseball throw, imagine a situation in which the teacher gives the instructions for the throw in English, but not all the subjects understand English. The scores of the non-English-speaking subjects could be systematically depressed because the subjects do not comprehend what they are expected to do. Such systematic errors of measurement are related to validity. The validity of a test is lowered whenever scores are systematically changed by the influence of anything other than what individuals are attempting to measure. In this instance the teacher is measuring not only baseball throwing ability but also, in part, English comprehension.

To decide whether we are dealing with reliability or validity, we can first determine whether the errors being considered are random or systematic. If a teacher is giving the baseball throw test to a class and two balls are employed, one firm and one soggy, and it is purely a matter of chance who gets what ball, the variation due to the ball used is a reliability problem. The variation due to the ball represents random error that affects the consistency of the measurements. If a teacher calls class members to take the test in alphabetical order, and it is a rainy day, and the one baseball provided gets wetter with each successive throw, the variation due to the increasing wetness of the ball is a *validity* problem. Scores are increased for those students near the beginning of the alphabet and decreased for students near the end. The validity of the baseball throw scores is lessened because the scores reflect not only baseball throwing prowess but alphabetical order as well. This is an instance of *systematic* error that affects the validity of the measurement.

Reliability is concerned with how consistently you are measuring whatever you are measuring. It is not concerned with whether you are measuring what you intend to measure: that is the validity question. It is possible for a measuring instrument to be reliable without being valid. However, it cannot be valid unless it is first reliable. For example, if your bathroom scale weighs 5 pounds heavier than your doctor's scale (which is assumed to be valid or accurate), your bathroom scale is said to be reliable, but not valid. Therefore, each time you weigh yourself you will most likely mentally subtract 5 pounds from the reading to get your actual weight. However, to detect whether or not you have lost weight, you need only to notice if your weight has gone up or down. Likewise, if you consistently set your watch 10 minutes fast to help you be on time, your watch is reliable (always 10 minutes fast), but it is not valid.

As previously mentioned, reliability is affected by random errors, any factors that will result in discrepancies between scores in repeated administrations of a measuring instrument. Random errors arise from a number of sources. Errors may be inherent in the instrument itself. For example, if a test is very short, those subjects who happen to know the few answers required will get higher scores than they deserve, whereas those subjects who do not know those few answers get lower scores than they deserve. For example, if a test is given to assess how well students know the capitals of the 50 states, but only five questions are asked, it is possible that a student who only knows 10 capitals could get all five correct, whereas a student who knows 40 capitals could get none correct. In a short test luck factors in more than in a long test. If a test is so easy that everyone knows most of the answers, the subjects' relative scores again depend upon only a few questions, and luck is a major factor. If questions are ambiguous, "lucky" subjects respond in the way the examiner intended, whereas "unlucky" subjects respond in another, equally correct, manner; however their answers are scored as incorrect. True-false tests are often considered the least reliable type of test because of the possibility of guessing the correct answers. An individual who merely guesses an answer has a 50% chance of getting it correct, and it is unlikely that the individual will guess the same answer on a second administration. Multiple choice tests that provide more responses for individuals to select from tend to be more reliable. The scoring procedure also affects reliability. Precise scoring procedures enhance reliability, whereas vague scoring procedures depress it (Bartos, 1992).

The Coefficient of Reliability

We estimate a test's reliability by using correlational analysis. The most commonly used **correlation coefficient** for this purpose is the Pearson Product Moment Correlation Coefficient (Pearson r). It is symbolized as r_{tt} (or r_{xx}, r_{11}, etc.). The **coefficient of reliability** can range from 1.00, when there is no error in the measurement, to 0.00, when the measurement contains all error. This degree of error is indicated by the degree of departure of the correlation coefficient from 1.00. A measuring instrument has error and low reliability to the extent that the reliability coefficient is depressed below 1.00. For example, a test that has a reliability of .92 contains less error than a test with a reliability of .75. When the Pearson r is used as a reliability coefficient, it is not squared to obtain the percent of predictability (or the coefficient of determination), since the reliability coefficient directly indicates the proportion of variance in a set of scores that is attributable to true differences among them. For example, a reliability coefficient of .90 indicates that 90% of the variance in obtained test scores is due to true score variance in the attribute measured, while 10% $(1 - .90)$ is due to error.

Approaches to Reliability

A test is reliable to the extent that the scores made by an individual remain nearly the same in repeated measurements. There are two approaches to expressing the reliability of a set of measurements.

1. One approach indicates the amount of variation to be expected within a set of repeated measurements of a single individual. If it were possible to weigh an individual 200 times, we would get a frequency distribution of scores to represent his or her weight. This frequency distribution would have an average value, which we could consider the "true" weight. It would also have a standard deviation, indicating the spread. This standard deviation is called the standard error of measurement since it is the standard deviation of the "errors" of measuring the weight for one person. It is sometimes referred to as a confidence band. In polls, for example, you will hear such statements as, "In a recent poll of 200 American adults, 55% of them (plus or minus 3%) agreed with the president's plan to reform social security." The confidence band gives us a broader estimate since it takes into consideration the possible error involved. With psychological or educational data, we do not often make repeated measurements on an individual. But if we have a pair of measurements for each individual, we can estimate what the variation of scores would have been if we had made repeated measurements. We discuss the standard error of measurement in more detail later in this chapter.

2. Reliability of measurement also tells the extent to which each individual maintains the same relative position in the group. The person who scores highest on a test today should also be one of the highest scorers the next time the group takes the test. Each person in the group should stay in the same position. We can compute a coefficient of correlation between two administrations of the same test to determine the extent to which individuals maintain the same relative position. This coefficient is called a **reliability coefficient** (r_{xx}). Thus, reliability of a measure is indicated by a low standard error of measurement or by a high reliability coefficient. Table 9.1 shows that there is an inverse relationship between reliability and standard error of measurement. As the standard error of measurement decreases, the reliability coefficient increases. Likewise, as the standard error of measurement increases the reliability coefficient decreases. Table 9.1 also shows a positive relationship between standard deviation and standard error of measurement. As the standard deviation increases, so does the standard error of measurement.

The Reliability Indices

Reliability can be estimated by correlating the scores obtained by the same individuals on different occasions or with different sets of equivalent items. The procedures require two administrations of a test. Other procedures either artificially split one test into two parts or determine the internal consistency of the test. These procedures are described below.

Test-Retest Reliability. An obvious way to estimate the reliability of a test is to administer it to the same group of individuals on two occasions and to correlate the paired scores. The correlation coefficient obtained by this procedure is called a **test-retest reliability coefficient.** For example, a teacher may give a physical fitness test to a class during one week and administer the same test again the following week. If the test is reliable, each individual's relative position on the second administration of the test will be near his or her

Table 9.1   Standard Error of Measurement

The relationship between the reliability coefficient and standard deviation will yield the standard error of measurement.

SD	.95	.90	Reliability Coefficient .85	.80	.75
30	6.7	9.5	11.6	13.4	15.0
28	6.3	8.9	10.8	12.5	14.0
26	5.8	8.2	10.0	11.6	13.0
24	5.4	7.6	9.3	10.7	12.0
22	4.9	7.0	8.5	9.8	11.0
20	4.5	6.3	7.7	8.9	10.0
18	4.0	5.7	7.0	8.0	9.0
16	3.6	5.1	6.2	7.2	8.0
14	3.1	4.4	5.4	6.3	7.0
12	2.7	3.8	4.6	5.4	6.0
10	2.2	3.2	3.9	4.5	5.0
8	1.8	2.5	3.1	3.6	4.0
6	1.3	1.9	2.3	2.7	3.0
4	.9	1.3	1.5	1.8	2.0
2	.4	.6	.8	.9	1.0

Example: reliability coefficient   = .85
            standard deviation   = 8
            standard error of measurement   = 3.1

relative position on the first administration of the test. The reliability coefficient (r_{tt}) will be near +1.00. Any change in relative position from one occasion to the next is considered an error. If the test contains considerable error, the r_{tt} will be nearer to zero. As explained earlier, a reliability coefficient is an estimate of the proportion of observed variance in test scores that is true variance. The difference between the value of the reliability coefficient and +1.00 is an unbiased estimate of the proportion of error variance in a test. For example, a test-retest reliability of .80 on the physical fitness test indicates that our best estimate is that 80 percent of the observed variance is true variance, and 20 percent is error variance (Bartos, 1992).

The test-retest reliability coefficient, because it is indicative of the consistency of subjects' scores over time, is sometimes referred to as a coefficient of stability. It tells us whether we can generalize from the score a person receives on one occasion to a score that person would receive if the test were given at a different time.

A test-retest coefficient assumes that the characteristic being measured by the test is stable over time, so any change in scores from one time to another is due to random error. The error may be due to the condition of the subjects themselves or to testing conditions. The test-retest coefficient also assumes that there is no practice effect or memory effect. For example, students may learn something just from taking a test and thus will react differently on the second taking of the test. These practice effects from the first testing will not likely be the same across all students, thus lowering the reliability estimate. If the interval of time is short, there may also be memory effect. That is, students may mark a question the same way they had previously done just because they remember marking it that way the first time. This memory effect can be controlled somewhat by increasing the time between the first test and the retest. On the other hand, if the time between testings is too long, differential learning may be a problem. That is, students will learn different amounts during the interval, which would affect the reliability coefficient.

Because of the problems discussed above, the test-retest procedure is most appropriate for determining the reliability of tests that measure attributes that are stable over time, such as an aptitude test. It is not appropriate for measuring traits that fluctuate over time, such as emotions, or for measuring attributes that might be affected by exposure to previous test items, such as creativity.

Equivalent-Forms Reliability. The **equivalent-forms technique** of estimating reliability, which is also referred to as the **alternate-** or **parallel-forms technique,** is used when it is probable that subjects will recall their responses to the test items. Here, rather than correlating the results of two administrations of the same test to the same group, one correlates the results of equivalent forms of the test administered at essentially the same time (in immediate succession). The resulting reliability coefficient is called the **coefficient of equivalence.** This measure reflects variations in performance from one specific set of items to another. It indicates whether we can generalize a student's score to what the student would receive if another form of the same test were given. The question is: To what extent does the student's performance depend upon the particular set of items used in the test?

If subjects are tested with one form on one occasion and with another form on a second occasion, and their scores on the two forms are correlated, the resulting coefficient is called the **coefficient of stability and equivalence.** This coefficient reflects two aspects of test reliability: variations in performance from one time to another as well as variations from one form of the test to another. This is the most demanding and the most rigorous measure available for determining the reliability of a test. In this case, however, alternate forms reliability may be affected by error due to "time sampling" and "content sampling." The reliability of the alternate forms can be affected by random factors related to the passage of time between the two administrations. Additionally, the reliability is affected by content sampling differences. For example, although Tim may be knowledgeable about the items on Test A, he may know little about the specific questions on Test B. Likewise, the items on Test B may better represent Joe's knowledge than Test A. Subsequently, Tim will obtain a higher score on Test A, while Joe will receive a higher score on Test B. The interactions between Tim's and Joe's knowledge and the content of the two forms are likely to introduce error, resulting in a lower reliability coefficient.

Designing alternate forms of a test that are truly equivalent is the major challenge with this technique of estimating reliability. If this is not successfully achieved, then the variation in scores from one form to another could not be considered as error variance. Equivalent forms of a test are independently constructed tests that must meet the same specifications; that is, they must have the same number of items, form, instructions, time limits, format, content, range, and level of difficulty, but the actual questions are not the same. Ideally one should have pairs of equivalent items and assign one of each pair to each form. The distribution of the test scores must also be similar.

The equivalent-forms technique is recommended when one wishes to avoid the problem of recall or practice effect and in cases when one has available a large number of test items from which to select equivalent samples. It is generally considered that the equivalent-forms procedure provides the best estimate of the reliability of academic and psychological measures.

Split-Half Reliability.   It is possible to get a measure of reliability from a single administration of one form of a test by using split-half procedures. The test is administered to a group of subjects, and later the items are divided into two comparable halves. Scores are obtained for each individual on the comparable halves and a coefficient of correlation calculated for the two scores. If each subject maintains a very similar position on the two sections, the test has high reliability. If there is little consistency in positions, the reliability is low. This method requires only one form of a test, entails no time lag, and maintains the same physical and mental influences operating on the subjects as they take the two sections.

A problem with this method occurs with splitting the test to obtain two comparable halves. If, through item analysis, one establishes the difficulty level of each item, one can place each item into one of the two halves on the basis of equivalent difficulty and similarity of content. The most common procedure, however, is to correlate the scores on the odd-numbered items of the test with the scores on the even-numbered items.

The correlation coefficient computed between the two halves will systematically underestimate the reliability of the entire test. Longer tests are more reliable than shorter tests if everything else is equal. Therefore, the correlation between the odd 50 and even 50 items on a 100-item test is a reliability estimate for a 50-item test, not a 100-item test. If we want the reliability for a 100-item test, we would need to use a 200-item test. However, if a test is too long, error associated with fatigue may result. An alternative to making a test that is too long is to transform the split-half correlation into an appropriate reliability estimate for the entire test, using the Spearman-Brown prophecy.

$$= \frac{2(r)}{1+(r)} \qquad\qquad \text{(Equation 9.1)}$$

For example, if we find a correlation coefficient of .65 between two halves of a test, the estimated reliability of the entire test, using the Spearman-Brown formula, would be

$$= \frac{2(.65)}{1+.65} = .79$$

The Spearman-Brown procedure is based on the assumption that the two halves are parallel. Because this assumption is seldom correct, in practice the split-half technique with the Spearman-Brown correction tends to overestimate the reliability that would be obtained if test-retest or equivalent forms procedures were used. This should be borne in mind when evaluating the reliabilities of competing tests.

Split-half reliability is an appropriate technique to use in avoiding time-to-time fluctuation in estimating reliability and when the test is relatively long. The other techniques, such as test-retest or equivalent forms, are more appropriate for short tests.

The split-half procedure is not appropriate to use with speed tests since it yields spuriously high coefficients of equivalence. A speed test is one that purposefully includes easy items so that the scores are mainly dependent upon the speed with which subjects can respond. Errors are minor; most of the items are correct up to the point where time is called. If a student responds to 50 items, the student's split-half score is likely to be 25-25; if another student marks 60 items, that student's split-half score is likely to be 30-30, and so on. Since individuals' scores on odd and even-numbered items are very nearly identical, within-individual variation is minimized, and the correlation between halves will be nearly perfect. Thus other procedures are recommended for use with speed tests.

Measuring Internal Consistency Reliability

Several formulas have been developed for estimating the reliability of a test without splitting the test and employing correlational procedures. These procedures estimate reliability through determining how all items on a single test relate to all other items and to the test as a whole. Tests that have a high degree of *internal consistency* have items that are homogeneous, measure a single construct (e.g., anxiety), and correlate highly with each other (Krathwohl, 1993). Researchers often determine the reliability of a test through either the Kuder- Richardson Formula Number 20 (KR 20) or the Kuder-Richardson Formula Number 21 (KR 21). Since the calculations used with the KR 20 are so involved, the KR 21 was developed to closely approximate the reliability coefficient generated by the KR 20 (Crowl, 1993). In order to obtain an estimate of the reliability using the KR 21 you only need the mean, the variance and number of test items.

KR21 $\quad r = \dfrac{Ks^2 - \overline{X}\left(K - \overline{X}\right)}{s^2\left(K - 1\right)}$ (Equation 9.2)

Where

$\quad r$ = reliability of the whole test

$\quad K$ = the number of items in the test

$\quad s^2$ = the variance of the scores

$\quad \overline{X}$ = the mean of the scores

Example

$$K = 100$$

$$s^2 = 54.3$$

$$\overline{X} = 82$$

$$r = \frac{100(54.3) - 82(100 - 82)}{54.3(100 - 1)}$$

$$r = \frac{5430 - 1476}{5375.7}$$

$$r = \frac{3954}{5375.7}$$

$$r = .74$$

The Kuder-Richardson formulas are designed to be used only with tests whose items are scored as either correct or incorrect. In the event your measuring device has items that take on several scores (e.g., very often, often, sometimes, rarely, never), often referred to as a Likert scale, you need to use Cronbach's alpha (Crowl, 1993). Cronbach's alpha is conceptually related to the Kuder-Richardson formulas.

A   C   T   I   V   I   T   Y

9.1 Reliability

1. What is the reliability for the total test if the split-half reliability is .70?
2. What is the reliability of a test where

$$K = 100$$

$$s^2 = 30$$

$$\overline{X} = 70$$

Interpretation of a Reliability Coefficient

The interpretation of a reliability coefficient should be based on a number of considerations. Certain factors affect reliability coefficients, and unless these factors are taken into account, any interpretation of reliability will be superficial.

The reliability of a test relates to the length of the test. As mentioned previously, the longer the test, the greater its reliability. A test usually consists of a number of sample items, which are, theoretically, drawn from a universe of test items. We know from what we have studied about sampling that the greater the sample size, the more representative it is expected to be of the population from which it is drawn. This is true also of a test. If it were possible to use the entire universe of items, the score of a person who takes the test would be the individual's true score. The greater the length of the test (that is, the greater the number of items included in the test), the more representative it should be of the true scores of the persons who take it. Since reliability is the extent to which a test represents the true scores of individuals, the longer the test, the greater its reliability, provided that all the items in the test belong in the universe of items.

Reliability is in part a function of group heterogeneity. The reliability coefficient increases as the spread of heterogeneity of the subjects who take the test increases. Conversely, the more homogeneous the group is with respect to the trait being measured, the lower the reliability coefficient will be. One explanation of reliability is that it is the extent to which we can place individuals, relative to others in their groups, according to certain traits and qualities. Such placement is easier when one is dealing with measures that fall in a large range rather than those that fall in a small range. It does not take a sensitive device to determine the placement of children in a distribution according to their weights when the age range of these children is from 5 to 15. In fact, this placement is possible with some degree of accuracy, even without using any measuring device. It does take a sensitive device, however, to carry out the same placement if all those who are to be compared and placed in the distribution are 5 years old. Thus the heterogeneity of the group with whom a measuring instrument is used affects the reliability of that instrument. The more heterogeneous the group used in the reliability study, the higher the reliability coefficient.

This fact should be kept in mind when selecting a standardized test. The publisher may report a high reliability coefficient based on a sample with a wide range of ability. However, when the test is used with a group having a much narrower range of ability, the reliability will be lower.

The reliability of a test is in part a function of the ability of the individuals who take the test. A test may be reliable at one level of ability but unreliable at another level. The questions in a test might be difficult and beyond the ability level of those who take it, or the questions might, on the other hand, be easy for the majority of the subjects. This difficulty level affects the reliability of the test. When a test is difficult, the subjects guess on most of the questions, and a low reliability coefficient will result. When it is easy, all subjects provide correct responses on most of the items, and only a few more difficult items discriminate among subjects. Again we would expect a low reliability.

There is no simple rule by which one can determine how difficult, or how easy, a test should be. It depends on the type of test, the purpose, and the population for which it is being constructed.

Reliability is in part a function of the specific technique used for its estimation. Different procedures for estimating the reliability of tests result in different coefficients of reliability. The equivalent-forms technique gives a lower estimation of reliability than either test-retest or split-half procedures because in the equivalent-forms technique form-to-form as well as time-to-time fluctuation is present. The split-half method, on the other hand, results in higher reliability coefficients than do its alternatives because in most tests some degree of speed is involved, and to that extent the reliability coefficient is overestimated. Thus, in evaluating the reliability of a test, one would give preference to a test whose reliability coefficient has been estimated by the equivalent-forms technique, rather than other techniques, when the reported reliabilities are similar. The same generalization would hold when comparing test-retest reliability with split-half. The same coefficient is more satisfactory if it results from the test-retest procedure rather than from the split-half method.

Reliability is in part a function of the nature of the variable being measured. Some variables of interest to researchers yield consistent measures more often than do other variables. For instance, most established tests of academic achievement have quite high reliabilities, whereas tests of personality variables have only moderate reliabilities.

Acceptable Reliability Coefficients

Different types of tests have different minimum levels of reliability. Perhaps the best response to the question of what is good reliability is that a good reliability coefficient is one that is as good as or better than the reliability coefficient of competing measures. For example, a spelling achievement test with a reliability of .80 is unsatisfactory if competing tests have reliability coefficients of .90 or better. A coefficient of .80 for a test of creativity would be judged excellent if other tests of the same construct have reliabilities of .60 or less. On average, however, achievement and aptitude tests generally have higher reliability coefficients than personality and interest scales because of the level of stability of the attribute being measured. Reliability coefficients in the .80s and .90s are considered adequate.

Standard Error of Measurement

As explained earlier in this chapter, the reliability, stability, or dependability of a test may also be expressed in terms of the standard error of measurement. The standard error of measurement provides an estimate of the range of variation in a set of repeated measurements of the same thing. Returning to our example of a baseball throw, we would expect with repeated administration, by chance, to obtain a number of different scores for the same individual. We would have a frequency distribution of scores. This frequency distribution has a mean, which is the best approximation of the true scores. The distribution also has a standard deviation, indicating the extent of the variation in the scores. Since this standard deviation is the standard deviation of the errors of measurement, it is called the standard error of measurement. If one were to construct a frequency polygon showing this distribution of scores, its shape would approximate that of the normal curve. Measurement errors are normally distributed; there may be many small errors but few large ones. The standard deviation of this distribution of error (the standard error of measurement) would give us an estimate of how frequently errors of a given size might be expected to occur when the test is used.

In many situations, one does not have repeated measures, but one can get an estimate of the standard error of measurement by using a chart such as Table 9.1 if one knows the reliability and the standard deviation.

The standard error of measurement can be interpreted like any other measurement of standard deviation. Let us assume that a test with a reliability coefficient of less than 1.0 is administered to an individual numerous times. Since the test is not totally reliable, the individual will obtain numerous scores normally distributed around a mean equal to the individual's true test score. The standard deviation of the distribution provides an index of the amount of measurement error, which we have been referring to as the standard error of measurement. The standard error of measurement is interpreted in terms of areas under the normal curve. More specifically, 68% of the individual's obtained scores will fall within +1.0 standard errors from the mean of the distribution, 95% of the individual's obtained scores will fall within +1.96 standard errors from the mean, and 99% of the individual's obtained scores will fall within +2.58 standard errors from the mean. (Note that for ease of discussion 95% and 99% are often related to 2 and 3 standard deviations respectively, but 1.96 and 2.58 are the accurate figures.) For example, if a subject demonstrated a score of 110 on the intelligence test where the standard error of measurement is 3, one could infer at the 68 percent confidence level that the subject's true score lies somewhere between 107 and 113. Or to state it differently, if the subject could be retested on this intelligence test a number of times, one could expect in about two-thirds of the retests a score between 107 and 113 would occur. Likewise, a score higher than 116 or lower than 104 will only occur about five times in a hundred.

Since, practically speaking, a test is never actually administered an infinite number of times to an individual, we usually administer a test only once to an examinee and use the resulting obtained score to estimate the true score. The standard error of measurement is then used to construct a confidence interval within which the individual's true score is likely to fall given the obtained score. The standard error of measurement is calculated using the following formula:

$$SE_{meas} = SD_t \sqrt{1 - r_{tt}} \qquad\qquad\text{(Equation 9.3)}$$

Where

SE_{meas} = standard error of measurement
SD_t = standard deviation of the test
r_{tt} = reliability of the test

Let us assume for this example that that the standard deviation is 8 and the reliability is .85. We get a SEM of 3.1.

$$8\sqrt{1 - .85} = 8\sqrt{.15} = 8(.39) = 3.1$$

We can double-check the standard error of measurement that we computed with the one found in Table 9.1. Note that we find 3.1 in the chart as well.

Let us say that Jim got a score of 75 on this test. We can pretty confidently determine that his true score fell in the following band(s):
Since *68%* of scores fall plus and minus one standard deviation we can say that there is a 68% chance that his true score fell between 71.9 and 78.1.

Score   (# of standard deviations) (SEM)

$$75 \pm (1)(3.1) =$$
$$75 \pm \quad (3.1) = 71.9 - 78.1$$

Since *95%* of scores fall plus and minus approximately two standard deviations *(actually, the accurate number to use is 1.96)* we can say that there is a 95% chance that his true score fell between 68.92 and 81.08.

Score   (# of standard deviations) (SEM)

$$75 \pm (1.96)(3.1) =$$
$$75 \pm \quad (6.08) = 68.92 - 81.08$$

Since *99%* of scores fall plus and minus approximately three standard deviations *(actually, the accurate number to use is 2.58)* we can say that there is a 99% chance that his true score fell between 67 and 83.

Score   (# of standard deviations) (SEM)

$$75 \pm (2.58)(3.1) =$$
$$75 \pm \quad (8) = 67 - 83$$

In conclusion, one looks for a low standard error of measurement or a high reliability coefficient as an indication of a test's reliability.

A   C   T   I   V   I   T   Y

9.2

Standard Error of Measurement

1. Find the SEM for a test that has a reliability coefficient of .84 and a standard deviation of 10.
2. Assuming Jill got a score of 80 on the exam, what is the range of her true score given the following confidence levels?
   a. 68
   b. 95
   c. 99

Measurement as It Relates to Research Proposals

The researcher needs to propose well in advance of collecting the data how the data will be measured and collected. The data may be measured by standardized means (e.g., standardized tests) or through nonstandardized methods (e.g., in terms of frequency counts, grade point averages, etc.). The researcher needs to choose a measurement that is valid and reliable for the particular dependent variables.

Measurement as It Relates to Program Assessment and Evaluation

In Chapter 8 we described a two-pronged approach for data collection and measurement. The first phase, examining how the program was implemented, was presented in Chapter 8. Here we discuss the second phase, data collection and measurement of the program as it was carried out. Again, the matrix suggested by Heppner et al. (1999) is a useful tool and includes the following categories: "(a) sources of information, (b) needed resources, (c) data collection, (d) time line, and (e) data analyses" (p. 498). See Table 9.2. Any number of tools to gather data (e.g., surveys, focus groups, etc.) as discussed in Chapter 5 may be used. Using the same scenario dealing with the educational fair for postsecondary technical schools, assume that a phone survey is used. Let us suppose that, prior to the educational fair, the researcher surveyed the students as to their postgraduation plans and determined those students who indicated a preference for attending a postsecondary technical program. The researcher then decided to use those students who indicated interest in attending a technical school as the population. The researcher further decided to measure the success of the program in terms of the number of students from this population who attended the educational fair and successfully enrolled in a technical school as opposed to number of students in the population who did not attend the educational fair but successfully enrolled in a technical school.

Table 9.2   An Evaluation Planning Matrix for Program Assessment

Evaluation Questions	Sources of Information	Needed Resources	Data Collection Methodology	Time Line	Data Analyses
How many students enrolled in a technical school?	Students who indicated interest in a technical school	Phone, list of students, forms for recording information	The researcher will call each graduate who indicated interest in a technical school	September following graduation	Inferential statistics

In order to give meaning to the data that is collected, the last column of the matrix, data analysis, indicates how the data will be interpreted. In this particular example inferential statistics (as opposed to the descriptive statistics discussed in Chapters 7 and 8) will be used. Inferential statistics are discussed in Chapter 10.

Measurement as It Relates to Grant Proposals

Measurement as it relates to grant proposals occurs in the evaluation process. The evaluation, which provides a means of accountability for the project, should be tied closely to the objectives (which were discussed in Chapter 5). Researchers base evaluations on the objectives of the project. The evaluation may either measure the project's current effects—how it is doing—(a formative evaluation) or the project's ultimate effects—how well it meets its objectives (a summational evaluation). The overall purpose is to identify changes that have occurred from before the implementation of the project. Many of the components discussed in the previous section related to program evaluation pertain to the evaluation of the grant proposal.

According to Lauffer (1983), the U.S. Department of Education developed several recommendations for designing project evaluations. Some of the most relevant points include: (a) the necessity for the objectives of the project to be measurable; (b) the importance of selecting measures that specify how the data will be collected, analyzed, and reported; (c) the use of multiple measures, rather than a single measure, if possible; and (d) the use of well-established measures when feasible.

According to Karges-Bone (1994), the evaluation is often called the "weak link" in grants because so many proposals lack a cogent, rational plan for assessing and reporting the results. Your evaluation will appear tight, neat, and clear when you: (a) establish whether the objectives that you set were met, (b) state the degree to which you were successful in meeting the goals and objectives, (c) report how you documented the outcome of the project, and (d) clearly present the data that illustrates the outcome of the project.

Worksheet 9.1

1. The following are scores of a group of subjects on a standardized depression scale and on a researcher-made scale. The researcher wants to determine if there is a significant relationship between the two scales. Is there? Find the correlation using either the Pearson Product Moment Correlation or the Spearman rho. See computer printouts in Figure 9.1.

Subject	Standardized Scale (X)	Researcher-Made Scale (Y)
A	18	28
B	18	30
C	17	30
D	17	26
E	16	28
F	16	24
G	15	22
H	15	20
I	14	26
J	14	22
K	13	24
L	13	18
M	12	20
N	12	18

2. Suppose the data given in question 1 were the scores of subjects on one test, with the X column representing the first half of the test and the Y column representing the second half of the test. With this information, calculate the reliability coefficient for the entire test.

3. With the information arrived at in question 2 and given the standard deviation of the test in question 2 as 7.00, what is the standard error of measurement for this test at the 99th, 95th and 68th confidence interval?

4. If you gave a test and wanted to find its reliability quickly and had the following information about the test, could you derive a reliability coefficient? K, X, s^2

5. Find the reliability coefficient of a test given the following data.

$$K = 50, \bar{X} = 29, s^2 = 64.89$$

Correlations

Correlations

		STANDARD	RESEARCH
STANDARD	Pearson Correlation	1.000	.821**
	Sig. (2-tailed)	.	.000
	N	14	14
RESEARCH	Pearson Correlation	.821**	1.000
	Sig. (2-tailed)	.000	.
	N	14	14

**. Correlation is significant at the 0.01 level (2-tailed).

Nonparametric Correlations

Correlations

			STANDARD	RESEARCH
Spearman's rho	STANDARD	Correlation Coefficient	1.000	.821**
		Sig. (2-tailed)	.	.015
		N	14	14
	RESEARCH	Correlation Coefficient	.821**	1.000
		Sig. (2-tailed)	.000	.
		N	14	14

**. Correlation is significant at the .01 level (2-tailed).

Figure 9.1 Computer Printouts

Worksheet 9.2

1. The following set of scores was generated from a test, given to children, measuring social skill development. What is the reliability of the test, and what is the SEM? ($K = 100$)

87
84
81
76
73
68
63
63
61

60

59

54

54

50

2. The following set of scores was generated from a scale measuring leadership ability. Find the following: ($K = 100$)

    a. The reliability coefficient

    b. The SEM for the scale

    c. The 95% confidence interval for the score of 77

85	70
84	68
81	65
80	65
77	61
74	58
74	58
71	

3. If you have a test with a standard deviation of 6 and a reliability of .85, what would be the confidence intervals for a raw score of 50 at the 68, 95, and 99% confidence intervals? Explain what those intervals mean.

P R O C E S S G O A L	Research Proposal

Selecting the Measure For the Dependent Variable

Define a process goal for selecting the measure for the dependent variable:

    I will consider which type of measure will be most reliable and valid by:

        Reexamining my literature review to see what measures have been used in related studies

        Locating possible standardized tests through electronic databases (such as *Mental Measurement Yearbooks*), references in the literature, test catalogues, etc.

        Examining the psychometric properties of possible standardized tests through electronic databases, references in the literature, test catalogues, the test manuals, etc.

continues

continued

I will determine if I will use a standardized test or some other objective measure (e.g., grade point average, frequency count, etc.).

I will summarize the measurement device following the example in the sample proposal.

Write your own process goal to help you finalize the measurement section.

P R O C E S S G O A L	Program Assessment and Evaluation

Measurement of the Program

Define a process goal for selecting the measure for the dependent variable:

I will consider which type of measure will be most reliable and valid for the evaluation of the program by:

Reexamining my literature review to see what measures have been used in related studies

Reexamining my objectives and basing my evaluation on them

I will design a matrix for each question or problem to be examined in the assessment, which will include the following categories: (a) sources of information, (b) needed resources, (c) data collection methodology, (d) time line, and (e) data analysis.

Write your own process goal to help you finalize the measurement section.

P R O C E S S G O A L	Grant Proposal

Measurement Related to Evaluation

Define a process goal for selecting the measure for evaluation:

I will consider which type of measure will be most reliable and valid for the evaluation of the grant project by:

Reexamining my literature review to see what measures have been used in related studies

Reexamining my objectives and basing my evaluation on them

I will decide if I will conduct a formative evaluation or a summative evaluation.

I will incorporate the following criteria where feasible:

Objectives that are measurable

Measures that specify how data will be collected, analyzed, and reported

The use of multiple measures

The use of well-established measures

Write your own process goal to help you finalize the measurement section.

Summary

In this chapter we presented a theoretical understanding of reliability since reliability is a critical consideration in the measurement devices used to determine the significance of research. We discussed the two dimensions of reliability, dependability over time and internal consistency in terms of the degree of consistency with which a test measures whatever it is evaluating. We further discussed reliability in terms of the standard error of measurement, which provides an estimate of the range of variation in a set of repeated measurements. We provided formulas for estimating reliability, as well as practice exercises. The process goal guidelines assisted students in the selection of the measurement tools to use in their particular proposals.

Key Terms

alternate-forms technique
correlation coefficient
coefficient of equivalence
coefficient of reliability
coefficient of stability
  and equivalence
equivalent-forms
  technique

internal consistency
parallel-forms technique
random error
random errors of
  measurement
reliability

systematic errors of
  measurement
test-retest reliability

10

Inferential Statistics

Thus far we have dealt with **descriptive statistics**, methods that allow us to describe and to summarize our observations. When we use descriptive statistics, we talk about the data we have. In the field of counseling and student affairs, however, there will often be times when we want to consider data we do not have or cannot observe in its totality (e.g., an entire population). In those cases we use what we observe in samples and what is known about sampling error to reach fallible but reasonable decisions about populations. The science of making reasonable decisions about populations based on what we infer from samples is called **inferential statistics.** Inferential techniques are customarily more complex than descriptive methods and, in most instances, make use of descriptive statistics such as the mean, median, and standard deviation (Bartos, 1992).

Inferential statistics allows us to draw from **sample data** inferences, which have wider generalizability. The goal of counseling and student affairs research is to develop a science of behavior for the field. This science of behavior should consist of systematically organized statements of verified relationships between variables in counseling and student affairs. When we discover the nature of the relationship between these variables we can make meaningful predictions regarding these phenomena—indeed we can truly become scientists in our field.

Unfortunately, in the attempt to establish the precise nature of the relationship between variables, the counselor or student affairs professional must usually conduct research with relatively small samples of a population. For example, we may wish to study the relationship between students' secondary-school programs and their subsequent achievement in college. To investigate this relationship, we could select a sample of college students and then collect data regarding their college performance and certain aspects of their secondary-education program. We are not interested only in this sample of students, however. We wish to discover the nature of relationship between variables so that the relationship may be generalized to an entire population or universe from which the sample was drawn.

In our discussion of samples and populations it is important to point out some specific terminology used in each case. It is interesting that one technical definition of the word statistic is "a measure based on a *sample.*" For example, a standard deviation computed from sample data is called a *statistic*. Measures based on populations, rather than samples, are called parameters. If one could determine, for example, the standard deviation of IQ scores for all 9-year-olds in the world, that standard deviation would be called a *parameter*. Another way of thinking of inferential statistics is to think of these techniques as ways of making estimates about the nature of the parameters or "real values" in the population. An easy way to remember these relationships is statistic is to sample as parameter is to population.

Of course, we rarely have access to parameters in our field, for it is far too difficult to obtain data from an entire population. Furthermore, in most cases it would be extremely wasteful of time, energy, and resources to obtain parameters directly, particularly when with large samples the parameters can be estimated quite accurately.

The symbols used to represent parameters are different from those used to represent statistics. We present several different symbols for statistics and parameters in Table 10.1.

statistic — sample
parameter — population

Table 10.1 Differences in Symbols used with Sample and Population Data Measures

Sample Statistic Symbol	Measure	Population Parameter Symbol
$\overline{X}$	Mean	M
s	Standard Deviation	σ
s^2	Variance	σ^2

Once we are satisfied with the representativeness of the sample, we are in the position to test a particular hypothesis concerning the relationship between variables. This is called *hypothesis testing*.

Hypothesis testing involves three basic steps: (1) defining the statistical and null hypotheses; (2) selecting, calculating, and evaluating the appropriate statistical test; and (3) deciding whether to retain or reject the statistical hypotheses (Bartos, 1992).

Defining the Statistical and Null Hypotheses

In Chapter 4 we discussed **statistical (or alternative)** and **null hypotheses.** Researchers define these statistical and null hypotheses, which are mutually exclusive and exhaustive, and in a later step attempt to test them. If, for example, the null hypothesis is retained, then the alternative hypothesis is automatically rejected. Likewise, if the null hypothesis is rejected, the alternative hypothesis is accepted.

Suppose that an instructor has developed a Web-based course in research and statistics and wants to research its effectiveness in terms of students' final exam scores as compared to a traditional research and statistics course. A possible alternative hypothesis (H1) is: There will be a statistically significant difference in final exam scores of graduate students who take a Web-based research and statistics course as opposed to graduate students who take a traditionally taught research and statistics course. The alternative hypothesis (H1) predicts a relationship between independent and dependent variables. The null hypothesis (H0) would be: There will be no statistically significant difference in final exam scores of graduate students who take a Web-based research and statistics course as opposed to graduate students who take a traditionally taught research and statistics course. The nondirectional null hypothesis is always expressed in terms of no relationship between independent and dependent variables. According to the null hypothesis, any observed difference between sample and population means will be due to sampling error rather than to the effects of the independent variable(s). Since our example is nondirectional **("two-tailed")** it can only state whether the null hypothesis is true or false. On the other hand, a directional **("one-tailed")** null hypothesis can also predict whether the population parameter estimated by the obtained statistic will be greater than or less than the parameter specified by the null hypothesis.

You may be wondering why we refer to nondirectional hypotheses as two-tailed and directional hypotheses as one-tailed. This is because the ends of a normal curve (i.e., where the curve approaches the baseline) are called the "tails" of the distribution (Borg & Gall, 1983). Later in the chapter we will explain tails more fully in a discussion on the level of significance.

Suppose that the instructor randomly assigns 50 counseling and student affairs students to the Web-based course and 50 counseling and student affairs students to the traditional course. At the end of the course, the instructor administers a final exam to all of the students and finds that the mean for those students taught in the traditional classroom is higher than the mean for those students taught through the Web course. How do we interpret this difference? How much difference in the means is necessary to account for a statistically significant difference?

We could account for the difference by declaring that either the method of teaching caused the difference or the difference occurred by chance. Even though the subjects were randomly assigned to the treatments, it is possible that through chance the students in the traditional classroom were more intelligent, more highly motivated, or for some other reason were more likely to learn the material better than the students in the Web-based course, no matter how they were taught.

The difference between the groups, therefore, could be a result of a relationship between the variables—method of teaching and mastery of the concepts—or it could be the result of chance alone (e.g., sampling error). To determine how much difference in the means is necessary to account for a statistically significant difference, we need to proceed to Step two.

Selecting, Calculating, and Evaluating the Appropriate Statistical Test

We will analyze the data using an appropriate statistical test. We need the correct test in order to minimize possible Type I and Type II errors (discussed later in the chapter). We need to choose the test based on the parameter of interest and the number and nature of the independent and dependent variables.

First, we need to determine the number of independent and dependent variables in the study. (For statistical purposes, moderator variables are considered as independent variables.) Next, we must determine the measurement scale of each variable: nominal, ordinal, interval, or ratio. Figure 10.1 provides more specific information.

We can see in Figure 10.1 that if *both* independent and dependent variables are interval measures, correlation techniques (parametric correlations) may be employed. Tests such as T-test and analysis of variances are used when independent variables are nominal or ordinal and the dependent variable is interval. Ordinal measurement generally calls for the use of nonparametric techniques, with a chi-square analysis recommended for a combination of nominal independent and nominal dependent variables. More complex statistical procedures such as multivariate analysis of variance (MANOVA) or factor analysis are needed when more than one dependent variable is analyzed simultaneously.

Statistical Tests Are Categorized as Either Parametric or Nonparametric

Parametric Tests. **Parametric tests** are used to test hypotheses about certain population parametrics such as means, variances, differences between means, etc. In order to use parametric tests, the data being measured must be interval or ratio and the following assumptions must be met: (a) the variable of interest is normally distributed in the population; (b) when more than one sample is used in a study, the variances of the populations from which the samples were drawn are equal; and (c) randomization was used in drawing observations from the population, resulting in observations that are independent.

Type and Number of Independent Variables

Type and Number of Dependent Variables		Interval 1	Interval More than 1	Ordinal 1	Ordinal More than 1	Nominal 1	Nominal More than 1	
Interval	0		Factor analysis	Transform ordinal variable into nominal and use C-1, or transform the interval variable into ordinal and use B-2, or transform both variables into nominal and use C-3				Row 1
Interval	1	Correlation	Multiple correlation			Analysis of variance (or t-test)	Analysis of variance	Row 1
Interval	More than 1	Multiple correlation						Row 1
Ordinal	0	Transform ordinal variable into nominal and use C-1, or transform the interval variable into ordinal and use B-2, or transform the interval variable into nominal and use C-2			Coefficient of concordance			Row 2
Ordinal	1			Spearman correlation Kendall's tau		Sign test, median test, U-test, Kruskal-Wallis	Friedman's two-way analysis of variance	Row 2
Ordinal	More than 1							Row 2
Nominal	0						Chi-square	Row 3
Nominal	1	Analysis of variance (see C-1)		Sign test, median test, U-test, Kruskal-Wallis		Phi Coeff., Fisher exact test, Chi-square		Row 3
Nominal	More than 1	Analysis of variance (see C-1)		Friedman's two-way analysis of variance				Row 3
		Column A		Column B		Column C		

Figure 10.1 Choosing the Appropriate Statistical Test

The t-test and the analysis of variance (ANOVA) are examples of parametric tests. While the t-test compares the means of two groups, ANOVA compares two or more means and also can make comparisons within groups. For example, if a researcher compared mean scores on a depression scale between a group of clients taking medication only and a group of clients in therapy, only then the researcher would use the t-test. However, if the researcher also used a third group of clients who had a combined treatment of medication and therapy, the researcher would need to run an ANOVA.

These two examples of parametric tests are listed below as well as other tests that are extensions of ANOVA. For example, MANOVA is a form of ANOVA used when there is more than one dependent variable. ANCOVA can be used when there is a need to control for an extraneous variable, such as pretest scores. Note that these are just a sample of the extensive list of parametric tests.

T-test: Parametric test used to assess the differences between two means when data are scaled on an interval or ratio scale of measurement.

Analysis of variance (ANOVA): A parametric test used to assess the difference between group means. It involves partitioning the total variance into components. In

[handwritten: one way ANOVA]

a one-way ANOVA, for example, the total variance is partitioned into between-groups variance and within-groups variance. It is used when data on the dependent variable are scored on an interval or ratio scale of measurement.

Multivariate analysis of variance (MANOVA): A form of the ANOVA used when a study involves more than one dependent variable

Analysis of covariance (ANCOVA): An extension of the ANOVA used to increase the efficiency of the analysis by statistically controlling the variability of the dependent variable due to the effects of an extraneous variable. ANCOVA involves obtaining scores on the extraneous variable and using the scores to adjust scores on the dependent variable.

While parametric tests are much more **powerful** (i.e., a researcher is more likely to reject a false null hypothesis when using a parametric test) than nonparametric tests, the criteria that needs to be met in order to use them is much more rigorous than nonparametric tests.

Nonparametric Tests. Nonparametric tests are much more flexible than parametric tests, yet they tend to be less powerful (a researcher is less likely to reject a false null hypothesis as a result of using a nonparametric test). Nonparametric tests are designed for data that is nominally scaled or ordinally scaled. An example of nominally scaled data is the frequency count of the number of high-school graduates who went on for postsecondary education versus the number of graduates who did not. An example of ordinally scaled data is the rank order of individuals' stress levels as self-reported on a psychological test. Nonparametric tests do not require meeting the above assumptions related to the distribution of the population; thus they are referred to as "distribution-free" tests. When parametric tests can be legitimately used, parametric tests are preferred over nonparametric tests, since the latter are less sensitive to the magnitude of the differences between measures because of the less informative data (nominal or ordinal data) used. Examples of nonparametric tests are the chi-square, the Mann-Whitney U test, the Wilcoxon test, and Kruskal-Wallis test, which are described below:

[handwritten margin note: nominal or ordinal less powerful]

Chi-square test: A nonparametric inferential statistical test that assesses the difference between observed and expected frequencies. It is used with nominally scaled data or any other data reported in terms of frequencies.

Mann-Whitney U test: Nonparametric technique that assesses whether the ranks of observations of one group are equal to the ranks of observations of another group. It is used when the study involves two independent groups and the data are rank-ordered.

Wilcoxon matched-pairs signed-ranks test: Nonparametric test that assesses the probability that the ranks of the positive differences between scores of matched pairs are equal to the ranks of the negative differences between scores of matched pairs. It is used when the study involves two correlated groups and rank-ordered data.

Kruskal-Wallis test: Nonparametric technique that assesses whether the sums of ranks of observations for all groups are equal. It is used when the study involves one independent variable, two or more independent groups, and rank-ordered data.

Making a Decision

Researchers analyze the data from a study using the selected statistical test. From the results, researchers determine where the sample statistic lies in the theoretical sampling distribution to determine the likelihood that it is attributable to chance or the experimental treatment. This process is best explained through an understanding of probability.

Probability

Central in the rationale underlying inferential statistics is the notion of **probability.** Since the researchers wish to generalize from sample phenomena to population phenomena, they would like to be fairly sure that what is observed in the sample is not a function of mere chance alone. It is possible to determine statistically with considerable precision the likelihood that a sample phenomenon is attributable to chance. Probability statements associated with sets of coin tosses can illustrate this. As we know, the chance of a coin landing heads up, when tossed, is one out of two. However, the likelihood that a tossed coin will come up heads two times in a row is only one out of four. Similarly, the chance of obtaining three heads out of three coin tosses is only one out of eight. The probability of getting 10 heads out of 10 coin tosses is only 1 in 1,024. All of these probabilities can be determined from a distribution of statistical probabilities used in a fashion similar to that of the normal curve. In the case of coin tosses, we use statistical probability distribution based on two choices (heads or tails). By using such curves we can determine what the probability is that an observed set of events or a mere extreme set of such events can be attributed to chance alone.

In a coin tossing example, we might visualize a situation in which two people are betting for cups of coffee, with the loser buying the beverage. Imagine that one of the individuals does all the coin flipping. Perhaps the other decides to call tails every time, figuring to win approximately half of the wagers. If the coin turned up heads 10 times in a row, the person who called tails would obviously have to buy more than the expected share of coffee. Further, since we have just seen that the probability of getting 10 consecutive heads is 1/1,024, the loser might begin to suspect that there was something suspicious about the coin—or the person flipping it!

In a similar fashion, the statistician determines the probability that an observed research phenomenon or one more extreme is attributable to chance alone. If the probability is rare, for example, only 1 in 100, then the phenomenon is usually attributed to something *other* than chance—ordinarily the experimental conditions under investigation. It is the experimenter, incidentally, who decides what is a "rare" event in any given investigation (Bartos, 1992).

Statistical Significance

When a statistical test reveals that the probability is rare that a set of observed sample data is attributable to chance alone, this result is labeled as **statistically significant.** For example, if two group means are so different that only one time in one thousand would we find such a difference by chance alone, it is said that the difference is a statistically significant one. By statistically significant we mean that the observed phenomenon represents a significant departure from what might be expected by chance alone.

An example involving the use of the normal curve may help clarify the notion of statistical significance. Certain statistical tests yield a value, representing the chance probability, which is interpreted from the baseline of the normal distribution. For example, certain statistical models for testing mean differences yield z values (of which you are familiar). Suppose one such formula produces a z value of +2.70. From a chart of the normal curve (see Figure 10.2) we can determine that a z value will occur by chance alone in a normal distribution less than 1% percent of the time, since the distribution is cut off in the tail at the right of the curve by an ordinate erected at +2.70 standard deviation units. Such a z value is statistically significant; that is, a significant departure from what might be expected by chance alone. Under such circumstances, therefore, the observed mean difference would be attributed to something other than chance, usually the experimental conditions.

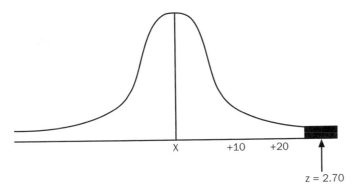

Figure 10.2 Statistical Significance Represented on a Normal Distribution

Many of the tests we may be using yield values other than standard scores, such as the z score described above. The above referenced t-test yields a t value, the ANOVA yields an F value, and the chi-square yields a x^2 value. These values indicate where the obtained sample statistic falls with regard to the theoretical sampling distribution regions: the **rejection region** and the **retention region.** The *rejection region* contains the values that are unlikely to occur by chance alone. If the statistical test yields a value in the rejection region, the null hypothesis is rejected, and the alternative hypothesis is accepted. On the other hand, the *retention region* contains those values that are likely to occur. If the statistical test provides a sample statistic in the retention region, the null hypothesis is retained, and the alternative hypothesis is rejected.

When the chance probability of an event's occurrence is 5 in 100, we say that the event is significant at the .05, or 5% level. In other words, we are saying that 5% of the theoretical sampling distribution represents the rejection region, which is defined by alpha (α) or the level of significance, and the remaining 95% represents the retention region. The same reasoning is true for any probability level. The value of **alpha** is set by a researcher in the proposal-planning phase, prior to collecting and analyzing data. When results of a study are "significant at the .01 level," we can say that the sample statistic falls within the region of values that have only a 1% probability of occurring if the null hypothesis is true. Sometimes the symbol p is used to represent the probability. Often the symbol is used as follows: $p < .05$, to indicate the probability of the event's occurrence (by chance) is less than ($<$) 0.05. Conversely, a symbol scheme of $p > .05$ would indicate that the probability was greater than .05. The probability of obtaining a z value of +2.70 in the example described earlier is less than 1 in 100; thus the probability level for the $z < 0.01$. Another way of stating this is to say that the z value is significant beyond the 0.01 level.

What significance levels should be used in rejecting null hypotheses? There are several schools of thought regarding this question. It has been conventional in behavioral science research work to use the 0.05 and 0.01 levels of significance. (Of course, if a statistical test yields a result which is significant at the 0.01 level, it is also significant at the 0.05 level.) These are the significance levels usually reported in the research literature. Some researchers contend that these arbitrary levels should be maintained; otherwise, researchers might be inclined to reject null hypotheses with 0.06, 0.09, 0.10, 0.12 or similarly varied significance levels. Such a practice, they contend, would lead to chaotic interpretations of hypotheses whereby a researcher might "stretch" a probability level in order to support a research hypothesis the researcher favored. Others argue that the level of significance should be a function of the hypothesis tested. They claim that in certain instances a very stringent level of significance, such as 0.001, should be employed; however, in other situations lower levels of significance, perhaps 0.25, for example, are acceptable.

Proponents of the latter view offer illustrations, such as a situation in which parenting groups for parents of preschoolers are being tested, with an experimental group versus a control group. Perhaps a year later the experimental group attains a mean performance in communicating skills with their children that is better than the control group, but only at the 0.30 level of significance. Advocates of unconventional significance levels argue that this level of significance would be totally acceptable, if there were no other method available for parent education. In other words, they contend that using a program based on 70 to 30 odds is better than no program.

In other situations, their argument continues, the level of significance might be set as low as 0.0001. For example, if a great sum of money is spent on new programming, the program should demonstrate its efficacy so that there is even less than 1 chance in 10,000 these results are accidental.

One- and Two-Tailed Tests

The researcher must decide if the test is to be conducted as **one- or two-tailed test.** This, again, is determined in the planning phase and is dictated by whether the hypotheses are directional (one-tailed) or nondirectional (two-tailed). The one and two tails refer to the tails of the probability curves from which the value yielded by the statistical test is interpreted. You will recall that we interpreted a z value of +2.70 as significant beyond the 0.01 level. A value of +2.70 falls in the right tail of the normal curve distribution. What should be done with a z of −2.70? This value, too, is significant beyond the 0.01 level, even though it falls in the left rather than the right tail of the curve.

In a well-conceived research investigation, the experimenter can often make a prediction as to the precise type of a relationship that will be observed. These predictions are usually based on prior research related to the hypothesis under analysis, or upon some type of theoretical rationale. For example, an investigator contrasting the efficacy of two diversity programs might test the research hypothesis (H1) that Group A's performance will be superior to that of Group B. Stated in the form of a null hypothesis (H0), the phrasing would be that Group A's performance will be equal to/or less than that of group B. Symbolically, using mean performance as the statistic, this null hypothesis would be expressed as $X0_1 \le X0_2$.

When researchers do not make a prediction, they allow for the possibility of a statistical result that may be either positive or negative, (e.g. a −z or a +z). Hence, they must use a two-tailed test to interpret their result, as in Figure 10.3. In such a case, the rejection region is equally divided between the two tails of the theoretical sampling distribution. For example, when the level of significance is .05, 2.5% (.05/2 = .025) of the rejection region lies within the positive tail and 2.5% lies within the negative tail. If researchers make a directional prediction regarding the outcome of their investigation, they are permitted to use a one-tailed test of significance, such as those depicted in Figure 10.4. In a one-tailed test, the entire rejection region lies in either the positive or negative tail of the distribution.

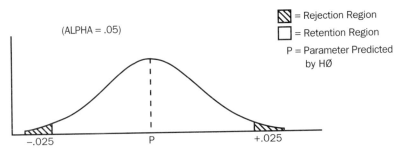

Figure 10.3 Theoretical Sampling Distribution for Two-Tailed Tests

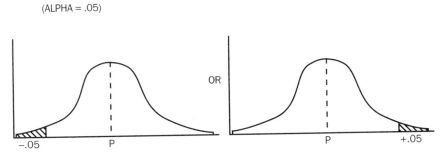

Figure 10.4 Theoretical Sampling Distribution for One-Tailed Tests

By using one-tailed tests, the researcher will more often reject a null hypothesis if the direction of the difference or relationship is the same as he or she predicted. Since all of the rejection area is in one tail, the value yielded by the significance test need not be as large, that is, as far from the mean, in order to be statistically significant.

For example, in the case of the normal curve, a z value must be at least as large as plus or minus 1.96 to be significant at the 0.05 level. If the researcher makes a directional hypothesis, e.g., predicts a positive z value, then the z need only be +1.65 in order to reject the null hypothesis when $p < 0.05$. This difference is illustrated in Figure 10.5.

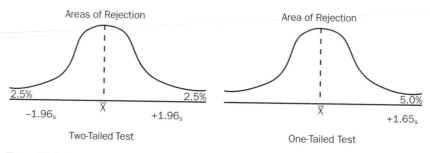

Figure 10.5   Comparing the Rejection Area in Two-Tailed and One-Tailed Tests

It is apparent that one-tailed tests are more powerful than two-tailed tests. On the basis of sample data, the hypothesis under consideration is either accepted or rejected and, if possible, results are generalized to the population.

Critical Values

In the section entitled, "Statistical Significance," we stated that when two group means are so different that the difference could not occur by chance alone, it is said that the difference is a statistically significant one. Is a 10-point difference in means significant? Or must it be 20 points? What constitutes a statistically significant difference?

To illustrate this concept we describe below an adapted version of a demonstration that a colleague, Dr. Mark Kiselica of the College of New Jersey, uses to explain this concept.

Imagine that we have before us two clear pitchers of water and a jar of Tang® orange juice drink. As we add a couple of granules of Tang® to the pitcher on the right, we ask you to please raise your hand as soon as you think there is a difference between the two pitchers of water. (More than likely your hand will go up almost immediately). If we were able to discuss what made the two pitchers of water different, you would probably say that the one on the right had a slight orange hue to it, that it has sugary granules in it, etc. If we asked you if the pitchers of water were statistically significantly different from each other, you would probably say no. Next, we would continue to add more Tang® to the pitcher on the right and ask you to raise your hand when you thought the two pitchers were statistically significantly different from each other. If your class responds as former classes have, hands would go up sporadically until nearly all hands were up. At that point we would discuss what criteria people used to determine that the two pitchers of water were significantly different. The most common response is that the difference occurs when the pitcher of water attains the familiar orange color of Tang®. The answer we look for is for students to indicate that there is a statistically significant difference when the amount of Tang® needed to make a pitcher of Tang®, as prescribed in the directions on the jar, is added to the pitcher. In other words, the manufacturer's directions serve as the critical value. Likewise, researchers can access **critical value tables** to determine whether or not a value is statistically significant.

Since researchers do not know by merely looking at raw scores or descriptive statistics if the groups vary significantly; they analyze the data with the statistical test they select. When researchers conduct a statistical test, the result is a value (e.g., t, F). Researchers use the value to decide where in the theoretical sampling distribution the sample statistic lies by comparing the value to a critical value table. Critical value tables (such as Table 10.2) are often included in statistics textbooks. Identification of the appropriate critical value is usually based on: (a) the level of significance, and (b) the degrees of freedom.

Table 10.2   Critical Values of t

Df	Level of significance for one-tailed test			
	.05	.25	.01	.005
	Level of significance for two-tailed test			
	.10	.05	.02	.01
1	6.3138	12.7060	31.8207	63.6574
2	2.9200	4.3027	2.9649	9.9248
3	2.3534	3.1824	4.5407	5.8409
4	2.1318	2.7764	3.7469	4.6041
5	2.0150	2.5706	3.3649	4.0322
6	1.9432	2.4469	3.1427	3.7074
7	1.8946	2.3646	2.9980	3.4995
8	1.8595	2.3060	2.8965	3.3554
9	1.8331	2.2622	2.8214	3.2498
10	1.8125	2.2281	2.7638	3.1693
11	1.7959	2.2010	2.7181	3.1058
12	1.7823	2.1788	2.6810	3.0545
13	1.7709	2.1604	2.6503	3.0123
14	1.7613	2.1448	2.6245	2.9768
15	1.7531	2.1315	2.6025	2.9467
16	1.7459	2.1199	2.5835	2.9208
17	1.7396	2.1098	2.5669	2.8982
18	1.7341	2.1009	2.5524	2.8784
19	1.7291	2.0930	2.5305	2.8609
20	1.7247	2.0860	2.5280	2.8453
21	1.7207	2.0796	2.5177	2.8314
22	1.7171	2.0739	2.5074	2.8188

continues

Table 10.2 Critical Values of t (continued)

	Level of significance for one-tailed test			
	.05	.25	.01	.005
	Level of significance for two-tailed test			
Df	.10	.05	.02	.01
23	1.7139	2.0687	2.4999	2.8073
24	1.7109	2.0639	2.4922	2.7969
25	1.7081	2.0595	2.4851	2.7874
26	1.7056	2.0555	2.4786	2.7787
27	1.7033	2.0518	2.4727	2.7707
28	1.7011	2.0484	2.4671	2.7633
29	1.6993	2.0452	2.4620	2.7564
30	1.6973	2.0423	2.4573	2.7500

Table Value: If the t value you generate is *equal to or greater than* the Table Value, it is *statistically significant* and you *reject* the null hypothesis.

Degrees of Freedom: number in groups minus the number of groups (e.g., two groups of 16 each, 16 + 16 – 2 = 30 degrees of freedom).

Let us assume that the mean course grade for counseling and student affairs students who took the traditional research and statistics course was 85, while the mean course grade for the same population of students who took a Web-based research and statistics course was 90. The means definitely differ from each other. Is the difference statistically significantly different? Let us say that we conduct a t-test on the data and obtain a t value of 2.56. Assuming that there were 28 degrees of freedom, and that it was a two-tailed test with 5% level of significance, the chart would give us a critical value of t (or "manufacturer's directions") equal to 2.0484. Since the t value provided by the t-test is greater than the value given in the critical value table, we will reject the null hypothesis. In other words, the value provided by the t-test exceeds the critical value, and we conclude that the obtained sample statistic lies within the rejection region; thus we reject the null hypothesis. If the value produced by the t-test had been less than the critical value, we would have concluded that the sample statistic lies within the retention region, and we would have retained the null hypothesis.

A C T I V I T Y

10.1

T-Values

Look up the critical value in the following cases. Would you reject or retain the null?

1.	t = 2.30	two-tailed test	20 degrees of freedom	$p = 0.01$
2.	t = 1.80	one-tailed test	26 degrees of freedom	$p = 0.05$
3.	t = 1.80	two-tailed test	26 degrees of freedom	$p = 0.05$

Critical Values and Computer Analysis

Researchers do not need to use critical value tables when statistical analysis is done by computer. The computer analysis provides the value and its associated level of significance, as shown in the accompanying computer printout, Figure 10.6. All that the researcher has to do is to notice whether or not the alpha related to the value is lower than the alpha that the researcher has established. If that is the case, then the researcher rejects the null hypothesis. If the alpha associated with the value is greater than the alpha set by the researcher, then the researcher retains the null hypothesis.

T-Test

Group Statistics

GROUP		N	Mean	Std. Deviation	Std. Error Mean
SCORES	1.00	15	74.9333	7.2749	1.8784
	2.00	15	68.5333	8.1404	2.1019

Independent Samples Test

		t-test for Equality of Means			
		t	df	Sig. (2-tailed)	Mean Difference
SCORES	Equal variances assumed	2.270	28	.031	6.4000
	Equal variances not assumed	2.270	27.653	.031	6.4000

Figure 10.6 Critical Values as Reported in Computer Analyses

This concept sometimes confuses students, since the value resulting from the statistical test must be *greater than or equal to* the critical value in order to reject the null. Through computer analysis, however, the alpha associated with the value from the statistical test must be *less than or equal to* the researcher's alpha. The confusion may disappear when students notice the relationship between the critical value and the alpha in the critical values chart (Table 10.2). Notice that there is an inverse relationship between alpha and critical value. The lower the alpha, the higher the critical value. Therefore, it makes sense that in order to reject the null, we must obtain an alpha that is lower than the alpha established by the researcher or a value that is higher than the tabled critical value.

Degrees of Freedom

Degrees of freedom are the number of values that are "free to vary" in a statistical calculation. A simple example may help to clarify this concept. Let us say that $N = 5$ and the mean equals 6. Let us further say that we know four of the five values. They are 10, 8, 2, and

1. What must the fifth value be? It must be 9 in order to bring the total to 30, which when divided by 5 equals a mean of 6. In this example there were four degrees of freedom because the first four values could have been anything (they were "free to vary") but the fifth one had to be the value 9.

Each type of statistical test varies in the way the degrees of freedom are calculated. The degrees of freedom for a t-test are calculated by the number in groups minus the number of groups. For example, if there are two groups of 24 subjects each ($24 + 24 - 2 = 46$ degrees of freedom). The degrees of freedom for chi-square analysis are figured by the number of groups minus one. Therefore, if there are two groups, there would be one degree of freedom ($2 - 1 = 1$).

Type I and Type II Errors

When researchers decide to reject or retain the null hypothesis, their decision may be either right or wrong. If the null hypothesis is true, the researcher is correct in retaining it and in error in rejecting it. The rejection of the true null hypothesis (stating no significant difference) is labeled a **Type I error.**

If the null hypothesis is false, the researcher is in error in retaining it and correct in rejecting it. The retention of a false null hypothesis is labeled a **Type II error.** Table 10.3 summarizes the four possible states.

Let us consider some possible consequences of the two types of errors in our sample.

Type I Error. An investigator conducts a study within the Department of Counseling at a large state university and declares that there is a relationship between teaching method (traditional classroom and computerized) and the mastery of the research and statistics concepts for graduate students of counseling and student affairs. The investigator, therefore, recommends the computer-based method as the better one. The Department of Counseling invests in a computer lab for the instruction of this course. After all this expenditure of time and money, the students from the Department of Counseling do not appear to score any higher in the research and statistics section on a national certification exam. Subsequent experiments do not produce the results observed in the original investigation. Although the ultimate truth or falsity of the null hypothesis is still unknown, the evidence supporting it is overwhelming. The original investigator is embarrassed and humiliated, and the Department of Counseling has spent unnecessary funds.

Type II Error. The researcher concluded that the difference between the two groups may be attributed to luck and that the null hypothesis is probably true. The researcher declares that one method of instruction is as good as the other.

Subsequent researchers conclude that the computerized instruction is better than the traditional instruction, and counselor education programs that change from traditional classroom instruction to computer-based instruction report impressive gains in students' scores on national exams. Although the ultimate truth still remains unknown, evidence supports the research hypothesis. The original researcher is embarrassed (but probably not humiliated). The research and statistics course remains as it has always been.

Type I errors typically lead to changes that are unwarranted. Type II errors typically lead to maintenance of the status quo when a change is warranted. In the field of counseling and

Table 10.3 Systematic Representation of Type I and Type II Errors

		The real situation (unknown to the investigator) is that the null hypothesis is:	
		true	false
The investigator, after making a test of significance, determines that the null hypothesis is:	true	investigator is correct	investigator makes Type II error
	false	investigator makes Type I error	investigator is correct

student affairs, researchers generally consider the consequences of a Type I error more serious than the consequences of a Type II error, although there are certainly exceptions to this.

Recall that all scientific conclusions are statements that have a high probability of being correct, rather than statements of absolute truth. How high must the probability be before a researcher is willing to declare that a relationship between variables exists? In other words, how unlikely must the null hypothesis be before one rejects it? The consequences of rejecting a true hypothesis, a Type I error, vary with the situation. Therefore, investigators usually weigh the relative consequences of Type I and Type II errors and decide, before conducting their experiments, how strong the evidence must be before they would reject the null hypothesis. This predetermined level at which a null hypothesis would be rejected is called the **level of significance.**

Of course, one could avoid Type I errors by always retaining the null hypothesis or avoid Type II errors by always rejecting it. Neither of these alternatives is productive. If the consequences of a Type I error would be very serious but a Type II error would be of little consequence, the investigator might decide to risk the possibility of a Type I error only if the estimated probability of the observed relationship's being due to mere luck is one chance in a thousand or less. This is called testing the hypothesis at the .001 level of significance. In this case the investigator is being very careful not to declare that a relationship exists when there is no relationship. However, this decision means the acceptance of a high probability of a Type II error, declaring there is no relationship when in fact a relationship does exist.

If the consequences of a Type I error are judged not to be serious, the investigator might decide to declare that a relationship exists if the probability of an observed relationship's being due to mere luck is 1 chance in 10 or less. This is called testing the hypothesis at the .10 level of significance. Here the investigator is taking only moderate precautions against a Type I error, yet is not taking a great risk of a Type II error.

Practical Significance

Up to this point we have talked about statistical significance; however, when results achieve statistical significance they may not always achieve practical significance. According to Borg and Gall (1983), one of the most common and serious misinterpretations of the test of significance is to confuse the statistical significance with the practical and theoretical significance of the research results. "Statistical significance does not imply practical significance" (Minium,

Clarke, & Coladarci, 1999, p. 212). Marlow (2001) refers to practical significance as clinical significance. She states that clinical significance is reached when the specific goal of a particular intervention is attained. For example, she says that when the practical goal is to increase a child's school attendance from 50% to 90%, anything below this goal may not be of clinical significance, although it may be statistically significant. Likewise, if the goal is to decrease "cutting" behavior in a female adolescent from 50% of the time when she is depressed to no incidence of cutting behavior, a decrease to 20% may be statistically significant but not clinically significant. On the other hand, a university may implement a million-dollar recruitment program to increase diversity on campus. The administrators may find that, while the program has brought in a higher percentage of freshmen with diverse backgrounds, the numbers are not statistically significant. However, they may conclude that the resulting increase in diversity on the campus is practically significant and justifies continuing the costly program.

T-Test

Researchers test a null hypothesis in numerous ways. The t-test is among the most widely used parametric test. The t-test is used to determine just how great the difference between two means must be in order for it to be judged significant, that is, a significant departure from the differences which might be expected by chance alone. Another way of stating the function of the t-test is to say that, through its use, we test the null hypothesis that two group means are not significantly different; that is, the means are so similar that the sample groups can be considered to have been drawn from the same population.

If you plan to use a t-test in analyzing a study, we encourage you to take advantage of one of the many statistical computer packages available to run your analysis. Most likely one of the first prompts that will come up will be an inquiry as to which type of t-test you want to run (e.g., t-test for independent samples, t-test for dependent samples). Researchers choose among the various t-test equations, depending on the samples in their study. One such t-test is the **t-test for independent samples,** which is used when comparing two groups of people on one measure. An example would be if you were to compare the final exam scores of a group of graduate students who took a traditional research and statistics course with a group of graduate students who took a computer-based research and statistics course. On the other hand, you would use the **t-test for dependent samples** when comparing one group of people on two measures, such as a pretest and posttest.

Since it is beyond the scope of this book to present all the various t-test equations, we are going to present only one, the **two-sample t-test.** We have chosen this particular equation because it is the easiest one to use in hand computation. As mentioned earlier in the book, we think that when you work by hand through a statistical analysis, you gain a better understanding of the results obtained through a computer analysis.

The *two-sample t-test* actually tests whether the two population means are equal (Norusis, 1993). As an example, Norusis cites a study conducted by Davis and Ragsdale, 1983) in which the researchers asked couples to rate, on a scale of one (definitely want to buy) to seven (definitely do not want to buy), their likelihood of buying various products. Low scores indicate those subjects who are more likely to be buyers. Of the 100 couples, 50 received questionnaires with pictures of the products (picture group), while the remaining 50 couples received questionnaires without photos (nonpicture group). The nonpicture group ($N = 50$) had a mean score of 168, while the picture group ($N = 48$, due to the failure of two couples to complete the questionnaire) had a mean score of 159. It appears that couples who saw pictures indicated a greater likelihood to purchase products than those who did not see pictures. By using the two-sample t-test, we are not asking whether the two sample means are equal, but whether the two population means are equal—not just those actually studied.

According to Norusis (1993, p. 254), "To test the hypothesis that, in the population, buying scores for the two questionnaire types are the same, the following statistic can be calculated:"

$$t = \frac{\overline{X}_1 - \overline{X}_2}{\sqrt{\dfrac{s_1^2}{N_1} + \dfrac{s_2^2}{N_2}}}$$
(Equation 10.1)

where $\overline{X}_1$ = mean of group 1
$\overline{X}_2$ = mean of group 2
s_1^2 = variance of group 1
s_2^2 = variance of group 2
N_1 = subjects in group 1
N_2 = subjects in group 2

Setting statistical notions aside for a moment, common sense tells us that when analyzing the probability that a mean difference between two groups is significant, an experimenter should first examine the following three factors: (a) the magnitude of the difference between the two means, (b) the degree of "overlap" between the two groups as revealed by the variability of each group, and (c) the number of subjects in the two samples. These three factors will be examined more carefully in the following discussion.

Other things being equal, the larger the value of t, the greater the probability that a statistically significant mean difference exists between the two groups under consideration. An examination of the t-test model supplied in the formula will reveal that if the two group means were absolutely identical, there would be no difference between them. Hence, a zero in the numerator of the formula would yield a zero t value. Generally speaking, the larger the difference between the two means, the greater will be the value of t (greater in the absolute sense, i.e., regardless of the algebraic sign). Thus, we may ordinarily conclude that the larger the t value, the less the probability is that the difference between the two means occurs from mere chance.

Although the size of t necessary for statistical significance varies with the sizes of the samples involved, it may assist you to see how large it must be in order to be significant at the 0.05 level when the sample size varies. In Table 10.2 you can see that as the number of degrees of freedom becomes larger, a smaller t value is sufficient to reject the null hypothesis. Degrees of freedom reflect the size of the sample.

However, this "larger the t, greater the significance" notion is complicated by the denominator of the t formula. This is as it should be, since the mere fact that two means differ tells one very little, until something is known about the variability of the two groups under consideration. Obviously, there must be some mean difference present, or it would be immediately concluded that there is no significant difference between the identical means of the two groups.

Group Variability

In addition to the actual mean difference, a factor of considerable importance in determining whether to accept or reject the null hypothesis is the variability of the groups involved. If the variances of the two groups are particularly great—that is, there is much spread in the distributions—relatively small mean differences between two groups will result in considerable overlap between the two distributions, such as in Figure 10.7. With so much overlap between the groups, one might be reluctant to conclude that the means of the two distributions were really different.

However, with smaller standard deviations in the samples concerned, the identical mean difference might be judged to reflect a real population mean difference. For example, consider the situation depicted in Figure 10.8.

In Figure 10.8 small standard deviations exist for the two groups under consideration, whereas in Figure 10.7 large standard deviations were present. In both cases an equivalent mean difference (10 units) occurred, but in the second instance one would be willing to place much more confidence in the assertion that the two samples were *not* drawn from the same population, since the groups are so clearly distinct.

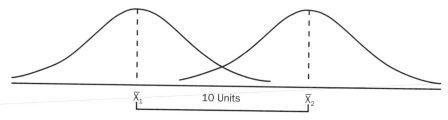

Mean difference of 10 units between two groups with relatively large standard deviations

Figure 10.7 Comparison of Two Groups with Large Standard Deviations

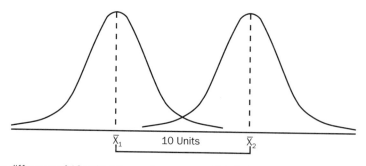

Mean difference of 10 units between two groups with relatively small standard deviations

Figure 10.8 Comparison of Two Groups with Small Standard Deviations

The notion generalizes to the principle that, other factors being equal, the smaller the variances of the two groups under consideration, the greater the likelihood that a statistically significant mean difference exists.

Sample Size

The third factor to be considered in testing for a significant mean difference is the size of the samples involved. To illustrate the necessity of taking sample size into account, we will employ an extreme example. Suppose the efficacy of a novel counseling approach were tested by using the new approach with only two individuals. A conventional method might also be employed with only two control subjects. Even if the means of the two "groups" differed by as much as 100 points, one would be unlikely to decide with much confidence that the new approach was greatly superior to the conventional approach. The size of the sample, of course, is an extremely important determinant of the significance of the difference between means, for with increased sample size, means tend to become more stable representations of group performance. The larger the sample, the greater confidence one can place in a relatively minor difference between the means. With an extremely small sample, therefore, one should be reluctant to place confidence in even large differences between two means.

To illustrate, common sense suggests that three factors are of importance in considering the significance of differences between the means of two groups: (1) the magnitude of the difference between the two means, (2) the size of the samples involved, and (3) the variability of the two groups. Now by reexamining the equation for the t-test, you will see that what we described from a common-sense viewpoint is actually incorporated in the formula itself. We will now use the data from the product questionnaire study to decide whether the two population means were equal. You will recall that group one had 50 subjects and a mean of 168, while group two had 48 subjects and a mean of 159.08. According to Norusis (1993) the variances for the groups were 21.787^2 and 27.564^2, respectively. Plugging these values into the equation the t value equals 1.77.

$$t = \frac{168.0 - 159.08}{\sqrt{\dfrac{21.787^2}{50} + \dfrac{27.564^2}{48}}} = 1.77 \qquad\qquad \text{(Equation 10.2)}$$

Norusis (1993) reports that the associated probability is 0.08. Since this probability is greater than 0.05, the null hypothesis that there is no difference in mean buying scores in the population for the two types of questionnaires is not rejected. We accept that the mean buying scores in the population are equal for the two types of forms.

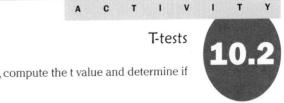

A C T I V I T Y

T-tests

10.2

Using the two-sample t-test and the following data, compute the t value and determine if you will reject or retain the null hypothesis.

continues

continued

Group 1	Group 2
$N = 16$	$N = 16$
Mean = 80	Mean = 70
$s = 2$	$s = 3$

Use two-tailed test, $p < .05$.

Chi-Square Test

The **chi-square (x^2) procedure** is one of the most widely used nonparametric tests. It is used to test hypotheses about the independence of frequency counts in various categories. Chi-square allows an individual to estimate the probability that observed frequencies differ from expected frequencies through chance alone.

Let us assume that high-school counselors in a large district decide to research an intensive prevention program that they introduce in their schools for seniors who are at risk for dropping out of school. They identify 100 at-risk seniors and randomly assign them to either the experimental or control group. They use chi-square to analyze if the number of students graduating after involving themselves in the intensive program (experimental group) differs from the number of students who graduate who were in the control group. The null hypothesis is "There will be no statistically significant difference in the graduation rate of at-risk high-school seniors who receive an intensive prevention program and those at-risk high-school seniors who receive the regular academic program."

The chi-square equation is given in equation 10.3.

$$x^2 = \Sigma \frac{(O - E)^2}{E}$$

where
x^2 = chi-square O = Observed frequencies
Σ = sum of E = Expected frequencies   (Equation 10.3)

Let us assume that out of the original 50 students assigned to the experimental group 40 graduate, while 20 of the original 50 students assigned to the control group graduate. In Table 10.4 the number of graduates from each group is considered the number observed. Since the null hypothesis states that there will be no statistically significant difference in the number of students graduating, it would be expected that the same number of graduates would occur in both the experimental and control groups. Therefore the sum of the observed column is divided evenly between both groups in the expected column (60/2 = 30). These figures are entered in the expected column, and the sum is given. Note that the sum of the expected frequencies is equal to the sum of the observed frequencies.

In the next column the expected frequencies are subtracted from the observed frequencies. The results are squared in the next column in order to get rid of any negatives. Next the squared result is divided by the expected frequency. Finally the last column is added to obtain the chi-square.

Table 10.4 Chi-Square Example

Group	Observed	Expected	$O - E$	$(O - E)^2$	$\dfrac{(O-E)^2}{E}$
Exp.	40	30	10	100	3.33
$(N = 50)$					
Cont.	20	30	−10	100	3.33
$(N = 50)$					
Sum	60	60	0	200	6.66
			$x^2 = 6.66$		

In order to decide if you will retain or reject the null hypothesis, you need to consult the critical value chart for chi-square, Table 10.5. Use $p < .05$.

Table 10.5

Critical Values of x^2
Level of Significance

Df	.20	.10	.05	.02	.01
1	1.642	2.706	3.841	5.412	6.635
2	3.219	4.605	5.991	7.824	9.210
3	4.642	6.251	7.315	9.837	11.341
4	5.989	7.779	9.488	11.668	13.277
5	7.289	9.236	11.070	13.388	15.086
6	8.558	10.645	12.592	15.033	16.812
7	9.803	12.017	14.067	16.622	18.475
8	11.030	13.362	15.507	18.168	20.090
9	2.242	14.684	16.919	19.679	21.666
10	3.442	15.987	18.307	21.161	23.209

Table Value: If the x^2 value you generate is *equal to or greater than* the Table Value, it is *statistically significant* and you *reject* the *null* hypothesis.

Degrees of Freedom: number of groups −1

As previously stated, the degrees of freedom for chi-square is the number of groups minus one. In this case $2 - 1 = 1$. When we look on the critical value chart, we see that for an alpha of .05, a critical value of 3.841 is needed. Since 6.66 is greater than the critical value, we reject the null. Thus, there is a statistically significant difference in the graduation rates of at-risk seniors who receive an intensive prevention program when compared with those at-risk seniors receiving the regular academic program. The computer printout is presented in Figure 10.9.

A   C   T   I   V   I   T   Y

10.3 Chi-square

Using the same scenario above, conduct a chi-square test where the observed graduates from the experimental group = 40 and the observed graduates from the control group = 30. Use $p < .05$.

NPar Tests
Chi-Square Tests
Frequencies

GROUP

	Observed N	Expected N	Residual
1.00	40	30.0	10.0
2.00	20	30.0	−10.0
Total	60		

Test Statistics

	GROUP
Chi-Square[a]	6.667
df	1
Asymp. Sig.	.010

Figure 10.9 Computer Printout of Chi-Square Analysis

Inferential Statistics in Research Proposals, Program Assessments and Evaluations, and Grant Proposals

Earlier in the chapter we discussed the selection of the appropriate statistical test (with the aid of the information in Figure 10.1) for running an analysis of the research data in a research study. In program assessment and evaluation, the same considerations apply.

You will recall that the last column of the evaluation matrix requests a specific plan for data analysis. If you are providing descriptive statistics, then you will want to consult Chapters 7 and 8. If you are planning to examine the nature of the relationship between these variables in order to make meaningful predictions regarding these phenomena, you will want to select the appropriate inferential analysis. Likewise, if evaluation is a part of the grant proposal, you must determine in advance how you will collect and analyze the data.

In all cases, you need to decide what data is to be collected and how it will be analyzed well before the first data is even collected. Therefore, every aspect of the evaluation and analysis needs to be carefully planned well in advance, from how the data will be organized and recorded to how it will be treated statistically.

Worksheet 10.1

1. The following sets of scores were derived from posttests on experimental and control groups. Answer the following questions based on these raw scores (assuming samples):
   a. What is the reliability coefficient of the instrument used? ($K = 100$) Use data from the experimental group.
   b. What is the approximate SEM for the experimental group?
   c. What is the t value of the two groups? ($p < .05$, one-tailed)*
   d. Would you accept or reject the null hypothesis?

Experimental	Control
86	80
83	80
83	76
81	74
80	74
78	73
76	71
76	70
74	68
73	68
71	63
70	61
68	58
65	58
60	54

*The computer analysis for 1-c appears in Figure 10.6.

P R O C E S S G O A L	Research Proposal

Choosing the Statistical Analysis

Define a process goal for finalizing Chapter 3:

> I will choose the appropriate statistical method by:
>
>> Rereading the section in Chapter 10 about selecting the appropriate statistical test
>>
>> Determining if my sample meets the strict assumptions needed to use a parametric test
>>
>> Determining how many independent and dependent variables I have and their measurement scales
>
> I will write the research design and procedures section of Chapter 3 by using the sample proposal as a guide.
>
> I will formulate a reasonable time line for carrying out the research.

Write your own process goal to help you finalize Chapter 3 of your research proposal.

P R O C E S S G O A L	Program Assessment and Evaluation

Choosing the Statistical Analysis

Define a process goal for finalizing the program assessment and evaluation proposal:

> I will choose the appropriate statistical method to evaluate the program by:
>
>> Rereading the section in Chapter 10 about selecting the appropriate statistical test
>>
>> Determining if the program I will be measuring meets the strict assumptions needed to use a parametric test
>>
>> Determining how many independent and dependent variables I have and their measurement scales
>
> I will finish the program assessment and evaluation proposal by finalizing the evaluation section.
>
> I will formulate a reasonable time line for carrying out the program assessment and evaluation.

Write your own process goal to help you finalize your program assessment and evaluation proposal.

P R O C E S S G O A L	Grant Proposal

Finalizing the Evaluation Plan

Define a process goal for finalizing the grant proposal:

I will determine if my grant proposal will include an evaluation component by:

Reviewing other successful grant proposals to see if they had this aspect built into them

Rereading my proposal to see how I would include an evaluation plan

If I determine that an evaluation component is to be included, I will choose the appropriate statistical method by:

Rereading the section in Chapter 10 about selecting the appropriate statistical test

Determining if my program meets the strict assumptions needed to use a parametric test

Determining how many independent and dependent variables I have and their measurement scales

I will write the evaluation plan for my grant proposal.

I will formulate a reasonable time line for carrying out the grant proposal.

Write your own process goal to help you finalize your grant proposal.

Summary

Inferential statistics is the science of making reasonable decisions with limited information. In this chapter we introduced you to the way researchers use what they observe in samples and what is known about sampling error to reach fallible but reasonable decisions about populations. Further, we discussed the null hypothesis, a basic tool of inferential statistics. Additionally, this discussion included hypothesis testing, probability, levels of significance, Type I and Type II errors, one- and two-tailed tests, choosing the appropriate statistical test, and parametric and nonparametric tests. We discussed statistical significance as well as practical significance. We provided a detail explanation of the t-test, as an example of a parametric test, as well as the chi-square test, a nonparametric test. We included practice exercises for you to learn how to compute and analyze t-tests and chi-square tests.

Key Terms

alpha

chi-square (x^2) procedure

critical value table

degrees of freedom

descriptive statistics

directional test

hypothesis testing

inferential statistics

level of significance

nondirectional test

nonparametric test

null hypothesis

one-tailed test

parametric test

powerful

probability

rejection region

retention region

sample data

statistical (or alternative)
  hypothesis

statistically significant

t-test for dependent
  samples

t-test for independent
  samples

two-sample t-test

two-tailed test

Type I error

Type II error

11

Reporting Results and
Statistical Literacy

Congratulations on the completion of your project, either the research proposal, program assessment and evaluation, or grant proposal! As previously mentioned, the purpose of developing these plans is to allow you to apply your knowledge of research and statistics. The actual implementation of these proposals is beyond the scope of this book; however, in the following discussion we would like to acquaint you with the process of reporting your findings. Additionally, we would like to provide you practice in understanding research findings as reported in the literature. We will attempt to accomplish this through the presentation of an article, presented in Appendix A, "Teaching and Learning with Humor: Experiment and Replication" (Ziv, 1988), which presents two studies concerning the use of humor in the teaching of statistics and psychology. We especially like this article since, like us, the author has attempted to combine some humor in the teaching of statistics. We will guide you through the first part as a learning experience and then provide you with an activity in part two which allows you to check your own statistical literacy.

Comparing Proposals and Final Reports

Although proposals and final reports differ, they are conceptually related. The quality of an intended study can be determined through the proposal. A well-written proposal provides the basis for a sound final report since the two documents overlap significantly. While proposals describe the problem you plan to research, the significance of the problem, a review of related literature, and your plan for gathering and analyzing the data; final reports summarize those areas as well as emphasize the results and provide a discussion of the implications of the findings. Since the proposal provides a systematic plan for your study, the more closely you carry out the proposal, the easier it will be to conduct your study and write up your final report. In the case of a research proposal, the transition from the proposal to a final report usually only involves minor revisions in the first three chapters. These revisions are primarily related to the verb tense of the documents. As you will recall, you wrote the proposal in the future tense since you wrote the proposal prior to the implementation of the project. However, you are to write the final report in the past tense since you will be summarizing what actually took place. For example, in the proposal you would write, "The groups will be formed through simple random sampling." In the final report, however, you would write "The groups were formed through simple random sampling." Although not specifically discussed here, program assessment and evaluations and grant proposals go through similar transformations in the writing of their final reports.

Final Reports

Sections of final reports are discussed below. You are also encouraged to consult the latest version of the *Publication Manual of the American Psychological Association* (APA, 2001).

Title Page

Final reports begin with a title page, which includes the title of the project, and the author's name and institutional affiliation, as well as a running head. You should make your title no longer than 15 words (Crowl, 1993) and choose the terminology carefully since the words in the title determine how the report will be indexed. Running heads are an abbreviation of the title, and you should place them at the top of each page.

Abstract

The abstract is a concise summary of your study, which should be less than 120 words (APA, 2001). Like the title, the abstract is used for indexing purposes, so you must choose the terminology carefully. It should include a statement of the problem, the methodology used, the results of the study, and a summary of the implications of the study. Although the abstract appears at the beginning of the report, you can write it only upon the completion of the study.

Introduction, Problem Statement, Hypotheses, Significance of Study

The introductory section or chapter serves many functions. It should tell the question to be researched, the hypotheses, and why the study is important. After reading this section the reader should have a good understanding of what the problem is and what its ramifications are (Leedy, 1997). A clear understanding of the problem and its significance will help the reader to later comprehend the findings and to judge the merits of the study. If you have introduced the problem by subdividing it into subproblems you should discuss each subproblem under a separate subheading. You should also introduce operational definitions that you use throughout the report. As mentioned above, the research proposal provides a good model for this section of the final report. You can easily write the final report by revising the introductory section of the research proposal from future to past tense.

Review of the Literature

The review of the literature provides a summary of the literature related to your present study. It should provide a synopsis of the research conducted in your area of inquiry. The discussion should not be presented as a series of disjointed studies, but rather in a manner that links the results in a meaningful way back to the hypotheses. If you uncover conflicting findings in your review of the literature, you should provide a careful examination of the variations and possible explanations for the differences. It is important that you report the major research in the field, taking care to paraphrase and reference the findings rather than providing a series of quotations. Ultimately you should explain how your study adds to the existing literature and fills in "a gap" in the related research. Wiersma (1991) states that a knowledgeable reviewer is one who can select appropriate information, connect it together and present it as background information for the problem, and then relate the ideas in the literature with the research problem. This section should not be affected by actually carrying out the study; therefore, little modification in the proposal's literature review will be needed for its use in the final report. In terms of length, Wiersma states that dissertation reviews generally contain at least 35 double-spaced pages.

Methodology

You should clearly explain this section of the report so that a reader could replicate the study if desired. Since you spell out the methodology in detail in the proposal, you can merely reflect any adjustments you had to make in actually carrying out the study in the final report. In theses or dissertations the descriptions should be very detailed since the writer is demonstrating mastery of the methodology. The methodology section is divided into four parts, each with its own subheading.

Subjects.   In this section you are to report how many subjects participated in your study as well as how many subjects were originally scheduled. For example, if you distributed surveys, indicate the rate of return. Demographics such as sex, age, grade level, ethnic background, and any kind of exceptionality should be reported. In the event you have more than one group, you are to indicate how many participants composed each group and how you assigned participants to the groups.

Design of the Study. In this section you are to include a written account of the treatments or interventions used. It is important that you clearly discuss the number and length of the treatments. In addition you should describe any testing periods, if applicable, including pretests.

Materials. In this section you should describe all materials that you used, including all equipment and the names of all standardized, as well as researcher-made, instruments, including information on reliability, validity and other information related to standardization.

Procedure. In this section you describe in detail the treatments or interventions used, the duration and intensity of the interventions, etc. Additionally, you describe the process you followed for collecting data.

Results

In this section you are to present the results in a form consistent with the type of study. For example, in quantitative studies you are to present data generated from statistical analysis, whereas in qualitative studies you would provide summary statements. When you use statistical analysis, you should report the statistical test applied. It is not necessary to present detailed information on findings that are not statistically significant; however, when reporting statistically significant findings, you should state the computed values of each statistic, the degrees of freedom, and the level of significance. For clarification you can report statistical data in tables and graphs. Specific details on reporting results in text and in tables and graphs are found in the most current version of the *Publication Manual of the American Psychological Association* (APA, 2001).

Discussion, Conclusions, and Implications

The primary focus of this section, which should link closely to the results section, should be your hypotheses. In this section you will discuss which of your hypotheses have been confirmed and which have not. You should then explain how your results fit in with or contradict prior findings. You will want to present any practical and theoretical implications from your study. It is also imperative that you discuss any weaknesses or limitations in your study. Some common limitations are related to: (a) the research approach, (b) the sampling method, (c) the response rate, (d) the reliability and validity of the data collection methods, (e) the internal and external validity, and (f) the interpretation of results. This discussion should relate back to the limitations you have identified in Chapter 1 of your proposal. Most discussions conclude with recommendations for further research in the area of inquiry.

Comparing Final Reports and Journal Articles

Length

Length is one characteristic that distinguishes the different types of reports. Technical reports submitted to funding agencies typically run a minimum of 100 pages (Wiersma, 1991). Theses and dissertations, reports of research that are carried out in conjunction with the pursuit of a masters or doctoral degree, are similarly at least 100 pages. Theses and dissertations can also appear in journals (although the content needs to be revised and reduced for that medium since journal articles typically range from 5 to 20 pages). Dissertations and lengthy reports usually are presented in chapters, while journal articles are organized with headings. A discussion of the components of journal articles follows. The components will be illustrated using the previously referenced article, "Teaching and Learning with Humor: Experiment and Replication" (Ziv, 1988).

Components of Journal Articles

Abstract. The abstract is a concise summary of the contents of the article. It is one of the most important sections of your article since the abstract is usually the first, and often the only, contact that individuals have with your article (APA, 2001). The abstract needs to be an accurate reflection of the contents of the study that reports, rather than evaluates, the findings.

In reading the abstract in the accompanying article, "Teaching and Learning with Humor: Experiment and Replication," you will find a brief summary of the two experiments described in this article. The author concisely describes the two experiments, the subjects and method of selection, and the results of the studies.

Introduction. The introduction section of the article opens by presenting the problem under study. Because of its prominent position in the paper, you do not need to label this section. In this section you identify the purpose of the study and what the existing research says about the problem under study. You will need to support the necessity of your study by presenting findings in the research that relate to your investigation as well as how your study will fill a gap in the literature. Your research hypotheses should proceed from the problem statement and your literature review. Additionally, in this section you will need to identify any technical terms crucial to the study.

It can be disheartening to think that the numerous pages you have written for Chapters 1 and 2 of your proposal are reduced in an article to just a few paragraphs! The bright side is that your careful planning and eventual development of those chapters allows you to demonstrate concisely the logical continuity between work that has been previously done with your own work. You will want to read the introductory section of this article before we continue our discussion of the introduction.

In Ziv's (1988) article we readily learn that using humor in teaching is the topic under study. Ziv briefly summarizes previous studies in this area and identifies the lack of research regarding this topic in natural, as opposed to artificial, settings. Additionally, Ziv recognizes that previous experiments have been short. None of the prior studies have involved more than one class lecture. This background information leads into the purpose of the study "to investigate the effects on student learning of judiciously used humor in teaching" (p. 7). Ziv further states the independent and dependent variables and provides some technical information related to humor as used in the experiments.

This particular study is unique in that it discusses two experiments. Therefore, its introduction presents an overview of the study as well as a specific introduction for each of the two experiments. In the introduction of experiment one Ziv (1988) immediately states the purpose and hypothesis of the experiment. Additionally, Ziv presents pertinent information from the literature that helps us understand how this particular experiment will add to the existing literature.

Method. Although the method section of the journal article cannot be as long as the same section in the proposal due to the limited space allowed, you will need to report how the study was implemented in as much detail as needed for the reader to be able to replicate it. As discussed above, this section is divided into four parts: subjects, design of the study, materials, and procedures. As you summarize this section, you need to include all pertinent information necessary for readers to carefully analyze the methods used. In order that our discussion of the application of these guidelines to the Ziv (1988) article makes sense, you will want to read the method section of experiment one.

In terms of describing the subjects in your own study, you should show how the subjects were sampled, describe the population that they represent, and provide descriptive information about the subjects. This allows the reader to analyze the study in terms of how the subjects represent the population (Wilkinson & McNeil, 1996). Ziv (1988), for example, tells us that two groups of students were randomly sampled and then assigned to their respective groups by a flip of a coin. In addition, the population is defined as students enrolled in an introductory course in statistics. Specific statistics describe the composition of each group.

The design of the study includes descriptions of the types and duration of treatment. You need to particularly explain the length of treatment since the duration has an impact on the study's effectiveness. According to Wilkinson and McNeil (1996), many nonsignificant results occur in studies because potentially effective results are not implemented for a long enough period of time. In the humor study, Ziv (1988) includes the design of the study along with the description of the subjects. Ziv tells us that the intervention is a statistics course and the length of treatment is the entire semester. Additionally, we learn that the same instructor taught both sections of this course. By using the same instructor, (holding this variable constant), extraneous error related to the instructor is minimized, which is a significant consideration. It appears that this experiment is a true experimental design since it meets the conditions for such a design, particularly in that the participants were randomly assigned to their groups. Because the study uses a posttest, but no pretest, it would be considered a posttest-only control type of design.

The materials section should particularly stress the measurement devices used and technical information about them, since they are most significant in testing the hypotheses. Ziv (1988) does report that the dependent variable was measured by a standardized statistical exam with a reliability of .91. The measurement was given as a posttest.

In the procedure section you describe each step in carrying out the study. When necessary, you are to include any instructions given to the participants. In addition you are to summarize the process you followed for collecting data, including the type of data, and where, when and how the data were collected. Ziv (1988) clearly describes the training in humor that the instructor received prior to the study and details how humor was employed in the course of the study. He includes in the study examples of the type of humor used in the teaching.

Results.   As in the final report, the results section of an article shows what the researcher discovered by conducting the study. You should present the results section so that it parallels the hypotheses. Tables and figures present data effectively, particularly in journal articles, where space is limited. While the tables and figures should contain all the data, the accompanying text only needs to summarize the significant or important results. At this time you will want to read the two concise paragraphs that contain the results of experiment one of the Ziv (1988) study. In reading the results section, you learn that an analysis of variance was used to analyze the posttest measurement. The means and standard deviations are presented in a table.

Although not the case in this particular article, tables presented in research articles will usually indicate statistically significant differences by asterisks or superscripts as shown in Table 11.1. Computer printouts will often provide the actual levels of significance in the tables they generate as well.

The second paragraph of the results section states one significant finding. A main significant effect was found between groups (meaning the experimental and control groups). In analyzing the results sections, you will want to ask yourself whether the experiment appears to have internal and external validity. You will recall that internal validity is the degree to which observed changes in the dependent variables are due to the independent variables as opposed to other, extraneous variables. Often a researcher or consumer of the research will conclude that the experiment has internal validity if and when the statistical analysis results in a statistically significant gain. According to Borg and Gall (1983) we cannot safely infer cause and effect unless we know that extraneous variables have been adequately controlled. If it is apparent to us that the researcher has painstakingly made every effort to control for these errors, we can say that it appears that the experiment has internal validity, but we can never be completely confident. In our review of experiment one, in reference to the threats

Table 11.1   Means and Standard Deviations of Final Exam Scores for Computer-Based Course and Traditional Course in Research and Statistic.

	Computer-Based		Control	
	M	SD	M	SD
Males	95.5[a]	5.2	82.3	10.2
Females	90.2	6.6	88.1	8.5

[a]$p < .01$

to validity, we can acknowledge that the researcher took solid measures to control for the threats (e.g., used random sampling, used a standardized test with high reliability, used the same instructor for both groups, etc.). We can be fairly confident that experiment one had internal validity. External validity is the extent to which the results can be generalized to other persons, settings or situations. Multiple studies are usually used in determining external validity. Based on the limited information that we have regarding experiment one, the question regarding external validity is inconclusive.

In the results section, the author also provides the **effect size,** an index that quantifies the strength of the relationship between variables (Heppner, Kivlighan, & Wampold, 1999). Although researchers are reporting effect sizes in the literature on a more regular basis, effect size means are most often used in meta-analysis to suggest a relationship between category variables and the overall impact of the intervention. Glass (1976) defines meta-analysis as the application of a quantitative method to the problem by combining evidence from different studies. Meta-analysis draws reliable and general conclusions from a large body of literature about the impact of the interventions. Glass proposed an estimator of the population effect size based on the sample value of the standardized mean difference. The effect size is the difference in the means between the treatment and control group means, X_t and X_c, divided by the standard deviation of the control group, s_c. $Es = \dfrac{X_t - X_c}{s_c}$ The effect size for boys is $\dfrac{83.2 - 71.5}{12.2} = .96$, while the effect size for girls is $\dfrac{81.7 - 73.2}{13.2} = .64$, as stated in the article. Cohen (1988) offers the following guidelines for judging the magnitude of an effect size: .20, small; .50, medium; .80, large. In Ziv's (1988) study the effect size for the boys would be considered high, while the effect size for the girls would be medium.

Discussion. The discussion section of an article is similar to that of the final report although you may need to be more concise because of the space limitations. After presenting the results, you will want to evaluate them and summarize their implications. You will want to begin by stating whether or not your hypotheses have been supported. You should then explain how your results support or contradict prior findings. This will lead into the presentation of any practical implications from your study. You will also need to discuss any limitations in your study and recommendations for further inquiry.

Before continuing this dialogue about the discussion session, you will want to read the one provided by Ziv (1988), which follows experiment two, since the study involved experiment one and a replication. Ziv starts out the discussion with a strong assertion that the "two studies demonstrate clearly the contribution of teachers' use of humor to student learning" (p. 12), thus supporting the primary hypothesis. In the ensuing discussion Ziv cautions that the results are a function of the controlled conditions present in the study and discusses how these special conditions were specifically integrated into the study, based on prior research findings. The implications and recommendations made address educators' practical use of the findings in this study as opposed to suggestions for further research.

Statistical Literacy

11.1

Read experiment two of the Ziv (1988) study and respond to the following questions. You will want to check your responses against those found in Appendix F.

1. What is the purpose of this study?
2. Name the independent and dependent variable(s).
3. What is the N of this study?
4. Describe the population from which the subjects were drawn.
5. How were the subjects selected?
6. Describe the procedures used in this study.
7. What type of research design was used in this study?
8. What was used to measure the dependent variable? How would you rate the reliability of the measure?
9. What statistical test was used?
10. What were the means and standard deviations for each of the groups?
11. What statistic resulted from the analysis? How many degrees of freedom were there?
12. What was the level of significance?
13. What was the effect size? Try to hand compute it.
14. What conclusions might you make based on the results?
15. How did experiment two differ from experiment one?
16. Does this experiment have internal validity? Why or why not?
17. Looking back at experiment one, would you say that it has external validity? Why or why not?

Summary

Critical to the research process is the accurate summarization and reporting of results. In this chapter we exposed you to the process of reporting results in final report form as well as a journal article. Additionally, we presented you with a two-part study to practice understanding research findings as reported in the literature. After guiding you through the first part of the study as a learning experience, we provided you with an activity that allowed you to check your own statistical literacy. Although in your future research you will most likely encounter much more difficult literature, this activity sheet provides you with a guide for reading the literature since, as you learned, all research reports and journal articles follow a similar format.

Key Terms

effect size

Appendices

A Notice Regarding the Format
We Used in the Sample Proposals

You will find in the appendices that we present the qualitative research proposal in "copy" form, while we present the quantitative research proposal in "final" form. We did this to show you two different versions, since instructors vary in the requirements they set for a research proposal. According to APA (2001), the *Publication Manual* is intended primarily as a guide in the preparation of copy forms which will later become typeset journal articles, although some academic departments require students to follow its guidelines when preparing theses, dissertations, and student papers. Other academic departments require these documents in final form, the exact form in which they will reach their audience. Since theses and dissertations are submitted to their university, not to a journal, students must satisfy the requirements of the graduate school, even if the requirements differ from those in the *Publications Manual*. You will find that although the quantitative research proposal follows APA style in terms of writing style, references etc., the layout and headings meet our university's guidelines.

Appendix A

Research Article

Teaching and Learning with Humor:
Experiment and Replication
AVNER ZIV
Tel Aviv University

ABSTRACT. Two experiments concerning humor in teaching and learning in higher education are presented. The first study used relevant humor in a one-semester statistics course in an experimental group and no humor in a control group. One hundred sixty-one students participated, and the results showed significant differences between the two groups in favor of the group learning with humor. No significant sex differences nor interactions were found. The second experiment was a replication of the first one, using 132 students in a one-semester introductory psychology course. The students (all females) were divided randomly into two groups. Humor was used in one, and the same teacher taught the second group without using humor. Again, significant differences were found: The group studying with humor had higher scores on the final exam. Explanations for the ways in which humor in teaching can influence student learning are given.

HUMOR IN EDUCATION, as a research topic, is relatively new. Although more than 50 papers have been written praising the value of humor in teaching (Powell & Andersen, 1985), very few research projects have tried to verify empirically this widely accepted idea. Unfortunately, when such research has been carried out, results showed that the introduction of humor into the teaching process did not improve learning. In one article, Gruner (1976) reviewed nine research projects investigating humor in teaching. All except one reached the conclusion that humor had no influence on learning. These studies, as well as many others, were conducted in artificial experimental settings rarely resembling real educational situations. Nonetheless, these disappointing results have discouraged researchers in the field and, although many continue to write about the importance of humor in teaching and learning, empirical studies have waned.

Recently, there has been some renewed interest in research on the influence of humor in the educational processes in the United States and Europe. Two main research directions are most prominent. The first focuses on students' evaluations of teachers using humor in their classes, measuring affective outcomes. The second is directed toward investigating the influence of teachers' use of humor on student learning, measuring cognitive outcomes.

The affective outcomes were measured by such studies as the ones conducted by Bryant et al. (1980) and Ziv et al. (1986). Bryant et al. had students audiotape one lecture in 70 different courses at the University of Massachusetts to investigate the amount of humor used by teachers and how students evaluated them. They found that 80% of the lecturers used humor at least once, some as much as 13 times, and one even 16 times during a 1-hour lecture. Because this study was never replicated, one wonders if such an abundance of humorous elements in American college teaching does, in fact, exist, or if something funny was happening at the University of Massachusetts. Among the findings, the authors report that for male teachers, usage of humor is related positively to appeal, delivery, and teaching effectiveness. For female teachers, only hostile humor was associated with enhanced appeal, whereas usage of nonhostile humor was associated with loss of appeal.

In the Ziv et al. (1986) study, tenth-grade students in four different classrooms watched a videotaped lecture of a professional actor playing the role of a teacher. Four films were presented (one in each classroom), one of which was a control film in which no humor was used. The other three films contained (a) self-disparaging humor (directed toward the teacher himself), (b) other-disparaging humor (directed toward students), and (c) mixed humor (a combination of a and b). Results showed that the teacher using mixed humor received the highest evaluation on "appeal" and "originality" factors. The other-disparaging teacher was perceived as most powerful, and the teacher not using humor at all was perceived as the most systematic in his teaching method.

Concerning the cognitive outcomes, previous experiments have been short in duration, none exceeding the limits of one lecture. Zillmann, et al. (1980), for instance, worked with kindergarten and first-grade children to investigate retention of televised material in which humor was included. Pairs of children were shown small portions of video programs lasting only several minutes and were interviewed immediately afterwards as to their retention of the material. Wakshlag, Day, and Zillmann (1981) used first and second graders as subjects, showing them educational films in which differently paced humor episodes were introduced. Children were tested individually and left alone for 10 minutes, free to manipulate a television set on which they could choose the program they wanted to watch.

In experiments conducted in higher education, the influence of humor on learning has been investigated in conditions closer to real educational settings. Students listened to one lecture (live or videotaped), and their retention of the material or their subjective evaluations of teacher effectiveness was measured. Kaplan and Pascoe (1977), for example, investigated humor in learning by presenting to groups of students a 20-minute videotaped lecture in which different types of humor were included.

To the best of this author's knowledge, no systematic research on actual teaching in classrooms taking into consideration the time element of educational processes was carried out before 1979, when the first book of research on humor in education was published in France (Ziv, 1979). Table 1 summarizes the research projects investigating humor's influences on student learning.

The purpose of the present study was to investigate the effects on student learning of judiciously used humor in teaching. A one-semester university course was planned, with humor as the independent variable in the experimental group and learning as the dependent variable in both the experimental and the control groups. One main study and one replication were conducted. The importance of replication is known to all educational psychologists and stressed in most books on research methodology (Borg & Gall, 1981). Nevertheless, studies using replications of psychological experiments in educational settings are extremely rare, due mostly to the time element involved.

2

Theoretically, the effects of humor on learning were described in Ziv (1979). Briefly, the theoretical basis of the experiments is based on the attention-gaining and holding power of humor on one hand and the conditioning paradigm of association of learning and the hedonic effects of humor on the other. Elements such as the relevance, quantity, and ways of presentation of humor are parts of the strategies used in teaching.

Table 1   Published Research on Humor and Learning

Research	Subjects	Duration of experiment	Method of experiment	Humor's influence
Kilpela (1961)	College students	10 minutes	Audiotape	None
Taylor (1964)	College students	7 minutes	Audiotape	None
Gibb (1964)	College students	1 hour	Biology lecture	Positive
Youngman (1966)	College students	10 minutes	Audiotape	None
Gruner (1967)	College students	10 minutes	Audiotape	None
Gruner (1976)	College students	10 minutes	Audiotape	None
Kennedy (1972)	College students	10 minutes	Audiotape	None
Markiewicz (1972)	College students	15 minutes	Written speech	None
Hauck & Thomas (1972)	Children	15 minutes	Written task	Positive retention
Perreault (1972)	College students	7 minutes	Written advertisement	Positive
Curran (1972)	Children	15 minutes	Cartoons	Positive
Weinberg (1973)	College students	1 hour	Lecture	Positive for low anxiety
Kaplan & Pascoe (1977)	College students	1 hour	Lecture	Positive after 6 weeks
Chapman & Crompton (1978)	Children	15 minutes	Tapes and slides	Positive for recall
Zillmann et al. (1980)	Children	10 minutes	Video clips	Positive for attention
Ziv (1979)	Adolescents	Semester course	Lectures in high school	Positive
Davis & Apter (1980)	Children	20 minutes	Lectures and slides	Positive
Wakshlag, Day, & Zillmann (1981)	Children	10 minutes	Video clips	Positive for attention

EXPERIMENT 1

The objective of this study was to investigate the effects on student learning of teaching with humor in a one-semester course. The specific hypothesis was formulated as follows: Students learning with a teacher using relevant humor will obtain higher scores on a test measuring learning than those studying the same material with a teacher not using humor. Several research studies have reported differences between the sexes in their response to humor but not one on sex differences in learning when humor is used. However, these differences as related to differences in learning were never investigated. Because research results relating to sex differences in reaction to humor in educational settings were studied only in regard to the kind of humor used by teachers (Bryant et al., 1980), no specific direction for the sex differences in response to humor as related to learning can be predicted. Therefore, the hypothesis relating to sex differences is nondirectional.

Method

Subjects

Two groups of students enrolled in an introductory course in statistics were the subjects of the first study. The two groups were formed randomly, and both studied for an entire semester with the same teacher, an experienced instructor in statistics.

One group was composed of 82 students, 51 females and 31 males; the second, of 79 students, 46 females and 33 males. The total number of students involved in the experiment was 161. By coin flipping, the first group was chosen to be the experimental group and the second to be the control. The students were not aware that they were participating in an experiment.

Instruments

The only instrument used in this study was the final exam at the end of the semester. This was a standard objective statistics exam, with 50 multiple-choice questions (four possible answers for each) used for all statistics courses in the department. Reliability calculated using Kuder-Richardson 20 was .91.

The teacher, the same for both groups, was trained to use relevant humor in the experimental group and to teach exactly the same material, without the use of humor, in the control group.

Procedure

The instructor participating in the experiment took part in a special seminar ("Humor in Teaching") conducted in the teacher training department. It was offered as an elective course to teachers who wanted to learn something about their ability to use humor to improve their teaching. From the 61 teachers who registered for the seminar, 12 were selected on the basis of their scores on a sense of humor test. The test's reliability and validity are described elsewhere (Ziv, 1979). In their training, different

5

methods of improving their use of humor in teaching were employed (Ziv, 1979). The teachers researched and found jokes and cartoons relevant to the study of statistics (and, of course, other subjects they taught) and prepared some new ones. Below are two examples (a description of a cartoon and a joke):

1. While teaching about means and standard deviations, the teacher projected a slide of a cartoon prepared in advance on a screen. It showed an explorer in Africa, talking to a few native children who watch him somewhat surprised. Behind the explorer, and without his being aware of it, is a huge crocodile with a wide-open mouth, ready to swallow him. He, addressing the kids, says, "There is no need to be afraid of crocodiles; around here their average length is only about 50 centimeters." One of the children says to another, "This guy had better think about the standard deviation, too."

2. While teaching correlations and explaining that they do not show a causal effect (a correlation does not mean that one variable is the cause of the other), the teacher told the following story:

On a planet whose inhabitants had just discovered earth and who were invisible to earthlings, experts decided to study the behavior of humans. One of them planned to conduct a study on the differences between fat and thin people. He went to a cafeteria and watched and noted the coffee-drinking patterns of those coming in. He noted carefully the behavior of fat and slim people in their coffee-drinking behavior, calculated correlations on his data, and found a positive significant relation. He reported: "There is a positive correlation between coffee drinking and body weight. Fat people mostly drink coffee with 'Sweet and Low,' thin people mostly with sugar. Conclusion: Sugar makes humans thin, while 'Sweet and Low,' fattens them."

Based on previous research (Ziv, 1981), the quantity of humor for each lesson was carefully "dosed." It was decided that three to four jokes per lesson were the optimum dosage; more would risk transforming the teacher into a clown and students' attention would be diverted from the content of the lesson. It was also important not to employ humor "mechanically" and not to use exactly the same number of jokes in each lecture. In three lectures, chosen randomly during the semester, the teacher did not employ any humor at all. Moreover, jokes had to be presented in a special continuity with the concept learned (Ziv, 1979). The following sequence was followed:

1. The teacher taught a concept, in this case a statistical one. (The first example demonstrated the importance of knowing the standard deviation of a distribution, and the second, the noncausality of correlation coefficients.)
2. He illustrated the concept with a joke or a cartoon.
3. After the laughter, he paraphrased the concept learned.

Results

After 14 weekly lessons (the duration of a semester), objective standard exams were given to the two groups of students. ANOVA was calculated according to a 2×2 design (Group $\times$ Sex). The means and standard deviations are presented in Table 2.

One main significant effect was found—between groups: $F(1, 160) = 5.39$, $p < .01$. No significant differences between the sexes nor significant interaction were found. The effect size was calculated, and the results were .96 for boys and .64 for girls. These results show the high significance of the differences obtained (Cohen, 1969).

EXPERIMENT 2

The objective of this study was to replicate the findings of the first study. This is an operational replication (Lykken, 1968) using the same methodology with a different student population and with a different teacher. This kind of replication is necessary to verify the validity of obtained results, taking into consideration the teacher's personality and technique and the characteristics of the population. Frequently, a certain technique demonstrated by one teacher does not produce the same results when employed by another. This happens rather frequently in educational research. The desire to verify the possibilities of generalization of the findings from the first study was the reason that the second study was planned.

Because this is a replication, the methodology is similar and will be described only briefly.

Table 2 Means and Standard Deviations of Final Exam Scores for Experimental and Control Groups in Experiment 1

	Experimental		Control	
	M	SD	M	SD
Boys	83.2	11.7	71.5	12.2
Girls	81.7	12.3	73.2	13.2

Subjects

Two entire classrooms of students in a teacher's college in Tel Aviv, taking an introductory psychology course, were assigned randomly to one experimental and one control group. The experimental group was composed of 65 students, the control of 67, the entire sample totalling 132 students, all females.

Instruments

As in Experiment 1, an objective examination, containing 50 multiple-choice questions to which there were four possible answers, was used (reliability, KR 20 = .93).

Procedure

Another teacher, experienced in teaching this course at the college, participated in the previously described seminar for teachers where he learned how to utilize humor in teaching and where cartoons and jokes relevant for the psychology course were prepared.

Two examples of the humorous material used in the experiment follow:

1. The teacher told the following joke to the class:

One morning a man walks to his work and looks up a building. From a window on the eighth floor, a beautiful, charming, splendid, blonde, young woman looks at him. His heart thumping, he decides that this is the most wonderful woman he has seen in his life and he'll do anything to have her. He runs into the building, finds that the elevator doesn't work, and starts running up the stairs. First floor, second, third, . . . sixth, . . . seventh. By now, he has difficulty breathing, and his climbing is much slower. But, he continues, dreaming about the wonderful lady he's going to meet. Finally, a bit out of breath, he gets to the eighth floor. He rings. A huge, muscular, angry-looking man opens the door. "Can I see the blonde lady?"

Before he finishes the last word, the huge guy starts hitting him with tremendous blows on his face and body and finally a kick in the back that throws him a few floors down the hard stairs. Getting up with difficulty, our hero limps toward his work.

The next day, passing by the building, he looks up and there she is again, even more beautiful and smiling at him. He decides that whatever happens, he must have her. Into the building, running up the stairs. First, second, . . . fifth floor. It's rather difficult, hard to breathe, but he feels love and courage and goes on. Before her door, still breathing hard, he rings. The huge, muscular, angry-looking guy opens the door, takes a look at him, and starts beating him. This time, falling down the stairs of the entire building, his body feeling completely broken, his face badly bruised, he has barely the force to find a taxi and go to the hospital. After some stitches and bandages, he is sent home and ordered to stay in bed for 2 days.

The third day, he walks by the building, looks up . . . and there she is, even more wonderful than he remembered—splendid, sweet, and smiling at him. No hesitation! He starts up the stairs (he doesn't have the strength to run, but he climbs steadily). First, second. . . . Finally, again out of breath, he is at her door, he rings, and she opens the door. Looking at her in wonder he says, "Where is the big guy?"

2. A series of four cartoons, prepared in advance, was presented with a slide projector on a screen. On each cartoon, the head of the same extremely worried person was shown. On each cartoon, a different text was written above his head.

    A. I am worried, I am always worried.
    B. Every day something worries me; it's terrible.
    C. Now, what worries me today is even more terrible.
    D. Today I'm worried because nothing worries me.

Jokes, cartoons, and very short anecdotes were introduced by the teacher in relevant places. For instance, the first joke was told after explaining the concept of conditioning. When he finished the joke and after the students' laughter, he said, "Here's conditioning for you." Then he repeated the definition of conditioning that he explained before the joke. The series of four cartoons was introduced after the explanation of the concept of free-floating anxiety as opposed to situation anxiety.

At the end of the semester, the final test was administered to both groups.

Results

The analysis of the results was straightforward. The obtained results were: mean for the experimental group = 82 (SD = 12.4), for the control group = 72.5 (SD = 11.2) The t test computed was 3.58, df = 130, $p < .01$. The calculated effect size was .85 (highly significant according to Cohen, 1969).

GENERAL DISCUSSION

The results of the two studies demonstrate clearly the contribution of teachers' use of humor to student learning. However, it should be clear that these results are a function of the special conditions of the preparation of the teaching material and the teaching process itself.

The preparation of the material included finding and creating humorous stimuli relevant to the course taught. Earlier research demonstrated that retention of material illustrated by humorous examples is most effective when these examples are relevant to the material taught and the test items are related to it (Kaplan & Pascoe, 1977). Because tests should measure learning of the most important concepts taught in a course, the humorous examples used were related to these concepts. As Kaplan and Pascoe noted, their findings "can account for the inability of earlier research to demonstrate an effect of humor upon learning. The use of humor significantly increases recall for only those items based on humorous examples" (p. 65). Therefore, when planning a course, the main concepts should be delineated, and the humor related to these concepts, intending to make them clearer, should be interjected in the appropriate places. Good objective tests will, of course, measure the understanding of main concepts. The consideration of this

9

triple relation among main concepts, humorous illustrations, and test items should be kept in mind when preparing the inclusion of humor in teaching.

The "dose" of humor is important. Many pretests were done before arriving at the "optimal dose," which in a classroom is three to four instances per hour. It is interesting to note that in the Bryant et al. (1980) research the mean jokes per lecture of the 70 teachers taped was similar: three to four. However, as in the joke quoted previously in their research, one should look also at the variance. In the present research, care was taken to have lectures in which fewer than three humorous examples were used and that there were also lectures given to the experimental group where no humorous examples were used at all. This insured an intermittent schedule, which was proven to be more effective than a regular one in learning research (Biehler & Snowman, 1984).

The training of teachers in employing humor in the classroom is regretfully missing in the teacher training programs. Reviewing 14 widely used textbooks in educational psychology, this author did not find in the indexes any references to humor. In spite of this, there is accumulating evidence that students appreciate and enjoy learning with a teacher who uses humor (Tamborini & Zillmann, 1981; Woods, 1983). Teachers who teach well sometimes behave like good actors. Somebody writes the text for them, and they must make it lively and interesting in order to capture the audience's attention and, as all actors, they have to repeat the "performance" many times. Humor can be an efficient tool in the teachers' armamentarium. It is clear that humor as used in sarcasm can have negative effects and that humor is not among the most important qualities of a good teacher. However, like the proverbial grain of salt, it can definitely improve the quality of any elaborate meal.

These observations should help teachers or educational psychologists to use humor in teaching or research. Students have a different appreciation for teachers who use different kinds of humor (Ziv, Gorenstein, & Moris, 1986) and, depending on what their main objectives are, teachers can choose the kinds of humor that best serves these objectives. In this research, only "prepared" and "made to measure" humor was used. In using spontaneous humor, teachers can improve the climate of their teaching, though not always the learning of their students. However, not all teachers should be encouraged to use humor. Some, because of their personality, believe that humor may present a danger or are embarrassed by it (Ziv, 1984), in which case they had better not use it at all.

10

REFERENCES

Biehler, R. F., & Snowman, J. (1984). *Psychology applied to teaching*. Boston: Houghton Mifflin.

Borg, W. R., & Gall, M. D. (1981). *Educational research*. New York: David McKay Co.

Bryant, J., Comisky, P., & Zillmann, D. (1979). Teachers' humor in the college classroom. *Communication Education, 28,* 110–118.

Bryant, J., Comiskey, P. W., Crane, J. S., & Zillmann, D. (1980) Relationship between college teachers' use of humor in the classroom and students' evaluation of their teachers. *Journal of Educational Psychology, 72, 511–519.*

Chapman, A. J., & Crompton, P. (1978). Humorous presentations of material and presentation material: A review of the humor and memory literature and two experimental studies. In M. M. Grunneberg & P. E. Morris (Eds.), *Practical aspects of memory*. London: Academic Press.

Cohen, J. (1969). *Statistical power analysis for the behavioral sciences.* New York: Academic Press.

Curran, F. W. (1972). *A developmental study of cartoon humor and its use in facilitating learning.* Unpublished doctoral dissertation, Catholic University of America.

Davis, A. P., & Apter, M. J. (1980). Humor and its effect on learning in children. In P. McGhee & A. Chapman (Eds.), *Children's humor.* New York: Wiley & Sons.

Gibb, J. D. (1964). *An experimental comparison of the humorous lecture and non-humorous lecture in informative speech.* Unpublished master's thesis, University of Utah.

Glass, G. V. (1976). Primary, secondary and meta-analysis of research. *Educational Research, 10,* 3–8.

Gruner, C. R. (1967). Effects of humor on speaker ethos and audience information gain. *Journal of Communication, 17,* 228–233.

Gruner, C. R. (1976). Wit and humor in mass communication. In A. J. Chapman & H. C. Foot (Eds.), *Humor and laughter: Theory, research and applications.* London: Wiley.

Hauck, W. E., & Thomas, J. W. (1972). The relationship of humor to intelligence, creativity, and intentional and incidental learning. *Journal of Experimental Education, 40,* 52–55.

Kaplan, R. K., & Pascoe, G. C. (1977). Humorous lectures and humorous examples: Some effects upon comprehension and retention. *Journal of Educational Psychology, 89,* 61–65.

Kennedy, A. J. (1972) *An experimental study of the effects of humorous message content upon ethos and persuasiveness.* Unpublished doctoral dissertation, University of Michigan.

Kilpela, D. E. (1961).*An experimental study of the effect of humor on persuasion.* Unpublished master's thesis, Wayne State University.

Lykken, D. T. (1968). Statistical significance in psychological research. *Psychological Bulletin, 70,* 151–159.

Powell, J. P., & Anderson, L. W. (1985). Humor and teaching in higher education. *Studies in Higher Education, 10,* 79–90.

Markiewicz, D. (1972). *The effects of humor on persuasion.* Unpublished doctoral dissertation, Ohio State University.

Perreault, R. M. (1972).*A study of the effects of humor in advertising as can be measured by by-product recall tests.* Unpublished master's thesis, University of Georgia.

Tamborini, R., & Zillmann, D. (1981). College students' perception of lectures using humor. *Perceptual and Motor Skills, 52,* 427–432.

Taylor, P. M. (1964).The effectiveness of humor in informative speeches. *Central States Speech Journal, 5,* 295–296.

Wakshlag, J. J., Day, K. D., & Zillmann, D. (1981). Selective exposure to educational television programs as a function of differently paced humorous inserts. *Journal of Educational Psychology, 73,* 27–32.

Weinberg, M. D. (1973). *The interactional effect of humor and anxiety on academic performance.* Unpublished doctoral dissertation, Yeshiva University.

Woods, P. (1983). Coping at school through humor. *British Journal of the Sociology of Education, 4,* 111–124.

Youngman, R. C. (1966).*An experimental investigation of the effect of germane humor versus nongermane humor in an informative communication.* Unpublished master's thesis, Ohio University.

Zillmann, D., Williams, B. R., Bryant, J., Boynton, K. R., & Wolf, M. A. (1980). Acquisition of information from educational television programs as a function of differently paced humor inserts.*Journal of Educational Psychology, 72,* 170–180.

Ziv, A. (1979). *L'humor en education: Approche psychologique.* Paris: Editions Sociales Francaises.

Ziv, A. (1981). *The psychology of humor.* Tel Aviv: Yahdav.

Ziv, A. (1984).*Personality and sense of humor.* New York: Springer.

Ziv, A., Gorenstein, E., & Moris, A. (1986). Adolescents' evaluation of teachers using disparaging humor. *Educational Psychology, 6,* 37–44.

Appendix B

Sample Quantitative Research Proposal

The Effects Of Solution-Focused/Social
Interest Goal-Setting Sessions On Personal
Accomplishment And Goal Attainment

A Research Proposal Submitted to
Dr. Noel Lot
Midwestern University

In Partial Fulfillment of the Requirements
For CNS 600
Research and Statistics

by
Ernest Worker
December 15, 2002

TABLE OF CONTENTS

1

CHAPTER 1
THE PROBLEM AND PROCEDURES

INTRODUCTION

Schools, mental health agencies, universities and other institutions where counselors and student affairs professionals are employed are currently facing tremendous financial challenges (Ambrose & Lennox, 1988; George, 1984; Hayes, 1984; Lancaster, 1989; Ritchie, 1989; Wittman, 1988; cited in Gilchrist & Stringer, 1992). These authors identify the sources of the financial challenges as the growing number of service providers and scarce funding by governmental agencies. Because of these financial constraints, employers and fiscal agents who employ graduates of counselor education programs continually call for justification of programs and accountability (Schaffer & Atkinson, 1983). Accountability in counseling settings serves two important functions: (a) to demonstrate the effectiveness of the services, and (b) to provide information to revise and improve counseling services (Krumboltz, 1974).

As far back as the 1970s, authors have recommended that counselors engage in ongoing program evaluation to justify their programs (Atkinson, Furlong, & Janoff, 1979; Burck & Peterson, 1975; Pine, 1975; Pulvino & Sanborn, 1972; cited in Schaffer & Atkinson, 1983). Counselors have not responded enthusiastically to engaging in program evaluation. In surveys of graduates of counselor education programs, school counselors, more than those of other specialties, have identified program evaluation as the role they feel least qualified to perform (Bartlett & Thompson, 1971; cited in Schaffer & Atkinson), derive the least satisfaction from (Dietz, 1972; cited in Schaffer & Atkinson), and spend the least amount of time (Atkinson, Froman, Romo, & Mayton, 1977; Furlong, Atkinson, & Janoff, 1979; cited in Schaffer & Atkinson).

After reviewing related literature, Wheeler and Loesch (1981) concluded that counselors have responded poorly because of a lack of training. This finding that counselors are less satisfied in areas in which they feel incompetent or have little training is supported by a study conducted by LaFountain (1993). In her study involving 275 school counselors, she analyzed over 20 variables (e.g., size of caseload, years in profession, number of buildings served, etc.) as possibly contributing to counselor burnout. Her major finding was that counselors feel the most stress when they are asked to perform duties for which they have not been trained nor feel competent. Wheeler and Loesch noted that although counselor education students usually receive some instruction in experimental research and statistics, they often receive little or no training in program evaluation.

Hadley and Mitchell (1995) define program evaluation "as a form of applied research distinguished by its relationship to a service program" (p. 62). They state that a service program is a set of service activities that can be of any size, from a national organization's program to one's individual work with one client or student. An example of program evaluation involving a counselor's work with an individual client is tracking the client's progress in finding a healthy balance between work and relaxation. An illustration of program evaluation with an individual case in the field of student affairs might involve a resident director who monitors a student's progress toward achieving better roommate relationships through participating in peer mediation.

As illustrated above, measuring the outcome of goals that clients or students set would be an appropriate way for counselors and student affairs professionals to begin to engage in program accountability. According to Sprinthall (1971; cited in Gysbers & Henderson, 1994), counselor training has emphasized techniques rather than the measurement of the outcome these techniques produce in individuals. Gysbers (1969; cited in Gysbers & Henderson) stated that counselor training has a history of assuming that counseling techniques, particularly individual counseling, were difficult to learn and, therefore, the majority of training time was devoted to learning techniques. Learning how to measure counselee and program outcomes was not stressed, since counselor educators felt such things could be learned on the job. Among the various settings in which counselor education graduates become employed, goal setting and treatment planning are most highly stressed in the field of mental health.

According to Cheston (2000), for counselors to effectively intervene with clients, they need to develop a treatment plan with the client by outlining the desired goals.

> Once the goals are formulated, the counselor draws from knowledge of the relationship with the client to challenge, interpret, reflect, and support the client toward the therapeutic goals. The job is to assist the client by structuring the change process and using counseling knowledge to implement steps toward the goal. (p. 257)

The lack of studies regarding goal setting and outcome measurement in the current literature reinforces the reality that counselors and student affairs professionals receive little training in these areas.

The purpose of this study is to determine whether training in goal setting and outcome measurement will affect the feelings of accomplishment experienced by counselors and student affairs professionals. Additionally, specific variables that may affect the level of goal attainment of the clients or students with whom counselors and student affairs professionals work will be investigated.

RESEARCH QUESTIONS

1. What is the effect of goal-setting training on the level of perceived personal accomplishment of counselors and student affairs professionals?

2. What is the relationship between the level of goal attainment by students and clients and the following variables: the participation of their counselor or student affairs professional in goal-setting training, the degree to which the goal meets the criteria for process goals, and the level of social interest present in the goal?

3

RESEARCH HYPOTHESES

H1. There will be a statistically significant difference in the perceived level of personal accomplishment for counselors and student affairs professionals who participate in the goal-setting training as opposed to those who do not participate, as measured by the Personal Accomplishment Subscale (PAS) of the Maslach Burnout Inventory (MBI).

H2. There will be a statistically significant difference in the level of goal attainment by clients and students as measured by the goal attainment form, based on whether or not their counselor or student affairs professional participates in goal-setting training, the degree to which the goal meets the criteria for process goals, and the level of social interest present in the goal.

NULL HYPOTHESES

H01. There will be no statistically significant difference in the perceived level of personal accomplishment for counselors and student affairs professionals who participate in the goal-setting training as opposed to those who do not participate, as measured by the Personal Accomplishment Subscale (PAS) of the Maslach Burnout Inventory (MBI).

H02. There will be no statistically significant difference in the level of goal attainment by clients and students as measured by the goal attainment form, based on whether or not their counselor or student affairs professional participates in goal-setting training, the degree to which the goal meets the criteria for process goals, and the level of social interest present in the goal.

IDENTIFICATION OF VARIABLES

The variables for this particular study are:

Independent Variables.

1. Participation in goal-setting training by the counselors or student affairs professionals.

2. Participation in goal-setting training by the counselors or student affairs professionals, degree to which goal meets criteria for process goals, level of social interest present in goal.

Dependent Variables.

1. Level of personal accomplishment of counselors and student affairs professionals as measured by the PAS.

2. Level of goal attainment by clients or students as measured by the goal attainment form.

Control Variables. Graduates from the same counselor education program; years of experience (in this case at least three).

SIGNIFICANCE OF THE PROBLEM

Although counselors and student affairs professionals are expected to assess the progress of their clients and students more than ever before, there is debate as to how training programs can better prepare their graduates to carry out this function. Some authors criticize counselor education programs for spending too little instructional time in program evaluation, while other authors propose additional course work (Gilchrist & Stinger, 1992; Schaffer & Atkinson, 1983). Still other authors question the effectiveness of current on-campus training sites since they have not made modifications in proportion to the needs of the clientele (Ametrano & Stickel, 1999; Neufeldt, 1994).

After surveying counselor education programs to determine the ratio of required coursework emphasizing scientific research to that stressing program evaluation, Schaffer and Atkinson (1983) found that counselor education programs spend twice as much instructional time on scientific research as on program evaluation. The authors questioned how counselor education programs could justify devoting twice as much required instruction to scientific research as to program evaluation when master's degree graduates are seldom expected to conduct scientific research. They asserted that if master's degree programs in counselor education are to meet the accountability demands placed on them, there must be a greater emphasis on instruction in program evaluation.

Likewise, Gilchrist and Stringer (1992) suggest training in effective marketing to help meet increasing demands for counselor accountability. According to them, marketing procedures have much in common with program evaluation activities that measure counselor efficiency and effectiveness, since effective marketing requires systematic assessment of client satisfaction, treatment outcomes, service utilization, and public relations. Gilchrist and Stringer recommend that counselor educators include marketing concepts, practices, and ethics in counselor education preparation programs by infusing them into existing core courses. They outline how customer orientation could be discussed in courses that introduce students to the counseling profession, how ethical practices could be covered in ethics courses, and how needs assessment and program evaluation could be covered in research courses. Further they propose that issues such as public relations and funding procurement could be addressed in professional courses designed for specific specialties (e.g., school counseling, student affairs, community mental health). Wittman (1988), too, advocated incorporating training in marketing as part of the counselor education curriculum. According to Gilchrist and Stringer, however, counselor educators and practitioners have had mixed reactions to the idea. Gibson (1984, cited in Gilchrist & Stringer) stated that the majority of mental health professionals disdain marketing since they equate it with high pressure selling.

5

Although many counselor education programs use on-campus counseling laboratories to serve as training sites for their students, some authors question the effectiveness of such sites since many of them do not require the same level of accountability as off-campus sites nor have they made service modifications in proportion to the needs of the clientele. Neufeldt (1994), for example, has reported that the types of problems seen in on-campus training clinics have changed from developmental concerns to more severe disorders. Likewise, Myers and Smith (1995) surveyed counselor education programs with on-campus laboratories and identified several problems that they were not able to address, such as alcoholism and drug addiction, serious psychopathology, and violent clients. Fong-Beyette (1988) promoted the community mental health model as the most appropriate one for teaching counseling students to function within the present day health care system.

Hague (1989) asserts that since accountability in clinical practice is receiving renewed interest, those individuals preparing counselors for practice must stress the concept of "responsibility." He describes responsibility as having two meanings: (a) to be responsible in terms of having an obligation, and (b) to be able to respond and give an account of what one does and where one stands. He emphasizes the latter definition that discusses "response-ability" by stressing the importance of treatment planning. He notes that the counseling students become "unstuck" when they answer for themselves the question, "What do I want to achieve?" In these cases, the end clarifies the means. Clarifying goals of a single session or a whole treatment plan leads to three kinds of "response-ability":

1. Knowing the end clarifies the means to be chosen toward that end.
2. Knowing the goal clarifies the criteria for success that will be used, allowing a clear and happy termination when the goals have been reached.
3. Knowing the purpose clarifies another important responsibility: the legal and ethical responsibility of the client-counselor relationship. (p. 349)

With the current emphasis on accountability in settings that employ graduates of counselor education programs, it is evident that training programs need to make modifications in order to address this need. According to Whiston and Coker (2000, p. 243), "Increasingly, clinicians are required to document their treatment approach on empirical evidence. Counseling students, as compared with other mental health workers, may be at a disadvantage in this realm." This study will investigate the training of counselors and student affairs professionals in a goal-setting model, which will serve as an initial step in program evaluation. Given that individuals feel more stress on the job when asked to perform jobs in which they feel unprepared, this study will also address whether the training affects their level of personal accomplishment.

6

OPERATIONAL DEFINITIONS

The following are operational terms for this study:

Adlerian Psychology/Individual Psychology—a psychological theory introduced by Alfred Adler. The approach, which is a holistic, systematic, and goal-oriented, focuses on an understanding of an individual's lifestyle (approach to life).

Council for the Accreditation of Counseling and Related Educational Programs (CACREP)—an accreditation body that grants accreditation to counselor education programs.

Goal attainment—the degree to which a client or student achieves the stated goal.

Goal-setting training—a full-day training that will emphasize a solution-focused/social interest goal-setting approach. The trainings will stress the acquisition of knowledge, practicing of skills, and application of the model.

Goal statement/attainment form—a form completed by the counselor or student affairs professional that includes a statement of the established goal and an assessment of the level of goal attainment.

Personal Accomplishment Scale—a subscale of the Maslach Burnout Inventory, which was designed to measure components of the burnout syndrome.

Process goal—a type of goal used in solution-focused therapy. Unlike other goals that tend to focus on the result, process goals focus on what needs to be done in order to achieve an end result.

Program evaluation—"a form of applied research distinguished by its relationship to a service program" (Hadley & Mitchell, 1995, p. 62).

Service program—a set of service activities that can range in any size from a national organization's program to one's individual work with one client or student (Hadley & Mitchell, 1995).

Social interest—"The willingness to participate in the give and take of life and to cooperate with others and be concerned about their welfare" (Dinkmeyer, Dinkmeyer, & Sperry, 1987, p. 64).

ASSUMPTIONS

It is assumed that:

1. all the participants received similar goal-setting training from their graduate program.
2. the students and clients with whom the counselors and student affairs professionals work will be equally representative of one another in regard to level of motivation.
3. there will be consistency in the scoring among doctoral students on the goal statement/attainment forms.

7

LIMITATIONS

1. The goal statement/attainment forms have been developed by the researcher, and there is no reliability or validity data available.
2. A one-day training may not have the intensity needed to bring about significant changes in the counselors and student affairs professionals.
3. Since the counselors and student affairs professionals will be working with a wide range of individuals in terms of age, presenting issues, settings, etc., there are numerous factors, other than those being examined in this study, that can affect their goal attainment.

CHAPTER 2
REVIEW OF THE LITERATURE

INTRODUCTION

Graduates of counselor education programs are finding employment in settings that increasingly call upon them to justify their programs and to be accountable (Schaffer & Atkinson, 1983). No matter the setting, (e.g., schools, agencies, or universities), these professionals are being questioned by the public as to the worth, the quality, accessibility, and the costs of their programs. For example, community members question the test scores of students in their local schools, the rates of employability of college graduates, the waiting lists at community agencies, and the value of their tax dollars. Counselors and student affairs professionals are being asked to provide services in a goal-focused manner in which many have not received training or are not convinced is effective (Schaffer & Atkinson, 1983; Wheeler & Loesch, 1981). A review of the literature reveals a prevalent trend in the accountability movement and provides examples of the profession's response to it.

REVIEW OF SELECTED LITERATURE

The call for accountability in the counseling and student affairs fields readily parallels one another. It appears that as the population to be served expands and more tax monies are required, the public calls upon professionals to justify their services. For example, initial psychotherapeutic approaches, which have their roots in models of long-term assessment and treatment, were substantially voluntary and available only to individuals who could pay for them (Bitter & Nicoll, 2000). Eventually, outpatient counseling became available to individuals in the middle and lower classes with private medical insurance plans and governmental agencies bearing most of the expense. The control for cost of care has recently transferred to corporate managed care systems. Although these trends have made counseling available to almost everyone, the managed care system's cost-effective mandate that treatment be focused and time-limited has greatly challenged counselors (Bittner & Nicoll).

In school counseling (historically referred to as guidance) the focus in the 1920s–1950s was on personal adjustment, organized around a counselor-clinical model (Gysbers & Henderson, 1994). As the trend leaned toward serving *all* students through developmental programs, which began during the 1960s, there was an appeal for counselors to state goals and objectives in measurable outcomes. During that time, Wellman (1968) developed a model and a taxonomy of guidance objectives classified in three domains of educational, vocational, and social development, which served as the basis of several subsequent models in the late 1960s and early 1970s. The accountability movement intensified in the 1970s with a renewed interest in career development theory, research, and practice. In the 1970s the emphasis was on defining developmental guidance programs as programs in their own right. At about this same time, the application of systems thinking was employed with a focus on individual's behavioral objectives, alternative activities, program evaluation, and implementation strategies (Gysbers & Henderson).

Likewise, in years past, the college experience was generally available only to the financially and academically able and primarily involved academic instruction. In recent years a college education has become available to just about anyone who seeks it (Hodum & Martin, 1994). As Gordon (1984) states, "Student populations are changing from academically skilled, middle-class youths to students with a more complicated mix of academic preparation, age, socioeconomic backgrounds, and reasons for enrolling in college" (cited in Hodum & Martin, 1994, p. 2). As the student body on college campuses has diversified, student affairs professionals have had to alter their programs and services to meet the challenges this entails. According to Upcraft and Schuh (1996), the student affairs professionals' primary function is to provide services to students that contribute to students' academic goals. However, it's questionable to what extent the student affairs professionals are trained in providing assistance to students in establishing goals in ways that enhance accountability.

Since the accountability literature in the field of student affairs tends to examine the programmatic level, this literature review is primarily a survey of the counseling literature as it applies to treatment planning and goal setting. A review of the literature, however, reveals few published models. One such model is Ivey and Matthews' (1984) meta-model for structuring the clinical interview. The model "is based on genetic epistemology for interviewing structure and includes: developing rapport, gathering information, determining outcome, exploring alternatives and confronting incongruity, and generalizing and transferring training" (p. 237). The authors propose that the model facilitates counselors in planning sessions, developing case summary notes, and creating treatment plans. The step of determining outcomes is the one most related to this study. According to Ivey and Matthews, "A defined outcome tells both the counselor and client when a goal has been achieved. In the absence of a defined goal the counselor may move to a goal not in agreement with the client" (p. 239). By establishing goals, the client and counselor will know when counseling can be terminated. The meta-model provides guidelines for the establishment of "well-formed" goals (p. 240). Specifically, a well-formed goal is one that is clear, that is obtainable, and that the client has control over.

The meta-model provides a general framework that ensures that interviewing objectives are met for both the counselor and client. The plan includes a form, "Interview plan and objectives form," and counselors are asked to complete it before they meet the client but after they study the client's file. The form is designed around the five stages mentioned above. The questions that the counselor needs to answer in preparation for the defining outcomes stage are: "Where do you believe this client would like to go? How will you bring out the idealized self or world? What would you like to see as the outcome?" (p. 241).

The authors suggest that counselors can use the same procedure when developing a treatment plan. When gathering data, the counselor may want to develop a list of client concerns and assets followed by ideal outcomes. The counselor will then list treatment alternatives geared to meet client needs. Finally the counselor will want to plan how to help clients transfer what they have learned in counseling into their life. On the interview plan and objectives form, the counselor will list what will enable him or her to feel that the session was worthwhile. Although Ivey and Matthews' (1984) meta-model seems to offer a sound framework for helping clients develop measurable goals, no efficacy studies were found in the literature to support the model.

In the mid-1990s computer-assisted treatment planning became increasingly important in mental health settings according to Weaver et al. (1994). They cite Ormiston et al. (1989) who used a word-processing program to create templates of problems that could be individualized for patients. Additionally, they cite Weiss and Chapman (1993), who used a database program to develop treatment plans based on a list of 28 symptoms.

In the social services delivery system, new computer and rapid assessment technology models are being developed to measure client and family strengths and deficits as well as to provide an assessment of current services (Rapp, Dulmus, Wodarski, & Feit, 1998). Although this model is primarily an integrated human service delivery system model in the social services field, perhaps it could serve as a protocol for counselors to use.

Weaver et al. (1994) also describe a computerized treatment planner that has been distributed widely in Veterans Affairs Medical Centers for use in their mental health programs. The computerized plan replaced a paper-and-pencil version, which was organized into four areas: problems, manifestations, goals, and interventions. Previously, each time therapists wrote treatment plans, they had to think of the words to describe what a patient needed in each of these four areas. The computerized version was found to be much more efficient, since in reviewing hundreds of treatment plans they discovered that 80% of their content was consistent across therapists and diagnoses and would be captured in the form of prewritten lists. The lists are flexible in that new items can be added and old ones eliminated. A formal treatment plan that is consistent for the documentation requirement is printed along with a version for clients themselves. The treatment plan includes goals, a treatment-activities schedule, staff responsible for the activities, and space for signatures. The program is also capable of providing other treatment options and forms for updating or terminating treatment.

Although computerized treatment planning was found to be more efficient in terms of therapists' time, as reported in Veteran's Affair's project (Weaver et al., 1994), the literature offers little guidance for implementing computerized treatment planning. In addition, it appears that clients are quite removed from the goal-setting process, which is contrary to the approach offered by Ivey and Matthews (1984). Along those same lines, a review of the literature revealed no studies on the effect that computerized treatment plans have on client outcome.

According to Wilson (1996) a movement that is highly committed to empirical research, as outlined in the 1995 Report by the Task Force on Promotion and Dissemination on Psychological Procedures, is one that identifies particular treatments for specific clinical disorders. He states that the profession has relied too long on therapists' clinical judgment in forming individual treatment plans. Wilson promotes the need for identifying effective treatment for major clinical disorders by referencing a study that left treatment totally to clinical judgment. In the study by Kadden, Cooney, Getter, and Litt, (1989; cited in Wilson), therapists made clinical judgments regarding 33 clients in inpatient alcohol dependency treatment. Therapists had to decide whether the clients would benefit more from coping skills training or interpersonal psychotherapy. While 18 patients received the recommended treatment, 15 did not. Those patients who did not receive the recommended treatment improved more. According to Faust (1986; cited in Wilson) "Clinical experience is unrelated to accuracy in clinical judgment" (p. 242). Garfield (1996) argues that identifying particular treatments for specific clinical disorders overlooks the importance of common factors across different forms of therapy, ignores important patient variablilty, and undermines therapist skill and versatility.

It would appear, then, that counselors face a dilemma because traditional treatment plans aim for comprehensiveness without regard to cost (Schreter, 1994) while "managed care companies, state agencies, and program funders are requiring 'best practices' that is, those intervention models that are based on research evidence" (Sexton, 2000, p. 221). According to Schreter, managed care companies are requiring therapeutic interventions that are short-term, focused, goal-oriented, prescriptive, and occurring in segments over time. "The challenge is for clinicians to create innovated treatment approaches that adequately deal with patients' problems and promote change" (Schreter, p. 65).

One solution to this challenge is brief therapy. According to Koss and Butcher (1986), and Steenbarger (1992), brief therapy approaches are at least as effective as long-term approaches, as indicated by third-party observations, standardized measurements, and client self-ratings. Whiston and Coker (2000) also suggest that brief therapy is effective with certain clientele (e.g., individuals with fewer chronic substance abuse problems, who have a higher degree of motivation, and are self-referred). While therapists generally appear to prefer long-term therapies, clients prefer therapists who are active, direct, and who structure sessions and move to problem resolution, which are all characteristic of brief therapy (Budman & Gurman, 1988; Garfield, 1988; cited in Bitter & Nicoll, 2000).

Although brief therapy models differ, and even the approaches used by individual practitioners using the same model may vary from each other, five characteristics appear common to brief therapy approaches: (a) time constraints, (b) focus, (c) counselor directiveness, (d) looking at symptoms as solutions, and (e) the assignment of behavioral tasks (Bitter & Nicoll, 2000).

Solution-focused (SF) counseling is one type of brief therapy that offers a goal-oriented approach. SF counseling is an approach based on the work of Milton Erickson who used hypnosis to help individuals generate successful solutions in their lives (de Shazer, 1985). In SF counseling de Shazer found that he was able to get similar results by replacing the use of hypnosis with purposeful questioning, focusing on solutions rather than on problems, and identifying what individuals were already doing well. Because the approach focuses on successful solutions that clients are already using, it tends to be brief.

In SF counseling, counselors use solution-oriented talk to establish the goal-oriented nature of the approach. One way they do this is by asking clients up front what it is they would like to change or do differently.

SF counselors maintain that people present their beliefs about their situation through the language they use. SF counselors help individuals replace their impotent words with language that is more productive and within their control. To help clients come up with goals, counselors often end an initial session by asking the client to be "on the lookout" between that time and the next session for situations that they would want to happen more often. In the second session a processing of their "homework" helps them to develop goals. SF counselors also use hypothetical questioning to help clients set goals. One such hypothetical question is the miracle question, "Suppose that one night, while you were asleep, there was a miracle and this problem was solved. How would you know? What would be different?" (de Shazer, 1988, p. 5). Counselors will often point out to the client that miracles are not likely to happen and then ask them what they "will be doing" to get that to happen.

Counselors assist individuals in formulating their responses into process goals. Walter and Peller (1992) summarized the criteria for process goals. According to them, process goals should be (a) positive in presentation, specifying what the individual will be doing; (b) an active process (e.g., "I will exercise daily" as opposed to "I will lose 10 pounds"); (c) in the here and now; (d) specific; (e) within the individual's control; and (f) in the individual's language.

In a study by LaFountain and Garner (1996) SF groups appear to be a promising approach for helping students to attain their goals and to make significant gains. The authors conducted a study involving 177 students in SF groups and 134 in control groups. Because SF groups emphasize an individual's use of personal strengths to create solutions to difficulties, they used the Index of Personality Characteristics (IPC) to assess the effectiveness of the SF groups. The IPC is a 75-item scale that provides information about the personal and social adjustment of children. According to Bachelor (1992), the reported estimates of reliability for the eight subscales are adequate to excellent.

Pretest and posttest measures for students were analyzed for the IPC using an analysis of covariance (ANCOVA) in which the posttest means were compared using the pretest scores as covariates. The procedure compensated for pretest differences. Statistically significant differences were reported on the following scales: Nonacademic, Perception of Self, and Acting In. Nonacademic and Perception of

Self are both measures of self-esteem, while Acting In is a measure of coping. Additionally, the students' goal attainment was assessed by a rater who interviewed the counselors involved in the study. The rater assigned a number from one to five for each student. A one meant that there was little attainment of the goal, while a five indicated that someone outside of the group reported that the student had shown improvement beyond the group setting. Using this scale, 91% of the students demonstrated progress toward their goal. More specifically, 14% generalized their goal outside of the group to a significant degree, 42% generalized their goal outside of the group, 25% demonstrated significant improvement in the group, 10% showed improvement regarding their goal in the group, and 9% made little progress toward their goal.

In the process of analyzing the goals, the authors noticed that a pattern began to emerge. There seemed to be a relationship between the existence of social interest in the chosen solution and the level of goal attainment. LaFountain (1996) further studied this relationship in a post hoc analysis. Before describing the analysis, the author discussed social interest, a concept belonging to Individual Psychology (also known as Adlerian Psychology). Adlerian approaches focus on an understanding of an individual's lifestyle, which is the individual's subjective, socially constructed approach to life. Additionally, Adlerian approaches are holistic, systemic, and teleological (goal-oriented) (Bitter, Christensen, Hawes, & Nicoll, 1998). LaFountain stressed that SF therapy and Individual Psychology share many constructs such as their positive perception of mental health, their emphasis on movement toward goals, and the encouragement of clients' strengths. The concept of social interest, however, is unique to Individual Psychology.

In contrast to SF counseling, which offers very specific criteria for goal setting, social interest is a more general prescription for goal attainment. According to Ansbacher and Ansbacher (1964, p. 53), "The resulting persistent deficiencies of the life-style lead to failure because the problems of life are of a social nature (in society, occupation, love) and inexorably demand social interest for their successful solution." Dinkmeyer, Dinkmeyer, and Sperry (1987) discuss social interest in the following:

> Adlerian Psychology sees people as social beings who cooperate with others to realize their goals and function fully. Thus Adlerians believe that mental health can be measured in terms of one's social interest, the willingness to participate in the give and take of life and to cooperate with others and be concerned about their welfare. A typical Adlerian suggestion for people who are discouraged is to become involved in helping others and to look outward instead of inward. Social interest and concern for others are contrasted with self-interest and concern only for one's own good. (p. 64)

This concept of community and cooperation in striving for goals significantly separates out Individual Psychology from SF therapy.

With this definition in mind, LaFountain (1996) noticed that many of the students who had successfully achieved their goals had an element of social interest in their goals. An example of a solution with characteristics of social interest is one where a student wanted to improve her relationship with her mother by spending more time with her and talking with her. In another group, a student had a similar goal of wanting to improve her relationship with her mother. However, her solution did not promote social interest. She chose to stay away from her mother as much as possible to avoid arguments. Therefore, to examine this relationship between the existence of social interest in the student's chosen solution and the level of goal attainment, a post hoc analysis was done. This was done by comparing the level of goal attainment, rated from one to five (as described previously), with the level of social interest. To determine the level of social interest, two master's level students who had made presentations and written in the area of Individual Psychology independently assessed each student's goal to determine the existence of social interest. They used the definition of social interest given earlier by Dinkmeyer et al. (1987) as the standard by which they made their decisions as to whether or not the goal had an element of social interest. They shared agreement in their decisions in 151 (85%) of the cases. Only those cases upon which they agreed were used in the final data analysis.

Of the 151 cases, 128 met the criteria for social interest, while 23 did not. Due to the disproportional number of cases in each sample, a nonparametric test, the Mann-Whitney test, was used to conduct the analysis. The mean rank for those students who had social interest goals was 85.67, while the mean rank for those students who did not have social interest goals was 22.20, $U = 234.5$, $p = .0000$. From the results it appeared there was a significant difference in the degree to which students attained their goals. Those students who created solutions that involved social interest attained their goals to a statistically significant higher degree than those who had goals that were more self-serving. This is consistent with Dinkmeyer et al's (1987) statement that people need to cooperate with others in order to achieve their goals.

To further examine the influence of social interest on goal attainment, the goal-setting training workshop, which will be used in this study to examine the effect of goal-setting training on counselors and student affairs professionals, will include social interest in the solution-focused goal-setting training.

SUMMARY

A review of the counseling literature shows that there are few studies that discuss treatment plans and goal setting and even fewer that address the efficacy of these practices. The literature does discuss the challenges that counselors face as they attempt to balance ethical practice with the accountability demands placed on them.

Brief therapy appears to be one solution due to the supporting findings. One specific model, SF counseling, with its emphasis on defining goals, seems like a promising approach to teach counselors to use in goal setting, as an initial step in moving in the direction of program evaluation. This model seems appropriate as well for student affairs professionals, particularly in their individual work with students. As described, for the purposes of the goal-setting training, an approach will be used which will combine the concept of social interest with the SF strategies.

CHAPTER 3
METHODOLOGY

INTRODUCTION

This section of the research study will include the target population, method of sampling, stimulus materials, measurement devices, data collection methods, statistical methods, research design, and estimated time schedule.

The study involves the effects of goal-setting training sessions on master's level counselors and student affairs professionals in regard to both their clients' or students' level of goal attainment and their level of perceived professional competence. A true experimental posttest control group design will be used in this study.

TARGET POPULATION

The target population for this study are graduates from a large midwestern counselor education program that is accredited by the Council for the Accreditation of Counseling and Related Educational Programs (CACREP). All participants have at least 3 years of postgraduate experience in a counseling or student affairs setting where they regularly work with students or clients. Because of the diversity of the counseling program, the participants represent a wide range of cultural and socioeconomic backgrounds.

METHOD OF SAMPLING

The method of sampling in this study will be a stratified random assignment of all counselors and student personnel professionals who volunteer for the goal-setting sessions. Using a computer-generated random numbers program, the experimenter will randomly assign one-half of the participants from each stratum (school counseling, community mental health counseling, student affairs work, or college counseling) to each of the two situations: goal-setting session emphasizing a solution-focused/social interest approach or a control group.

STIMULUS MATERIALS

The experimental group will participate in a full-day (six hour) training that will emphasize a solution-focused/social interest goal-setting approach. The trainings will stress the acquisition of knowledge, practicing of skills, and application of the model. The format will be primarily interactive and will consist of a lecture/discussion and small group exercises. The session will end with instruction in completing the paperwork to document the goals of students and clients. The control group will meet for a half-hour to learn how to complete the paperwork for documenting the goals of their students and clients. The control group will be offered the combined solution-focused/social interest training at the conclusion of the study.

17

MEASUREMENT DEVICES

The measurement devices to be used in this study are the Personal Accomplishment Subscale (PAS) from the Maslach Burnout Inventory (MBI), and a goal statement/attainment form. The PAS will be used to measure participants' feelings of competence. Goal statement/attainment forms will be used to assess the level of social interest in the goals set by the student or client as well as to assess whether the student or client attains the goal.

The Personal Accomplishment Subscale. The PAS is a subscale of the MBI, which was designed to measure components of the burnout syndrome. The PAS specifically "assesses feelings of competence and successful achievement in one's work with people" (Maslach & Jackson, 1995, p. 2). The instrument is a self-report questionnaire on which individuals rate items using a six-point, fully anchored response format. Bodden (1985) concurred with the authors that the instrument is research-oriented and should not be used for individual diagnosis, but Bodden emphasized that the instrument appears to be the best available for operationalizing the burnout construct. Internal consistency was estimated by Cronbach's coefficient alpha and a .71 reliability coefficient was given for the PAS. A test-retest reliability coefficient of .80 for the PAS was also established. Maslach and Jackson presented substantial evidence for the validity of the MBI.

Goal statement/attainment form. The goal statement/attainment form will be developed by the researcher. Counselors and student affairs professionals will use one form for each student or client. Following the initial goal-setting session with each student or client, the counselors and student affairs professionals will complete the goal statement section of the form. In this section they will indicate their names, an identification number for the student or client, the date of the first meeting with the stated individual, the date the goal is written, and a complete statement of the goal developed by the student or client. The counselor or student affairs professional will complete the goal attainment section at one of the following times (whichever time comes first): when the client or student achieves the goal, upon termination of the meetings, or when 15 weeks elapse. The counselor or student affairs professional will indicate the date and describe in detail the status or progress of the client or student in regard to the goal.

DATA COLLECTION METHODS

Data will be collected on the PAS and the goal statement/attainment form. Both groups of participants will be given the PAS as a posttest. In addition, the goals of the students and clients will be assessed in regard to their attainment and level of social interest at the conclusion of the study. The researcher conducting this study will administer and score the PAS.

The researcher will train four doctoral-level counseling students in the assessment of goal attainment and level of social interest in the goal statements. The doctoral students will determine whether or not each goal is attained and indicate the level of attainment on a scale of one to five, as described in the LaFountain (1996) study. The doctoral students will use the method based on the Dinkmeyer, Dinkmeyer, and Sperry (1987) definition to evaluate the level of social interest (on a scale of one to five) present in the goal stated, also described in the LaFountain study. For example, a female student in the residence hall who involves herself in mediation sessions in order to work out a roommate difficulty and uses the skills learned in other situations as well would be given a five. Another student who has as her only goal to move out of the room to solve the roommate problem would be awarded a one.

The researcher will appoint one of the doctoral-level students as the lead doctoral student. The lead doctoral student will collect the completed forms from the participants and distribute them to the other doctoral students for assessment. The lead doctoral student will review the assessments made by the other three doctoral students. Only those cases will be used where at least two of those three doctoral students scored them identically in terms of goal attainment and level of social interest. When all tasks are completed and the data collected, the researcher will analyze and interpret the data.

STATISTICAL METHODS

For the purposes of analyzing the PAS, a t-test for independent samples will be used. In order to identify which variables predict goal attainment, a mutliple regression analysis will be conducted. A $p \leq .05$ level of significance will be used for all analyses in this study.

RESEARCH DESIGN AND PROCEDURES

The research design for this study will be a true random posttest control group design. An illustration of this design follows:

$$R \quad X \quad O$$
$$R \qquad O$$

The purpose of this study is twofold: (1) to examine the effect of the goal-setting training on the personal satisfaction of counselors and student affairs professionals, and (2) to assess which variables contribute to the attainment of the goals set by clients and students.

The experimental and control groups will be derived from volunteers who are graduates of a midwestern CACREP-accredited counseling program who have at least 3 years of experience in their fields and are actively working with students or clients. Each group will be determined through stratified random assignment, using a computer-generated program.

The experimental group will participate in a full-day training that will emphasize a solution-focused/social interest goal-setting approach. As previously stated, the format of the training will be primarily interactive and the emphasis will be on the acquisition of knowledge, practicing of skills, and application of the model. All participants (including the control group) will receive training in documenting

19

the goals for the purposes of the study. The control group will be offered the opportunity to take the entire training at the conclusion of the study.

As will be explained in the training, all participants (experimental and control) will complete a goal statement form for each student or client they plan to see for more than one session beginning in September and October 2002. Fifteen weeks after the counselor or student affairs professional has set a goal with an individual, the counselor or student affairs professional is to complete the goal attainment section of the form. The counselor or student affairs professional will complete the form earlier in the event that the individual stops seeing him or her or achieves the goal. At the end of February 2003, the researcher will administer the PAS to all participants as a posttest. After receiving training in the assessment of the goal statement/attainment forms, doctoral students will assess the forms under the guidance of a lead doctoral student. The researcher will score the PAS.

According to Campbell and Stanley (1963), this type of design controls for all internal validity factors (history, maturation, testing, instrumentation, regression, selection, mortality, and interaction) and the external validity factor of interaction of testing and treatment. Since randomization is used in the research design, it is assumed that initially the groups have equal variances; however, without a pretest it cannot be certain.

The researcher will analyze and interpret the data collected from the PAS and the goal assessment/attainment forms administered in this study. The results will determine the acceptance or rejection of the null hypotheses.

TIME SCHEDULE

1-02 Request permission to conduct research study.

5-02 Send out letters to potential participants.

6-02 Select experimental group and control group participants from volunteers.

7-02 Train doctoral students in the assessment of goal selection/attainment forms.

8-02 Conduct trainings for experimental groups. Hold meeting for control group participants.

9-02 Counselors and student affairs professionals complete goal statement forms for students and clients with whom they initially set goals this month.

10-02 Counselors and student affairs professionals complete goal statement forms for students and clients with whom they initially set goals this month.

1-03 Counselors and student affairs professionals complete goal attainment forms for students and clients with whom they initially set goals in 9-02.

2-03 Counselors and student affairs professionals complete goal attainment forms for students and clients with whom they initially set goals in 10-02.

		20
2-03	Counselors and student affairs professionals take the PAS.	
2-03	Researcher scores PAS.	
2-03	Doctoral students assess the goal statement/assessment forms.	
3-03	Research analyzes research results.	
4-03	Training sessions are held for control group members.	

21

REFERENCES

Ametrano, I. M., & Stickel, S. A. (1999). Restructuring the on-campus counselor education laboratory: Contemporary professional issues. *Counselor Education and Supervision, 38,* 280–292.

Ansbacher, H. L., & Ansbacher, R. R. (Eds.). (1964). *Superiority and social interest.* Evanston, IL: Northwestern University Press.

Bachelor, P.A. (1992). Review of Index of Personality Characteristics. In J. K. Kramer & J. C. Conoley (Eds.). *The eleventh mental measurements yearbook*, volume I (pp. 403–404). Lincoln, NE: University of Nebraska.

Bitter, J. R., Christensen, O. C., Hawes, C., & Nicoll, W. G. (1998). Adlerian brief therapy with individuals, couples, and families. *Directions in Clinical and Counseling Psychology, 8* (8), 95–112.

Bitter, J. R., & Nicoll, W. G. (2000). Adlerian brief therapy with individuals: Process and practice. *The Journal of Individual Psychology, 56* (1), 31–44.

Bodden, J. L. (1985). Review of Maslach Burnout Inventory. In J. V. Mitchell, Jr. (Ed.). *The ninth mental measurements yearbook*, volume I (p. 903–904). Lincoln, NE: University of Nebraska.

Campbell, D. T., & Stanley, J. C. (1963). *Experimental and quasi-experimental designs for research.* Chicago: Rand McNally.

Cheston, S. E. (2000). A new paradigm for teaching counseling theory and practice. *Counselor Education and Supervision, 39* (4), 254–269.

de Shazer, S. (1985). *Keys to solutions in brief therapy.* New York: Norton.

de Shazer, S. (1988). *Clues: Investing solutions in brief therapy.* New York: Norton.

Dinkmeyer, D. C., Dinkmeyer, D. C., Jr., Sperry, L. (1987). *Adlerian counseling and psychotherapy.* Columbus, OH: Merrill.

Fong-Beyette, M. L., (1988). Do counseling and marketing mix? *Counselor Education and Supervision, 27,* 315–319.

Garfield, S. L. (1996). Some problems associated with "validated" forms of psychotherapy. *Clinical Psychology: Science and Practice, 3,* 218–229.

Gilchrist, L. A., & Stringer, M. (1992). Marketing counseling: Guidelines for training and practice. *Counselor Education and Supervision, 31,* 154–162.

Gysbers, N. C., & Henderson, P. (1994). *Developing and managing your school guidance program* (2nd ed.). Alexandria, VA: American Counseling Association.

Hadley, R. G., & Mitchell, L. K. (1995). *Counseling research and program evaluation.* Pacific Grove, CA: Brooks/Cole.

Hague, W. J. (1989). Educating for response-able counseling. *Canadian Journal of Counseling, 23* (4), 340–345.

Hodum, R. L., & Martin, O. L. (1994). *An examination of college retention rates with a university 101 program.* Paper presented at the annual meeting of the Mid-South

Ed. Research Assoc., Nashville. (ERIC Document Reproduction Service No. 380036)

Ivey, A. E., & Matthews, W. J. (1984). A meta-model for structuring the clinical interview. *Journal of Counseling and Development, 63,* 237–243.

Koss, M. P. & Butcher, J. W. (1986). Research on brief psychotherapy. In S. L. Garfield & A. E. Bergin (Eds.). *Handbook of psychotherapy and behavior change* (3rd ed.; pp. 627–670). New York: Wiley.

Krumboltz, J. D. (1974). An accountability model for counselors. *Personnel and Guidance Journal, 52,* 639–646.

LaFountain, R. M. (1993). Trends that differentiate school counselors regarding burnout. *The Pennsylvania Counselor, 39* (5), 20–21.

LaFountain, R. M. (1996). Social interest: A key to solutions. *Journal of Individual Psychology, 52* (2), 150–157.

LaFountain, R. M., & Garner, N. E. (1996). Solution-focused counseling groups: The results are in. *The Journal for Specialists in Group Work, 21* (2), 128–143.

Maslach, C., & Jackson, S. E. (1995). *Maslach Burnout Inventory Manual.* Palo Alto, CA: Consulting Psychology Press.

Meyers, J. E., & Smith, A. W. (1995). A national survey of on-campus clinical training in counselor education. *Counselor Education and Supervision, 35,* 70–81.

Neufeldt, S. A. (1994). Preparing students to work with today's clinic clients. In J. E. Myers (Ed.). *Developing and directing counselor education laboratories* (pp. 83–90). Alexandria, VA: American Counseling Association.

Rapp, L. A., Dulmus, C. N., Wodarski, J. S., & Feit, M. D. (1998). Integrated human service delivery system: Public welfare model. *The Journal of Applied Social Sciences, 22* (2), 151–156.

Schaffer, J. L., & Atkinson, D. R. (1983). Counselor education courses in program evaluation and scientific research: Are counselors being prepared for the accountability press? *Counselor Education and Supervision, 23* (1), 29–34.

Schreter, R, K. (1994). Outpatient services: The clinician's view. In R. K. Schreter, S. S. Sharfstein, & C. A. Schreter (Eds.). *Allies and adversaries: The impact of managed care on mental health services* (pp. 60–68). Washington, DC: American Psychiatric Press.

Sexton, T. L. (2000). Restructuring clinical training: In pursuit of evidence-based clinical training. *Counselor Education and Supervision, 39* (4), 218–227.

Steenbarger, B. N. (1992). Toward science-practice integration in brief counseling therapy. *The Counseling Psychologist, 20* (3), 403–450.

Upcraft, M. L., & Schuh, J. H. (1996). *Assessment in student affairs: A guide for practitioners.* San Fransisco: Jossey-Bass.

Walter, J., & Peller, J. (1992). *Becoming solution-focused in brief therapy.* New York: Brunner/Mazel.

22

23

Weaver, R. A., Christensen, P. W., Sells, J., Gottfredson, D. K., Noorda, J., Schenkenberg, T., & Wennhold, A. (1994). Computerized treatment planning. *Hospital and Community Psychiatry, 45* (8), 825–827.

Wellman, F. E. (1968). *Contractor's report, Phase I, National Study of Guidance.* Contract OEG 3-6-001147-1147, Washington, DC: Department of Health, Education, and Welfare, Office of Education.

Wheeler, P. T., & Loesch, L. (1981). Program evaluation and counseling: Yesterday, today, and tomorrow. *Personnel and Guidance Journal, 59* 573–577.

Whiston, S. C., & Coker, J. K. (2000). Reconstructing clinical training: Implications from research. *Counselor Education and Supervision, 39* (4), 228–253.

Wittman, P. P. (1988). Marketing counseling: What counseling can learn from other health care professionals. *Counselor Education and Supervision, 27,* 308–314.

Wilson, G. T. (1996). Empirically validated treatments: Reality and resistance. *Clinical Psychology: Science and Practice, 3* (3), 241–244.

Appendix C

Sample Qualitative Research Proposal

Exploring the Role of Forgiveness in Eliminating Racism
Jan Arminio, Ph. D.
Shippensburg University

Chapter 1

In his poignant book *The Sunflower*, author Simon Wiesenthal relates his experience of being asked for forgiveness by a dying Nazi soldier (who killed numerous Jewish civilians, including shooting children jumping from a burning building) while Wiesenthal was a prisoner in a concentration camp. The soldier stated, "I know that what I am asking is almost too much for you but without your answer I cannot die in peace" (1969, p. 54). Wiesenthal asks the reader what they would have done. In the remainder of the book numerous religious, political, academic, and military scholars address Wiesenthal's question.

Unfortunately there are many episodes of horror in the history of our planet and most notably in the twentieth century (Shriver, 1995). In the aftermath of these episodes, many scholars, politicians, religious leaders, educators, and counselors are asking not only what role forgiveness plays in healing wounds from atrocities but also how forgiveness may lead societies to more just ways of living.

First, it is prudent to explore what forgiveness is. Shriver defined forgiveness as "an act that joins moral truth, forbearance, empathy, and commitment to repair a fractured human relation" (1995, p. 9). Murphy and Hampton (1988) defined forgiveness as the emotion of how one wronged feels toward the perpetrator. Forgiving is "forswearing my resentment toward the person who has wronged me—a change of attitude" (p. 21). It is essential to understand that forgiveness does not imply forgetting the wrong deed (Minow, 1998; Murphy & Hampton, 1988; Shriver, 1995; Wiesenthal, 1969) nor does forgiveness condone the deed (Bass & Davis, 1988; Flanigan as cited in Heller, 1998; Tobin, 1993). A school counselor wrote,

> There is a forgiveness that absolves us of guilt and seems to lessen our part in a certain event. There is also a deeper quest for forgiveness where we extend ourselves to another in requesting forgiveness. On a superficial level, asking for forgiveness may benefit only the asker. Forgiveness has a truer and deeper meaning that should be treasured by both the person asking for forgiveness and the forgiver. Granting forgiveness is very difficult and complex, as it demands a surrender and vulnerability that is often necessary to begin to rebuild relationships. (Truckenmiller, 1994)

Moreover, apologizing is not the same as asking for forgiveness. Asking for forgiveness is at a higher level of humility, repentance, and vulnerability. Apologies differ from asking for forgiveness in that they do not empower the wronged to decide when they emotionally can forgive the perpetrators. But apologies do offer an acknowledgement of responsibility, an important step in the process of forgiveness. For example, there are several groups engaged in a German-Jewish dialogue where ancestors of holocaust victims and ancestors of their Nazi perpetrators meet to discuss the intense pains of both the bloodline of the wronged and the perpetrator. In these discussions forgiveness is often requested and, when an individual is ready, given.

Shriver (1995) strongly believed that acknowledging wrongdoing, apologizing, and asking for forgiveness exposes atrocities of the past to "public discourse" (p. 154) with the hope that healing will occur and that atrocities will not be repeated.

This study seeks to explore how forgiveness is experienced on a day-to-day basis. Do culture, race, or other issues of identity influence one's perception of and experience with forgiveness? Is forgiveness a tool to becoming more just with each other? If so, should the topic of forgiveness be more fully utilized in multicultural education by counselors and student affairs professionals?

Chapter 2
Exploring the Phenomenon

To each journey participants bring preunderstandings. For me, this journey to better understand the lived experience of forgiveness, its influences, and its possible utility in creating a more just society, is no exception. Van Manen wrote, "it is better to make explicit our understandings … to hold them deliberately at bay even to turn this knowledge against itself exposing its shallow or concealing character" (1990, p. 47). Below are the preunderstandings I bring to this exploration. I gained these preunderstandings from previous journeys, literature, and the experiences of others as described to me and interpreted by me.

Being Called to the Phenomenon

On a previous journey, I embarked on a dissertation to better understand the life experience of white folks as they struggle to turn away from racism to a more just way of being. During my dissertation defense, a committee member asked why she did not read any reference to forgiveness in my study. I was surprised by her comment and was left momentarily speechless. I finally commented that none of my participants had mentioned forgiveness, thus the absence. She smiled and responded, "Well, the topic of your next study." Her statement nagged at me over the subsequent 7 years. I felt there was profound insight to be gained, as if I were about to embrace something but it was just beyond my reach. It was while reading about forgiveness that I came to realize what had been escaping me. Her question was geared not at what might a participant have said about forgiveness that I had failed to cover in my dissertation, but rather at why did I not comment on its absence. Just as forgiveness was not an experience in my participants' lives relevant enough to mention to me, it also was not relevant enough to me for me to notice its absence. When talking about turning from hate, discrimination, bias, and privilege, why was forgiveness not a relevant experience?

<u>Cultural Influences of Forgiveness</u>

In his thoughtful study of the forgiveness of enemies, particularly as it relates to the U.S., Shriver (1995) offered a resolution passed by the Charleston Colored People's Convention (passed in 1865), speeches and writings of U. S. civil rights activists (particularly Martin Luther King), and writings pertaining to the Pacific campaign of World War II as evidence that the likelihood of asking for and granting forgiveness is influenced by culture. In particular he wrote,

> Is there, in the culture of a significant segment of African Americans a predisposition toward, an ingrained gift for, injecting forgiveness into their political relations with the white majority of this country? The Charleston convention suggests that hypothesis. (p. 177)

The Charleston Colored People's Convention resolved that, "As American chattel Slavery has now passed forever away, we would cherish in our hearts no malice nor hatred toward those who were implicated in the crime of slaveholding" (p. 176). Yet, the response of white people to this resolution and to the nonviolent protests of Martin Luther King (which often were met with brutality) implies the statement, "Why aren't you nonforgiving like us?"

Moreover, Japan's cultural proclivity to "Let the past flow away like the river" (Shriver, 1995, p. 138) has impeded Japan's acknowledgement of wrongdoing during World War II as well as their going so far as to ask for forgiveness. To the contrary, it has been the value they place on harmony between Japan and its post-World War allies that has been the impetus to begin to debate acknowledging wrongdoing. Additionally, the West's notion of placing blame (combined with racism) encouraged the internment of Japanese Americans.

Religious Influences

Culture and religion are linked in such a way that one informs and influences the other. How does Shintoism influence the Japanese attitude toward the cultural value of harmony? How does Christianity influence the notions of forgiveness? Shriver wrote that Athena, in Greek mythology, first offered the idea of forgiveness when increasing retaliation for wrongdoing was the norm. The Hebrew Bible makes forgiveness more common and clearly forbids escalating retaliation (i.e., a tooth for a tooth, but only a tooth for a tooth). Jesus brought forgiveness to prominence. In fact, Shriver believed that Jesus sought to have forgiveness learned in a community setting, that forgiveness is "indispensable" in the role of social change (p. 35).

Yet, in Wiesenthal's *The Sunflower*, described above, Jewish scholars replied that Wiesenthal should not forgive the soldier, while the Christians and Buddhists replied that Wiesenthal should forgive the soldier. Certainly one's connection with a wrong influences one's meaning making about it as well as one's theology. If forgiveness is so prominent in Christianity, why the absence of asking for racial forgiveness by white Christians?

Public Apologies

There have been several instances of governments offering apologies that "acknowledge the fact of harms, accept some degree of responsibility, avow sincere regret, and promise not to repeat the offense" (Minow, 1998, p. 112). Examples include: the U.S. reparations to interned Japanese Americans and President Bush's signed letters of apology, President Clinton's apology to the survivors of a government study that withheld treatment to African American men with syphilis, Prime Minister Blair's apology for his government's role in the Irish Potato Famine, Prime Minister Howard's apology for the Australian government's theft of Aboriginal children from their families to be adopted by white families, Prime Minister Murayama's apology for the suffering Japan caused during World War II, German lawmakers' apology for the Holocaust, Canada's apology to its Native Americans for suppressing their culture, etc. (Minow, 1998). Also, governments have made apologies to individuals, such as President Chirac's apology to the descendents of Alfred Dreyfus, a Jewish army captain who was falsely accused of treason (Minow, 1998). Yet, these apologies do not ask for forgiveness. They are neither that humble nor that vulnerable.

Some see such apologies as futile because they cannot change the past. Shriver stated that such apologies allow for public discourse of wrongdoings, which promotes healing and hopefully diminishes the possibility of their repetition. I agree.

<u>Forgiveness as Process</u>

The literature is clear that there is a process necessary to yield forgiveness. Prior to being forgiven there must first be punishment (in the form of acknowledging the wrongdoing plus either a sense of guilt or a social sanction such as a fine or prison term, restitution, or reparations, and acceptance of responsibility) and atonement (the asking for forgiveness) (Minow, 1998; Murphy & Hampton, 1988; Shriver, 1995; Wiesenthal, 1969). Forgiveness is clearly a moral choice that does not condone the immoral act (Bass & Davis, 1988; Flanigan as cited in Heller, 1998; Tobin, 1993).

Yet, these apologies do not ask for forgiveness. I believe those making them are neither humble enough nor vulnerable. However, forgiveness is beginning to gain importance in healing as it becomes an emerging field of study (Heller, 1998) and a therapeutic tool (Bass & Davis, 1988; Tobin, 1993).

How is forgiveness experienced by individuals? In particular, how is forgiveness experienced in day-to-day multicultural interactions?

Chapter 3
Methodology

The method of travel on this present journey is phenomenological hermeneutics. Phenomenology is both a philosophy and research approach to study the nature of lived experience. Phenomenologists seek to gain greater understanding into a phenomenon as it is experienced, not as it is conceptualized (van Manen, 1990). Hermeneutics is the science of interpretation. In hermeneutic phenomenology the essence of the phenomenon is assumed to be veiled or implicit and must be explored to be better understood. Just as Hermes interpreted the Greek Gods to mortals, the researcher's role is "to come to a deeper understanding of what persons go through as they conduct their day-to-day life in the language of everyday life" (Hultgren, 1989, p. 50). Hermeneutic phenomenology brings implicitness to explicitness through phenomenological deconstruction, reflection, and hermeneutic recovery. The researcher, as the interpreter, is not an objective observer, but rather an active ingredient in the research process and as such is referred to in the first person.

A map for this journey will be van Manen's (1990) steps for conducting a hermeneutic phenomenological study. These are: turning to a phenomenon to which the researcher is seriously committed, investigating experience as it is lived rather than how it is conceptualized, reflecting on the essential themes that characterize the phenomenon, describing the phenomenon through the art of writing and rewriting, maintaining a strong and oriented pedagogical relation to the phenomenon, and balancing the research context by considering the parts within the whole (van Manen, 1990). Further instructions for the journey will be Brown's (1989) standards for interpretive inquiry.

Purposeful sampling will be used to gather insight into the phenomenon of race-related forgiveness. In this case, attendees at community race dialogues will be invited to participate. These people are considered information-rich participants (those most likely to elucidate the phenomenon) (Patton, 1990). Insights into both the asking for and granting of forgiveness, particularly as these experiences relate to race, will be explored.

Regarding how we travel, in meeting with participants I will evoke Gadamer's notion of conversation, rather than having our meetings take the form of an interview. Conversations take their own twists and turns, reaching their own conclusions. It is a process of coming to an understanding by opening up one to the other. The goal is to understand (not judge) what is said "so that we can be one with each other on the subject" (Gadamer, 1960/1992, p. 385). Approximately 25 people of various identities will participate. Some may be engaged in more than one conversation in order to clarify interpretations. Co-travelers will be asked to describe forgiveness, to give examples of asking for and granting forgiveness in general and in particular involving race, to speak about the role of forgiveness in eliminating oppression, and to address whether higher education should increase its focus on forgiveness as a healing tool, and if so, how.

Records of our journey will be in the form of audiotaped transcriptions of our conversations. They will be read a number of times until common themes emerge. Van Manen described themes as elements that occur frequently in the text (1990). They are not stand-alone elements, but rather strands woven together throughout the fabric of the phenomenon. Subsequently I will expose numerous examples that exemplify the identified themes. I will then convene a group of multicultural educators to serve in a "human science dialogue" for collaborative analysis (van Manen, 1990, p. 101). By reading many of the transcripts and through group conversation, the human science dialogue will confirm the trustworthiness of the emerging themes and add insight into the meanings that lay inherent in the lived experience of these participants.

Next will begin the essence of the hermeneutic phenomenologist's interpretations, the writing and rewriting of the exposed themes (van Manen, 1990). Veiled meaning is unveiled through writing and rewriting about the themes. With each writing, a layer of the lived experience will become more clearly exposed and better understood. Then, a more authentic description of their lived experience will be written.

I will give a draft of the analysis to each participant to assess whether my interpretations are accurate. If they are not, I will make alterations, which will result in a more authentic description of their lived experience.

Forgiveness 8

References

Bass, E., & Davis, L. (1988). *The courage to heal.* New York: Harper Perennial.

Brown, M. (1989). What are the qualities of good research? In F. Hultgren & D. Coomer (Eds.), *Alternative modes of inquiry* (pp. 257–297). Peoria. IL: Glencoe.

Gadamer, H. (1992). *Truth and method* (2nd ed.) (J. Weinsheimer and D. Marshall, Trans.). New York: Crossroad. (Original work published 1960).

Heller, S. (July, 17, 1998). Emerging field of forgiveness studies explores how we let go of grudges. *The Chronicle of Higher Education,* A18–A20.

Hultgren, F. (1989). Introduction. In F. Hultgren & D. Coomer (Eds.), *Alternative modes of inquiry* (pp. 37–59). Peoria. IL: Glencoe.

Minow, M. (1998). *Between vengeance and forgiveness: Facing history after genocide and mass violence.* Boston: Beacon Press.

Murphy, J. C., & Hampton, J. (1988). *Forgiveness and mercy.* Cambridge: Cambridge University Press.

Patton, M. Q. (1990). *Qualitative evaluation and research methods.* Newbury Park, CA: Sage Publications.

Shriver, D. W. (1995). *An ethic for enemies: Forgiveness in politics.* New York: Oxford University Press.

Tobin, E. (1993). *How to forgive yourself and others.* Liguori, MO: Liguori Publications.

Truckenmiller, K. (1994). *Multicultural journal.* Unpublished paper.

Van Manen, M. (1990). *Researching lived experience; Human science for an active sensitive pedagogy.* Albany, NY: State University of New York Press.

Wiesenthal, S. (1967). *The sunflower: On the possibilities and limits of forgiveness.* New York: Schoken Books.

Appendix D

Selected Standards Related to Research and Assessment

American Counseling Association
American College Personnel Association
National Association of Student Personnel Administrators

American Counseling Association
As approved by the Governing Council, April 1997
ACA Code of Ethics Preamble*

The American Counseling Association is an educational, scientific, and professional organization whose members are dedicated to the enhancement of human development throughout the life-span. Association members recognize diversity in our society and embrace a cross-cultural approach in support of the worth, dignity, potential, and uniqueness of each individual. The specification of a code of ethics enables the association to clarify to current and future members, and to those served by members, the nature of the ethical responsibilities held in common by its members. As the code of ethics of the association, this document establishes principles that define the ethical behavior of association members. All members of the American Counseling Association are required to adhere to the Code of Ethics and the Standards of Practice. The Code of Ethics will serve as the basis for processing ethical complaints initiated against members of the association.

The following section of the Code of Ethics is the most relevant to the area of research and assessment:

Section G: Research and Publication

G.1. Research Responsibilities

a. Use of Human Subjects. Counselors plan, design, conduct, and report research in a manner consistent with pertinent ethical principles, federal and state laws, host institutional regulations, and scientific standards governing research with human subjects. Counselors design and conduct research that reflects cultural sensitivity appropriateness.

b. Deviation From Standard Practices. Counselors seek consultation and observe stringent safeguards to protect the rights of research participants when a research problem suggests a deviation from standard acceptable practices. (See B.6.)

c. Precautions to Avoid Injury. Counselors who conduct research with human subjects are responsible for the subjects' welfare throughout the experiment and take reasonable precautions to avoid causing injurious psychological, physical, or social effects to their subjects.

d. Principal Researcher Responsibility. The ultimate responsibility for ethical research practice lies with the principal researcher. All others involved in the research activities share ethical obligations and full responsibility for their own actions.

e. Minimal Interference. Counselors take reasonable precautions to avoid causing disruptions in subjects' lives due to participation in research.

f. Diversity. Counselors are sensitive to diversity and research issues with special populations. They seek consultation when appropriate. (See A.2.a and B.6.)

G.2. Informed Consent

a. Topics Disclosed. In obtaining informed consent for research, counselors use language that is understandable to research participants and that (1) accurately explains the purpose and procedures to be followed; (2) identifies any procedures that are experimental or relatively untried; (3) describes the attendant discomforts and risks; (4) describes the benefits or changes in individuals or organizations that might be reasonably expected; (5) discloses appropriate alternative procedures that would be advantageous for subjects; (6) offers to answer any inquiries concerning the procedures; (7) describes any limitations on confidentiality; and (8) instructs that subjects are free to withdraw their consent and to discontinue participation in the project at any time. (See B.1.f.)

b. Deception. Counselors do not conduct research involving deception unless alternative procedures are not feasible and the prospective value of the research justifies the deception. When the methodological requirements of a study necessitate concealment or deception, the investigator is required to explain clearly the reasons for this action as soon as possible.

c. Voluntary Participation. Participation in research is typically voluntary and without any penalty for refusal to participate. Involuntary participation is appropriate only when it can be demonstrated that participation will have no harmful effects on subjects and is essential to the investigation.

d. Confidentiality of Information. Information obtained about research participants during the course of an investigation is confidential. When the possibility exists that others may obtain access to such information, ethical research practice requires that the possibility, together with the plans for protecting confidentiality, be explained to participants as a part of the procedure for obtaining informed consent. (See B.1.e.)

e. Persons Incapable of Giving Informed Consent. When a person is incapable of giving informed consent, counselors provide an appropriateexplanation, obtain agreement for participation, and obtain appropriate consent from a legally authorized person.

f. Commitments to Participants. Counselors take reasonable measures to honor all commitments to research participants.

g. Explanations After Data Collection. After data are collected, counselors provide participants with full clarification of the nature of the study to remove any misconceptions. Where scientific or human values justify delaying or withholding information, counselors take reasonable measures to avoid causing harm.

h. Agreements to Cooperate. Counselors who agree to cooperate with another individual in research or publication incur an obligation to cooperate as promised in terms of punctuality of performance and with regard to the completeness and accuracy of the information required.

i. Informed Consent for Sponsors. In the pursuit of research, counselors give sponsors, institutions, and publication channels the same respect and opportunity for giving informed consent that they accord to individual research participants.

Counselors are aware of their obligation to future research workers and ensure that host institutions are given feedback information and proper acknowledgment.

G.3. Reporting Results

a. Information Affecting Outcome. When reporting research results, counselors explicitly mention all variables and conditions known to the investigator that may have affected the outcome of a study or the interpretation of data.

b. Accurate Results. Counselors plan, conduct, and report research accurately and in a manner that minimizes the possibility that results will be misleading. They provide thorough discussions of the limitations of their data and alternative hypotheses. Counselors do not engage in fraudulent research, distort data, misrepresent data, or deliberately bias their results.

c. Obligation to Report Unfavorable Results. Counselors communicate to other counselors the results of any research judged to be of professional value. Results that reflect unfavorably on institutions, programs, services, prevailing opinions, or vested interests are not withheld.

d. Identity of Subjects. Counselors who supply data, aid in the research of another person, report research results, or make original data available take due care to disguise the identity of respective subjects in the absence of specific authorization from the subjects to do otherwise. (See B.1.g. and B.5.a.)

e. Replication Studies. Counselors are obligated to make available sufficient original research data to qualified professionals who may wish to replicate the study.

G.4. Publication

a. Recognition of Others. When conducting and reporting research, counselors are familiar with and give recognition to previous work on the topic, observe copyright laws, and give full credit to those to whom credit is due. (See F.1.d. and G.4.c.)

b. Contributors. Counselors give credit through joint authorship, acknowledgment, footnote statements, or other appropriate means to those who have contributed significantly to research or concept development in accordance with such contributions. The principal contributor is listed first and minor technical or professional contributions are acknowledged in notes or introductory statements.

c. Student Research. For an article that is substantially based on a student's dissertation or thesis, the student is listed as the principal author. (See F.1.d. and G.4.a.)

d. Duplicate Submission. Counselors submit manuscripts for consideration to only one journal at a time. Manuscripts that are published in whole or in substantial part in another journal or published work are not submitted for publication without acknowledgment and permission from the previous publication.

e. Professional Review. Counselors who review material submitted for publication, research, or other scholarly purposes respect the confidentiality and proprietary rights of those who submitted it.

American College Personnel Association
As presented by the ACPA Standing Committee on Ethics
And approved by the ACPA Executive Council, November 1992
Preamble*

The American College Personnel Association (ACPA) is an association whose members are dedicated to enhancing the worth, dignity, potential, and uniqueness of each individual within post-secondary educational institutions and thus to the service of society. ACPA members are committed to contributing to the comprehensive education of the student, protecting human rights, advancing knowledge of student growth and development, and promoting the effectiveness of institutional programs, services, and organizational units. As a means of supporting these commitments, members of ACPA subscribe to the following principles and standards of ethical conduct. Acceptance of membership in ACPA signifies that the member agrees to adhere to the provisions of this statement. This statement is designed to address issues particularly relevant to college student affairs practice. Persons charged with duties in various functional areas of higher education are also encouraged to consult ethical standards specific to their professional responsibilities.

Ethical Standards

Four ethical standards related to primary constituencies with whom student affairs professionals work—fellow professionals, students, educational institutions, and society—are specified. Those standards most closely related to research and assessment are included.

1.   Professional Responsibility and Competence.

Student affairs professionals are responsible for promoting student's learning and development, enhancing the understanding of student life, and advancing the profession and its ideals. They possess the knowledge, skills, emotional stability, and maturity to discharge responsibilities as administrators, advisors, consultants, counselors, programmers, researchers, and teachers. High levels of professional competence are expected in the performance of their duties and responsibilities. The ultimately are responsible for the consequences of their actions or inaction.

As ACPA members, student affairs professionals will:

1.2   Contribute to the development of the profession (e.g., recruiting students to the profession, serving professional organizations, educating new professionals, improving professional practices, and conducting and reporting research).

1.3   Maintain and enhance professional effectiveness by improving skills and acquiring new knowledge.

1.12 Use records and electronically stored information only to accomplish legitimate, institutional purposes and to benefit students.

1.13 Define job responsibilities, decision-making procedures, mutual expectations, accountability procedures, and evaluation criteria with subordinates and supervisors.

Source: Reprinted with permission of the American College Personnel Association (ACPA).

1.14 Acknowledge contribution by others to program development, program implementation, evaluation, and reports.

1.17 Gain approval of research plans involving human subjects from the institutional committee with oversight responsibility prior to initiation of the study. In the absence of such a committee, they will seek to create procedures to protect the rights and assure the safety of research participants.

1.18 Conduct and report research studies accurately. They will not engage in fraudulent research nor will they distort or misrepresent their data or deliberately bias their results.

1.19 Cite previous works on a topic when writing or when speaking to professional audiences.

1.20 Acknowledge major contributions to research projects and professional writings through joint authorships with the principal contributor listed first. They will acknowledge minor technical or professional contribution in notes or introductory statements.

1.21 Not demand co-authorship of publications when their involvement was ancillary or unduly pressure others for joint authorship.

1.22 Share original research data with qualified others upon request.

1.23 Communicate the results of any research judged to be of value to other professionals and not withhold results reflecting unfavorably on specific institutions, program, services, or prevailing opinion.

1.24 Submit manuscripts for consideration to only one journal at a time. They will not seek to publish previously published or accepted-for-publication materials in other media or publication without first informing all editors and/or publishers concerned. They will make appropriate references in the test and receive permission to use if copyrights are involved.

As ACPA members, preparation program faculty will:

1.28 Provide graduate students with a broad knowledge base consisting of theory, research, and practice.

2. Student Learning and Development.

Student development is an essential purpose of higher education, and the pursuit of this aim is a major responsibility of student affairs. Development is complex and includes cognitive, physical, moral, social, career, spiritual, personality and educational dimensions. Professionals must be sensitive to the variety of backgrounds, cultures, and personal characteristics evident in the student population and use appropriate theoretical perspectives to identify learning opportunities and to reduce barriers that inhibit development.

As ACPA members, student affairs professionals will:

2.7 Inform students about the purpose of assessment and make explicit the planned use of results prior to assessment.

2.8 Provide appropriate information to students prior to and following the use of any assessment procedure to place results in proper perspective with other relevant factors (e.g., socioeconomic, ethnic, cultural, and gender related experiences).

3. Responsibility to the Institution

Institutions of higher education provide the context for student affair practice. Institutional mission, policies, organizational structure, and culture, combined with individual judgment and professional standards, define and delimit the nature and extent of practice. Student affairs professional share responsibility with other members of the academic community for fulfilling the institutional mission. Responsibility to promote the development of individual students and to support the institution's policies and interests require that professional balance competing demands.

As ACPA members, student affairs professional will:

3.10 Evaluate programs, services, and organizational structure regularly and systematically to assure conformity to published standards and guidelines. Evaluations should be conducted using rigorous evaluation methods and principles, and the results should be made available to appropriate institutional personnel.

National Association of Student Personnel Administrators (NASPA)*

NASPA is an organization of colleges, universities, agencies, and professional educators whose members are committed to providing services and education that enhance student growth and development. The association seeks to promote student personnel work as a profession, which requires personal integrity, belief in the dignity and worth of individuals, respect for individual differences and diversity, a commitment to service, and dedication to the development of individuals and the college community through education. NASPA supports student personnel work by providing opportunities for its members to expand knowledge and skills through professional education and experience. The following standards were endorsed by NASPA at the December 1990 board of directors meeting in Washington D.C. We include those standards that are most relevant to research and assessment.

9. Integrity of Information and Research

Members ensure that all information conveyed to others is accurate and in appropriate context. In their research and publications, members conduct and report research studies to assure accurate interpretation of findings, and they adhere to accepted professional standards of academic integrity.

18. Assessment

19. Members regularly and systematically assess organizational structures, programs, and services to determine whether the developmental goals and needs of students are being met and to assure conformity to published standards and guidelines such as those of the Council for the Advancement of Standards for Student Services/Developmental Programs (CAS). Members collect data that include responses from students and other significant constituencies and make assessment results available to appropriate institutional officials for the purpose of revising and improving program goals and implementation.

———

*Source: Reprinted with permission of the National Association of Student Personnel Administrators (NASPA).

Appendix E

Table of Random Numbers

40083	85862	75029	84851	45378	81096	66261
72878	65716	25031	52788	53202	22208	34595
2948	62062	40868	88272	48546	96715	67351
78126	03385	69321	28599	96983	98704	00213
15367	42384	77829	83980	97112	58334	21013
91973	95443	69706	04601	13415	71722	05679
02185	86714	42967	05829	75659	77553	78730
37443	57970	53632	47735	35072	66686	47324
95004	62156	61649	81592	40098	30965	30926
48632	42266	16174	70775	11439	65949	13019
86074	59080	52694	36000	86487	12988	82982
96887	49310	97084	92599	38034	56557	71070
00881	79997	74625	20348	67786	49446	38343
95258	57351	66243	99371	44496	22813	73959
77273	20516	15076	87153	54957	62555	79877
00077	87077	13020	95738	69020	73744	61350
46767	20865	40115	93782	61179	64347	81132
22757	20970	74350	20094	70283	77464	99366
96659	10839	74407	76243	10761	05654	55075
20963	99921	47510	25482	84993	38439	30689
26883	44372	01467	31480	94827	22515	47820
61527	80240	61705	30247	79983	36088	45665
99966	89690	71521	37338	21707	14580	19324
08952	48373	98909	14092	25974	17195	00641
19134	37114	20634	71191	88997	60801	53394
11726	91375	22370	19279	63380	76274	09364
89493	40287	85988	16676	00252	03955	69120
53247	68616	00020	21726	01077	00226	45412
15055	81536	88914	47206	31644	04699	71462
56055	38061	26439	85019	02407	61592	25469
55146	13481	20563	75566	58689	13814	91812
10582	54557	26107	22206	09401	51209	47442
56788	45009	57815	28549	07146	05141	17927
82366	39517	26040	62127	77612	48832	05322
91393	91938	46175	12098	42971	39762	31505

Appendix F

Answers to Activities and Worksheets

Note: Answers may vary due to the method of rounding (using two decimal points or using the exact numbers arrived at with the calculator).

Activity 1.1

Study 1:

Independent Variable(s):	Participation in an intensive study skills program
Dependent Variables(s):	Graduation rate

Study 2:

Independent Variable(s):	Approach to play therapy
Dependent Variables(s):	Frequency of occurrence of encopresis
	Level of responsibility for cleanup

Study 3:

Independent Variable(s):	Level of knowledge of the position
	Attitude toward residential policies
	Ability level to handle conflicts
Dependent Variables(s):	Level of commitment to the resident assistant position

Activity 2.1

A sample response: Greg will need to use the process of individual random assignment to place the college students (who have been recently identified with AD/HD) into one of two groups. One group of students will receive the training, while the other group will not receive the training. After a specific amount of time elapses, Greg will measure the social skills level of each student.

Activity 2.2

1. quasi-experiment
2. ex post facto
3. critical research
4. true experiment
5. ethnomethodology
6. descriptive
7. phenomenology
8. correlational studies

Activity 3.1

1. Yes
2. Yes
3. No
4. No
5. No
6. Yes
7. No

Activity 3.2

The following are sample responses:

1. Will involvement in an intensive study skills program improve the graduation rate of at-risk seniors?
2. What is the effect of the type of approach to play therapy on the rate of occurrence of encopresis and the level of responsibility for cleanup by latency-aged children?
3. How do knowledge of the resident assistant position, attitude toward residential policies, and ability to handle conflict determine the commitment one has to the position of resident assistant?

[handwritten margin note: level of comm de on 1, 2, 3]

Activity 3.3

Independent: participation in social skills training
Dependent: level of social skills
A sample research question is:

> What is the effect of social skills training on the acquisition of social skills by young adults with ADHD who were first diagnosed in college?

Activity 5.3

1. c; 2. i; 3. a; 4. b; 5. l; 6. g; 7. d; 8. e

Activity 7.1

1. c; 2. a; 3. b; 4. b; 5. d

Activity 7.2

Mean = 5
Median = 5
Mode = 5
A scatter graph or scattergram is the most appropriate graph, since single dots are plotted to represent the values of single events on two variable scales.

Activity 7.3

The mean is 10.59, while the median and mode continue to be 5. This happens because the mean is sensitive to extremes. The distribution is positively skewed because the high extreme score is pulling the distribution and creating a tail on the right end of the distribution.

Activity 7.4

Population variance is 1.2.; population standard deviation is 1.10 (rounded). Sample variance is 1.33; sample standard deviation is 1.15 (rounded).

Activity 7.5

Mode = 10
Median = 10
Mean = 10
Standard deviation = 1.15

Activity 7.6

T = 53.3

Activity 7.7

Sam's z score is +2, Lynn's z score is +1, Bob's z score is –2
Sam has a t score of 70, a SAT-type score of 700, and a stanine score of 9
Lynn has a t score of 60, a SAT-type score of 600, and a stanine score of 7
Bob has a t score of 30, a SAT-type score of 300, and a stanine of 1

Activity 7.8

Terry, since Terry's standard score (z = 1.5) is the highest.

Worksheet 7.1 - Descriptive Statistics

1. $\bar{X} = 63.88$, or 64
   Median = 63
   $s^2 = 48.27$
   $s = 6.95$
   Percentile for a raw score of 66 = 69
   z for a raw score of 56 = –1.15
   t for a raw score of 59 = 42.81
   t for a raw score of 68 = 55.76
   Stanine for a raw score of 75 = 8

2. $\bar{X} = 76.69$ or 77
   Median $= 76$
   $s^2 = 54$
   $s = 7.35$
   Percentile for a raw score of $87 = 92$
   z for a raw score of $80 = +.41$
   z for a raw score of $68 = -1.22$
   t for a raw score of $68 = 37.76$
   Stanine for a raw score of $67 = 2$

Activity 8.1

3. The following could be possible correlation coefficients: $+.90, 0, -.55, -.33$
4. $-.70$
7. (a) 49%, (b) Forty-nine percent of the variance in graduate school G.P.A. and is explained by scores on the GRE, (c) 51%

Worksheet 8.1 – Correlation

1. $p = .72$
   percent of predictability $= 52\%$
2. $p = .98$
   Conclusion: Objective and essay tests yield same basic results.

Activity 9.1

1. .82
2. .30

Activity 9.2

1. 4
2a. 76–84
2b. 72.16–87.84
2c. 69.68–90.32

Worksheet 9.1

1. See computer printout. In both cases it comes out to .82.
2. .90
3. 68th (2.2), 95th (4.31), 99th (5.68)
4. Yes
5. .83

Worksheet 9.2

1. KR = .85, SEM = 4.57
2. (a) .76, (b) 4.5 (rounded), (c) 68–86 (rounded)
3. SEM = 2.32
   47.68–52.32
   45.45–54.55
   44.01–55.99

Activity 10.1

1. retain
2. reject
3. retain

Activity 10.2

Reject the null.

Activity 10.3

The $x^2 = 1.42$. Retain the null.

Worksheet 10.1

KR = .65
SEM is approximately 4.3
t value = 2.13. Reject the null.

Activity 11.1

1. The purpose of this study was to replicate the findings of experiment one.
2. The independent variable is the use of humor; the dependent variable is an objective exam.
3. $N = 132$. The experimental group was composed of 65 students, while the control group had 67 students.
4. The subjects were samples of the population of students in a teachers' college in Tel Aviv who were taking an introductory psychology course.
5. The researcher randomly assigned two entire classrooms to each of the two conditions. Intact groups were used.
6. Two entire classrooms of students were assigned randomly to one experimental group and one control group. The instructor, who had been trained in the humor seminar, offered an introductory psychology course to both groups of students. He added the judicious use of humor to the course he taught to the experimental group. No humor was used in the course offered to the control group.

7. Although you may have thought that this design was true experimental, since intact groups were formed before the random assignment occurred, the design would be considered quasi-experimental. It is a posttest-only control group design.

8. The posttest measure is an objective examination containing 50 multiple-choice questions. The reliability is .93, which is considered to be very good.

9. Statistical analysis was done using a t-test.

10. The mean for the experimental group is 82 with a standard deviation of 12.4. The mean for the control group is 72.5 with a standard deviation of 11.2.

11. The analysis resulted in a t = 3.58 with 130 degrees of freedom.

12. The level of significance is less than .01.

13. The effect size is .85, which is considered to be highly significant. (82 – 72.5/11.2).

14. There appears to be a statistically significant relationship between the use of humor in the teaching of psychology and achievement.

15. While experiment one had two independent variables, the use of humor and the sex of the subject, experiment two only had one variable, the use of humor.

16. Again, this experiment appears to have internal validity due to the careful planning that the author put into designing the study, but we cannot be absolutely certain.

17. Since this study is a replication of experiment one, and similar findings resulted, it appears that experiment one may have external validity. You would want to continue to replicate the study to verify it.

Appendix G

References and Additional Readings

REFERENCES

Adler, A. (1992). *What life could mean to you.* (C. Brett, Trans.) Oxford: Oneworld. (Original work published 1931.)

American Psychological Association. (2001). *Publication manual.* Washington, DC: Author.

ASCA Research Committee. (1992). *Action-oriented research desk guide for professional school counselors.* Alexandria, VA: Author.

Association for Advanced Training in the Behavioral Sciences. (1996). *National counselor examination review*, Vol. III (14th series). Ventura, CA: Author.

Association for Advanced Training in the Behavioral Sciences. (1988). *Preparatory course for the psychology license exam*, Vol. II. Ventura, CA: Author.

Baker, S. B. (1983). Suggestions for guidance accountability. *Pennsylvania Journal of Counseling*, 2, 52–69.

Baker, S. B. (1993, June). *Action research strategies for achieving accountability.* Paper presented at the annual conference of the American School Counselor Association, McLean, VA.

Barlow, D., Haynes, S. C., & Nelson, R. O. (1984). *The scientist practitioner: Research and accountability in clinical and educational settings.* New York: Pergamon Press.

Bartos, R. B. (1992). *Educational research.* Shippensburg, PA: Shippensburg University.

Borg, W. R., & Gall, M. D. (1983). *Educational research.* White Plains, NY: Longman.

Brown, M. (1989). What are the qualities of good research? In F. Hultgren & D. Coomer (Eds.), *Alternative modes of inquiry in home economics research* (pp 257–297). Peoria, IL: Glencoe.

Butler, L., Miezitis, S, Friedman, R., & Cole, E. (1980). The effect of two school-based intervention programs on depressive symptoms in preadolescents. *American Educational Research Journal*, 17, 111–19.

Campbell, D. T., & Stanley, J. C. (1963). Experimental and quasi-experimental designs for research. Chicago: Rand McNally.

Cherry, A. L. (2000). *A research primer for the helping professions: Methods, statistics, and writing.* Belmont, CA: Wadsworth/Thomson Learning.

Cohen, J. (1988). *Statistical power analysis for the behavioral sciences* (2nd ed.). Hillsdale, NJ: Erlbaum.

Coomer, D. & Hultgren, F. (1989). Considering alternatives: An invitation to dialogue and question. In F. Hultgren & D. Coomer (Eds.), *Alternative modes of inquiry in home economics research* (pp. xv–xxiii). Peoria, IL: Glencoe.

Crowl, T. K. (1993). *Fundamentals of educational research.* Madison, WI: Brown & Benchmark Publishers.

Darroch, V. & Silvers, R. J. (1982). *Interpretive human studies: An introduction to phenomenological research.* Lantham, MD: University Press of America.

Dillon, K. (1982). Statisticophobia. *Teaching of Psychology, 9,* (2), 117.

Gillies, R. M. (1993). Action research for school counselors. *School Counselor, 41* (2), 69–72.

Glaser, B., & Strauss, A. (1967). *The discovery of grounded theory: Strategies for qualitative research.* Chicago: Aldine.

Glass, G. V. (1976). Primary, secondary, and meta-analysis of research. *Educational Researcher, 5* (10), 3–8.

Glesne, C., & Peshkin, A. (1992). *Becoming qualitative researchers: An introduction.* White Plains, NY: Longman.

Glueck, S., & Glueck, E. (1957). *Unraveling juvenile delinquency.* Cambridge, MA: Harvard University Press.

Hadley, R. G., & Mitchell, L. K. (1995). *Counseling research and program evaluation.* Pacific Grove, CA: Brooks/Cole Publishing.

Heppner, P. P., Kivlighan, D. M., & Wampold, B. E. (1999). *Research design in counseling.* Belmont, CA: Wadsworth.

Herman, K. C. (1993). Reassessing predictors of therapist competence. *Journal of Counseling and Development, 72,* 29–32.

Karges-Bone, L. (1994). *Grant writing for teachers: If you can write a lesson plan you can write a grant.* Torrance, CA: Frank Schaffer Publications.

Knowles, L. (1974). Helping students learn basic inferential statistics. *College Student Journal, 8* (3), 7–11.

Krathwohl, D. R. (1993). *Methods of educational and social science research.* White Plains, NY: Longman.

Lauffer, A. (1983). *Grantsmanship* (2nd ed.). Beverly Hills, CA: Sage.

Leedy, P. D. (1997). *Practical research: Planning and design.* Upper Saddle River, N.J.: Prentice Hall.

Levin, J. R. (1982). Modifications of a regression toward the mean demonstration. *Teaching of Psychology, 9* (4), 237–38.

Liu, Y. C., & Baker, S. B. (1993). Enhancing cultural adaption through friendship training: A single case study. *Elementary School Guidance and Counseling, 28*, 92–103.

Lundervold, D. A., & Belwood, M. F. (2000). The best kept secret in counseling: Single-case (N=1) experimental designs. *Journal of Counseling & Development, 78,* 92–102.

Marlow, C. (2000). *Research methods for generalist social work* (3rd ed.). Belmont, CA: Wadsworth/Thomson Learning.

Minium, E. W., Clarke, R. C., & Coladarci, T. (1999). *Elements of statistical reasoning.* New York: John Wiley & Sons.

Morrell, J. P. (1996). *Grant writing basics.* Salem, OR: Energeia Publishing.

Norusis, M. J. (1993). *SPSS for Windows: Base system user's guide, release 6.0.* Chicago: SPSS, Inc.

Patton, M. Q. (1990). *Qualitative evaluation and research methods.* Newbury Park, CA: Sage.

Rosenthal, R., & Jacobson, L. F. (1968). *Pygmalion in the classroom: Teachers' expectation and pupils' intellectual development.* New York: Holt, Rinehart, & Winston.

Rosenthal, R., & Rosnow, R. (Eds.). (1969). *Artifact in behavioral research.* New York: Academic Press.

Rosenthal, R., & Rosnow, R. L. (1975). *The volunteer subject.* New York: John Wiley.

Rowh, M. (1992). *Winning government grants and contracts for your small business.* New York: McGraw-Hill.

Stanovich, K. E. (1991). *How to think straight about psychology* (3rd ed.). Glenview, Il: Scott, Foresman.

Terman, L. M. (1925). *Genetic studies of genius (Vol. 1), Mental and physical traits of a thousand gifted children.* Stanford, CA: Stanford University Press.

Upcraft, M. L., & Schuh, J. H. (1996). *Assessment in student affairs: A guide for practitioners.* San Francisco: Jossey-Bass, Inc.

Walter, J. & Peller, J. (1992). *Becoming solution-focused in brief therapy.* New York: Brunner/Mazel.

Whyte, W. F. (1989). Action research for the twenty-first century: Participation, reflection, and practice. [Special Issue] *American Behavioral Scientist, 32.*

Wiersma, W. (1991). *Research methods in education* (5th ed.). Needham Heights, MA: Simon & Schuster.

Wilkinson, W. K., & McNeil, K. (1996). *Research for the helping professions.* Pacific Grove, CA: Brooks/Cole Publishing.

Willett, J., & Singer, J. (1992). *Statistics for the twenty-first century.* New York: Mathematical Association of America.

Ziv, A. (1988). Teaching and learning with humor: Experiment and replication. *Journal of Experimental Education, 57* (1), 5–15.

ADDITIONAL READINGS

Bogdan, R. C., & Biklen, S. K. (1998). *Qualitative research for education: An introduction to theory and methods* (3rd ed.). Boston: Allyn & Bacon.

Cresswell, J. W. (1994). *Research design: Qualitative and quantitative approaches.* Thousand Oaks, CA: Sage.

Denzin, N. K., & Lincoln, Y. S. (Eds.). (1994). *Handbook of qualitative research.* Thousand Oaks, CA: Sage.

Kirk, J., & Miller, M. L. (1986). *Reliability and validity in qualitative research.* Beverly Hills, CA: Sage.

Marshall, C., & Rossman, G. B. (1995). *Designing qualitative research* (2nd ed.). Thousand Oaks: Sage.

Patton, M. Q. (1990). *Qualitative evaluation and research methods* (2nd ed.). Thousand Oaks, CA: Sage.

Pelto, P. J., & Pelto, G. H. (1978). *Anthropological research: The structure of Inquiry* (2nd ed.). New York: Cambridge University Press.

Fink, A. (1998). *Conducting research literature reviews: From paper to the Internet.* Beverly Hills, CA: Sage.

Fraenkel, J. R., Sawin, E. I., & Wallen, N. E. (1999). *Visual statistics: A conceptual primer.* Boston: Allyn & Bacon.

Kimmel, A. J. (1988). *Ethics and values in applied social research.* Beverly, CA: Sage.

Lipsey, M. W. (1990). *Design sensitivity: Statistical power for experimental research.* New York: Holt, Rinehart & Winston.

Murphy, E. R., & Myors, B. (Eds.). (1998). *Statistical power analysis: A simple and general model for traditional and modern hypothesis tests.* Hillsdale, N.J.: Lawrence Erlbaum.

Neuman, S. B., & McCormick, S. (Eds.). (1995). *Single-subject experimental research: Applications for literacy.* Newark, DE: International Reading Association.

Index

Note: Page numbers in italics refer to figures and tables.